BY JAMES G.W. MacLAMROC
GUILFORD COUNTY HISTORIAN &
PAST PRESIDENT OF THE MUSEUM.

FIRST COUNTY SEAT
GUILFORD COUNTY, NORTH CAROLINA
1771 - 1774

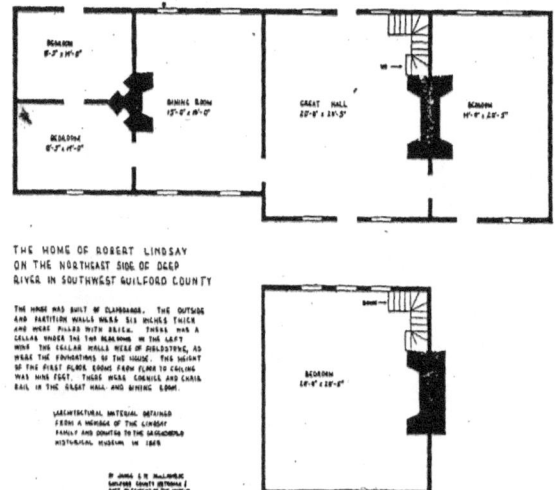

THE HOME OF ROBERT LINDSAY
ON THE NORTHEAST SIDE OF DEEP
RIVER IN SOUTHWEST GUILFORD COUNTY

THE HOUSE WAS BUILT OF CLAPBOARDS. THE OUTSIDE AND PARTITION WALLS WERE SIX INCHES THICK AND WERE FILLED WITH BRICK. THERE WAS A CELLAR UNDER THE TWO BEDROOMS IN THE LEFT WING. THE CELLAR WALLS WERE OF FIELDSTONE, AS WERE THE FOUNDATIONS OF THE HOUSE. THE HEIGHT OF THE FIRST FLOOR ROOMS FROM FLOOR TO CEILING WAS NINE FEET. THERE WERE CORNICE AND CHAIR RAIL IN THE GREAT HALL AND DINING ROOM.

ARCHITECTURAL MATERIAL OBTAINED FROM A MEMBER OF THE LINDSAY FAMILY AND DONATED TO THE GREENSBORO HISTORICAL MUSEUM IN 1969.

BY JAMES G.W. MacLAMROC
GUILFORD COUNTY HISTORIAN &
PAST PRESIDENT OF THE MUSEUM.

Courtesy "Diary of Elizabeth Dick Lindsay"
edited by Jo White Linn, 1975

GUILFORD COUNTY

DEED BOOK ONE

edited by
William D. Bennett, C.G.

Southern Historical Press, Inc.
Greenville, South Carolina

This volume was reproduced from
An 1990 edition located in the
The Publisher's Private Library,
Greenville, South Carolina

All rights reserved. No part of this publication may be reproduced, stored in a retrieval system, transmitted in any form, posted on to the web in any form or by any means without the prior written permission of the publisher.

Please direct all correspondence and orders to:

www.southernhistoricalpress.com
or
SOUTHERN HISTORICAL PRESS, Inc.
PO BOX 1267
375 West Broad Street
Greenville, SC   29601
southernhistoricalpress@gmail.com

Originally published: Raleigh, NC, 1990
Copyright 1990 by:
William D. Bennett
Raleigh, NC
Copyright Transferred 2018 to:
Southern Historical Press, Inc.
Greenville, SC
ISBN #0-89308-970-2
All rights Reserved.
Printed in the United States of America

GUILFORD COUNTY
DEED BOOK ONE

CONTENTS

Home of Robert Lindsay   ii

Maps   vi
    Lindsay's Home
    Guilford Courthouse
    Collet 1771
    Price-Strother 1808

Introduction   xi

Names in German Script   xv

Abbreviations   xviii

Deed Book One   1

Personal Name Index   91

Place Name Index   107

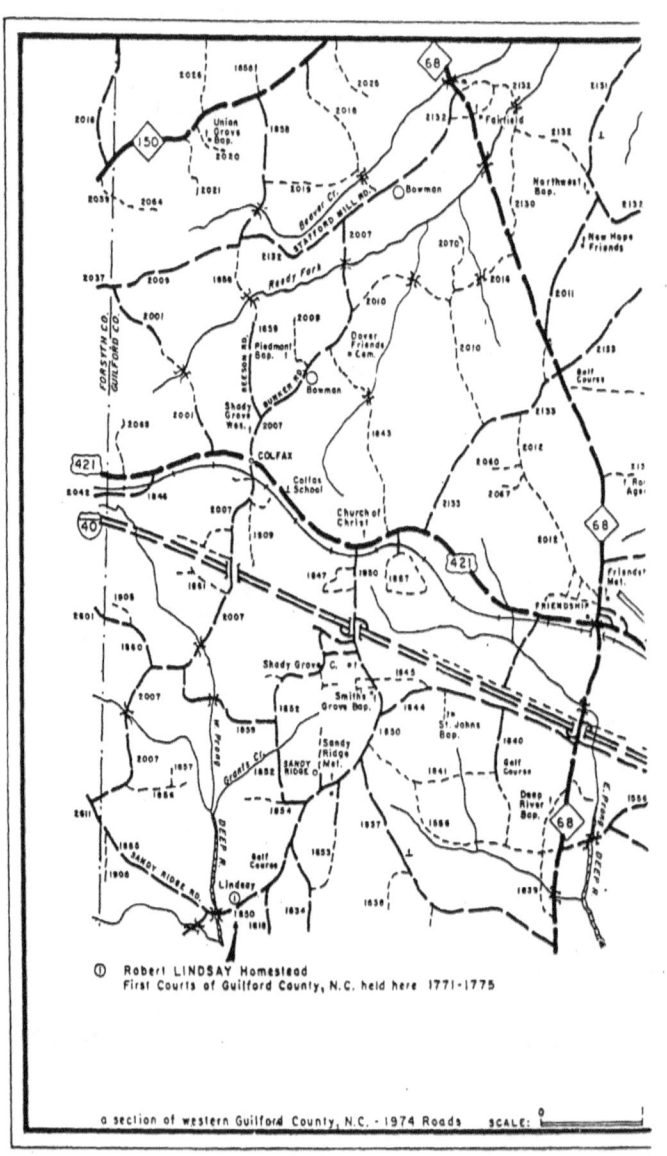

Courtesy "Diary of Elizabeth Dick Lindsay"
edited by Jo White Linn, 1975

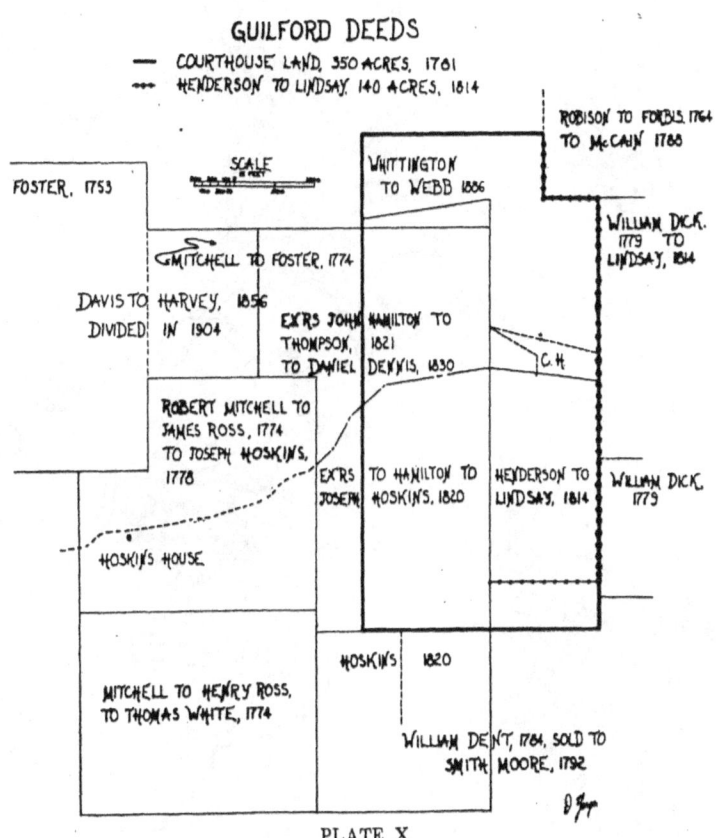

PLATE X
Martinville Lots and Plan — A Reconstruction (based on a sketch in the Taylor Report)

Guilford Courthouse Land

Courtesy "The Gray Family & Allied Lines", Jo White Linn, 1976.

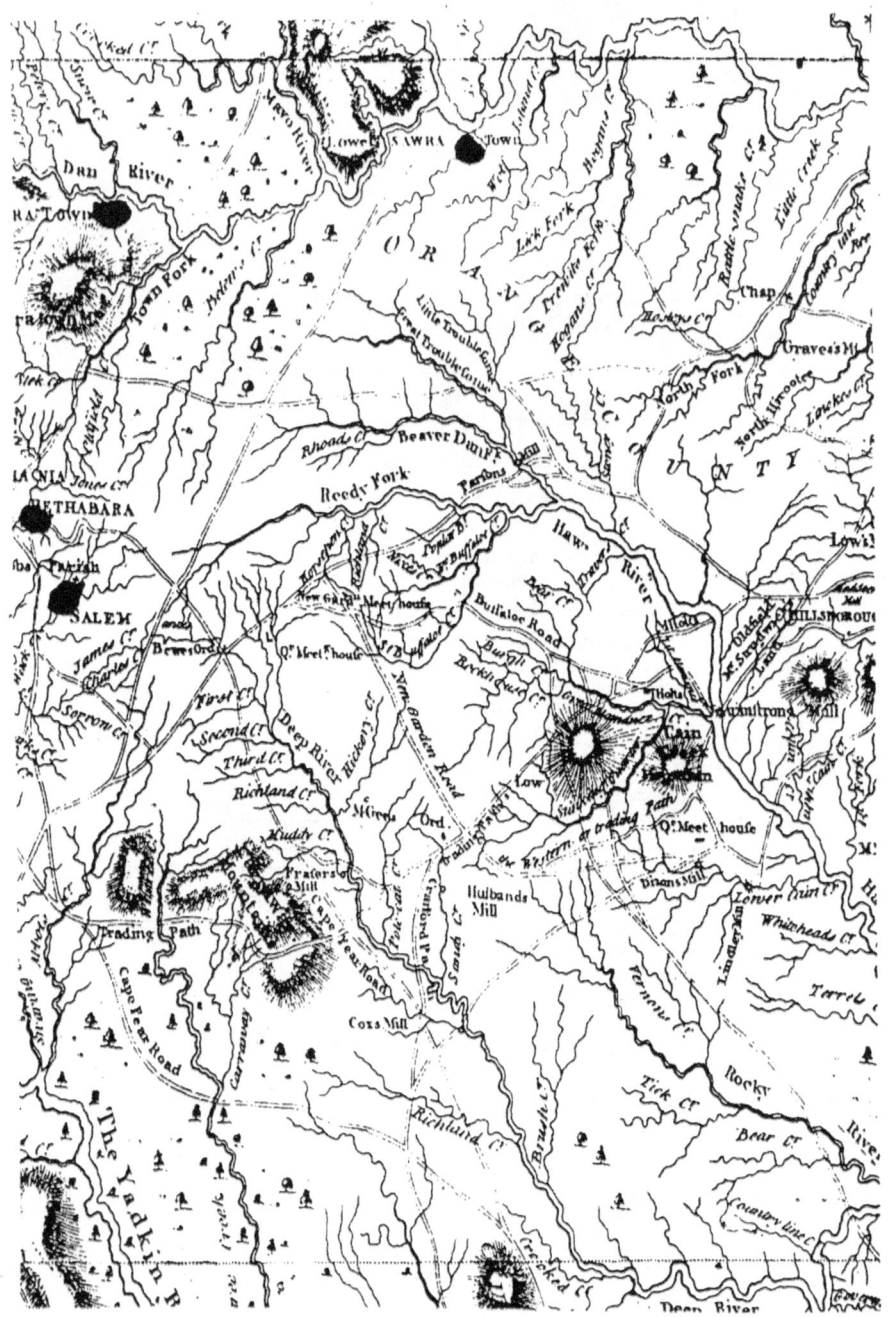

From the Collett Map 1770

Most of the information for this area was drawn from the notes and other records of William Churton.

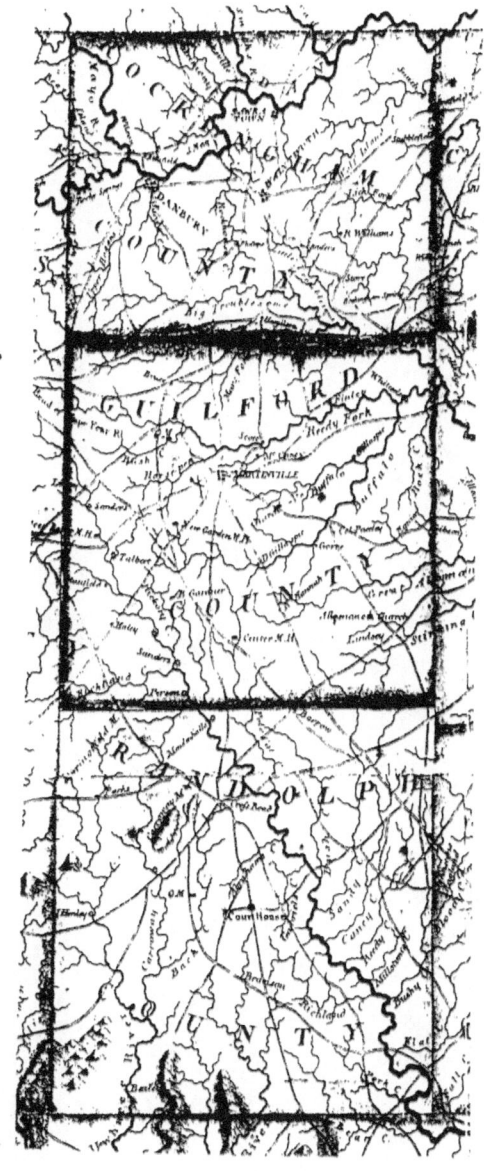

From the Price-Strother Map 1808

This was the first map of North Carolina based on a complete survey of the state. It is also the first state-wide map to delineate the county boundaries.

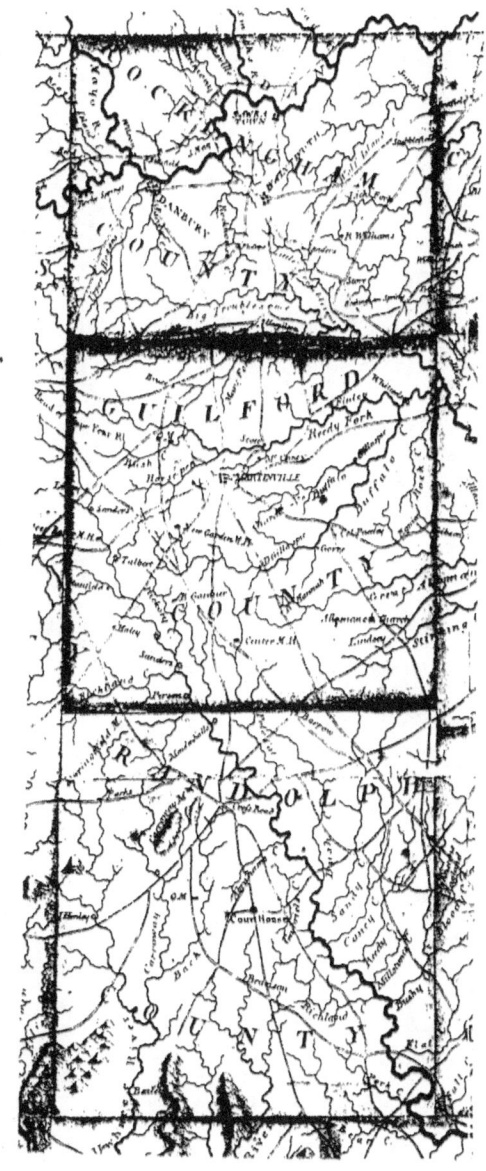

From the Price-Strother Map 1808

This was the first map of North Carolina based on a complete survey of the state. It is also the first state-wide map to delineate the county boundaries.

INTRODUCTION

Guilford County was formed in 1771 from the western part of Orange County and the eastern part of Rowan County and comprised the present counties of Rockingham, Guilford, and Randolph. It is interesting to note that the clerk became confused in recording the minutes of the General Assembly concerning the second reading of the bill calling for the organization of the new county. These are minutes for the session held on 7 January 1771 and reads as follows: "A bill for erecting part of Rowan County and part of Orange County into a separate County and Parish by the name of Chatham County and Unity Parish and other purposes. Read second time and passed." The transcript of these minutes can be found in Colonial Records of North Carolina, Vol. 8, page 352. Likewise, the clerk referred to the county to be formed from the southern part of Orange County as "Guilford County and St. Bartholomews Parish." On 26 January 1771 the bill was ordered enrolled in the statutes. This bill provided for the Act to become effective 1 April 1771 and the first court was ordered to meet at the home of Robert Lindsay.

Guilford County was one of four counties formed at this session of the General Assembly the others being Wake, Chatham, and Surry Counties. Some historians have considered the erection of the four counties an attempt to satisfy at least one of the demands of the Regulators: more representation. However, Gov. Tryon's formation of Guilford County seemd to have been for other purposes. In a letter from Gov. Tryon to Earl Hillsborough dated Newbern 12 March 1771, Tryon wrote, "The Acts for erecting four new counties seemed a measure highly necessary from the too great extent of the counties they were taken out of. The erecting Guilford County out of Rowan and Orange Counties was in the distracted state of this country a truly political division as it separated the main body of the Insurgents from Orange County, and left them in Guilford.

The Act for the establishment of Guilford County begins:

> "Whereas the great extant of the Respective Counties of Rowan & Orange renders the Attendance of the Inhabitants of part of Rowan County and the Inhabitamts of the upper part of Orange County to do Publick Duties in their respective Counties extremely difficult & expensive for remedy whereof
> Be it enacted by the Governor Council & Assembly and by Authority of the same that a line beginning at a point twenty five Miles due west of Hillsborough running Thence North to the Virginia line Then West to a point due North of the painted Springs Then South to Anson line Then along Anson & Cumberland lines to a point due South of the beginning --- be erected into a distinct County by the name of Guilford an Unity Parish."

At the same session of the Assembly which established Guilford County an act was passed for surveying the Surry, Rowan, and Guilford lines. Since the description refers to so many of the geographical locations found in the following deeds, the complete description of the Surry-Guilford line is presented:

> Beginning at a post oak standing in a hollow at a small distance from the Reedy Fork of Haw River and on the NW side, being the corner of Rowan County and Surry County, Running from thence N 3 miles to the Reedy Fork of Haw River, thence 4 miles to the waters of Belews Creek, Thence crossing said Creek to William Hannah's 7 miles, then crossing said Creek again at 10 miles at eleven miles crossing it again at a very high hill, at 40 poles crossing said creek at a fall and a fish trap at 13 miles and three-quarters crossed said creek again above John Southerland's, then crossed Dan River at the upper end of Lads Island through the lower end of Lads old clearing, thence crossing Dan River twice at Neals bent at a white oak on the north bank, then across the Danupper Road whewre a branch crosses said road about 4 miles from Carmichaels Ford on Dan River, thence by William Crumps on Bever Island Creek, crossing the same 26 miles crossing the forks of said Creek, thence by Charles Smiths whose house is in Guilford about thirty yards thence to the Virginia line to sundry white oak saplings about three quarters of a mile below Francis Holts on a small branch that runs into Crookit Creek, in all 22 miles one half a six pole."

A study of Guilford County Deed Book One calls attention to two ancient and antiquated customs and usages brought over from medieval England. The first of these customs is referred to as "Livery of seisin" or the act of delivering legal possesion of property. It was the appropriate ceremony at common law for transfering the corporal possessions of lands or tenements by a grantor to his grantee. It was 'livery in deed' where the parties went together upon the land, and there a twig or clod or other symbol was delivered in the name of the whole. If the property was a house in town, a key could be used as the symbol. In deeds this often referred to as "the livery of seisin by turf and twig." Where these references occurred in the original, tney have been omitted in these abstracts because they added no vital information.

The second antiquated custom was the use of "Lease and Release." This is a species of conveyance much used in England, said to have been invented by Serjeant Moore, soon after the enactment of the Statute of Uses in 1536. It is thus contrived. A lease for one year is made by the owner of the freehold. This, without any enrollment, makes the bargainor stand seized to the use of the bargainee, and vests in the bargainee the use of the term for one year, and then the statute immediately annexes the possession. Being thus in possession, he is capable of receiving a release of the freehold and reversion, which must be made to the tenant in possession, and accordingly the next day a release is granted to him. The lease and release, when used as a conveyance of the fee, have the joint operation of a single conveyance. The deed of release often contains a more detailed description of the property than the lease.

Because the microfilm copy of Deed Book 1 is almost illegible, these abstracts were prepared from the originals in the Register of Deeds' Office at the courthouse in Greensboro, North Carolina. The staff in the office is most courteous and cooperative. Anyone desiring xerox copies of pages from this or any other deed book can obtain copies for thirty-five cents each, plus postage, by writing to the Register of Deeds at the Courthouse in Greensboro.

The Public Register, in recording the deeds in Deed Book 1, found many deeds with names written in German script. While he tried to reproduce faithfully the script, the user should be aware that he was writing a script that was not native to him and in some instances erred in forming the various letters. Facsimiles of the names written in German script follow this introduction. An attempt has been made to reproduce the name in Roman letters where the name can be deciphered. Also included is the Anglicized version of the name, where it is known.

There is an excellent example in the names in German script to refute the idea that a man signing with a mark was illiterate. On page 354, Martin Stalley was a witness to a deed and signed his full name, John Martin Stalley, in German script. He was also a witness to the next deed that was recorded. In this deed, Stalley signed with a mark, "M".

In addition to deeds, there are several items of interest included in this deed book. On page 177, William Coltrane proved the dates of birth of his children mothered by his wife, Rachel Worthington. On page 321, Francis McNairy provided the record of his marriage and the dates of birth of his children. On page 468, James Hunter gave the rate of exchange for three foreign currencies. Doubloons were valued at six pounds, pistoles were valued at thirty shillings, and half jorgs were valued at three pounds four shillings.

"Your orator further sheweth, that during the late war, to wit, about the months of March or February Seventeen hundred and eighty one, the British Army, among the many Barbarous and wanton ravages commited in this County destroyed the greatest parts of the records of the said Court of Pleas and Quarter Sessions of the County of Guilford." Thus pleaded James McCollom in his suit against his brother concerning a lost will. [Salisbury District Superior Court Equity Enrolling Docket, p. 31.] On 23 September 1790, John McKibbons of Mecklenburg County testified, "During the ravages of the late war the records of the County of Guilford were in a great measure utterly destroyed by the enemy and the Books or Dockets containg the records relating to the trial herein before charged among others utterly lost and destroyed." [Salisbury District Superior Court Enrolling Docket, p. 49.]

Earlier, John Hamilton had testified, "The records of the said trials and the returns were destroyed with a large part of the records of the said Court of the County of Guilford by a detachment of the British Army during the late war." [Salisbury District Superior Court Enrolling Docket, p. 53.]

For historians and genealogists, the deeds of Guilford County serve an important function. Since the first ten years of the court minutes are missing, and since there are no extant tax lists for the county prior to 1815, the deeds supply proof of residence for many persons whose names do not appear else where. It is not unique that the deed book was saved. It was customary for the Public Register to maintain an office at a location other than the courthouse. In 1771 a bill was introduced in the General Assembly to require the Public Register to bring his books to the courthouse when the court was in session. The bill was rejected by the governor because it contained no provisiion requiring the Public Register to return the books to his office.

If the user is unable to find the name of interest in the deeds, marriage bonds, or wills, there is still one more place to search. Many years ago, the North Carolina State Archives felt it necessary to laminate a number of the General Assembly Papers. Where these papers needed to be folded, it was necessary to separate the document and re-attach the two pieces after lamination. Unfortunately, the names on some petitions were not properly identified and it was impossible to determine to which petition the names should be attached. In the loose General Assembly Papers for the 1773 Session there is a folder with a number of sheets of names from petitions. All the names in this folder are of people who resided in Guilford County.

NAMES IN GERMAN SCRIPT

P. 9	*David Lau*	David Lau - David Low
P. 23	*Conroth Stoehle*	Conrath Stoehle - Conrad Staley
P. 45	*Danl Lau*	Danl. Lau - David Low
P. 51	*Conrath Stehle*	Conrath Stehle - Conrad Staley
P. 51	*Jacob Gobl*	J[aco?]b Gobl - Jacob Goble
P. 83	*Johannes Haus*	Johannes Haus - John House
P. 84	*Conrath Stehle*	Conrath Stehle - Conrad Staley
P. 84	*Jonas Gobell*	Jonas Gobell - Jonas Gobel
P. 84	*Henry Glap*	[Henrich?] Glap - Henry Clap
P. 86	*Nicolaus Gobel*	Nicolaus Gobel - Nicholas Goble
P. 86	*Henry Glap*	[Henrich?] Glap - Henry Clap
P. 86	*Conrath Stehler*	Conrath Stehler - Conrad Staley
P. 91	*Hennrich Weitzel*	Hennrich Weitzel - Henry Whitsel
P. 142	*Niclans Kuntz*	Niclans Kuntz - Nicholas Countz
P. 201	*Conrath Stehle*	Conrath Stehle - Conrad Stally
P. 201	*[?]arin Stehle*	[?]arin Stehle - [Catherine?] Stally
P. 204	*Hennrich Weitzel*	Hennrich Weitzel - Henry Whitsel

P. 212 Bernhart Klab - Bernard [Barnabus] Clap

P. 213 Henderick Sig[?] - Henry Sigfret

P. 244 David Lau - David Low

P. 251 Jorg Vahlentin Klab
George Valentine Clap

P. 251 Bernhart Klab - Barnabus Clap

P. 253 Hennrich Weitzel - Henry Whitsel

P. 260 Hennrich Weitzel - Henry Whitsel

P. 260 Bernhart Klab - Barnabus Clap

P. 260 Saml. Klap - Saml. Clap

P. 271 Jacob Leyenberger - Jacob Lienbarger

P. 271 Jacob Griesohn - Jacob Gresson

P. 271 Frantz Leyenberger - Francis Lienbarger

P. 272 Jacob Leyenberger - Jacob Lienbarger

P. 272 Jacob Griesohn - Jacob Gresson

P. 272 Ger-g Leyenberger - George Lienbarger

P. 283 Michel ?itte - Michael Ricter

P. 353 George Schwartz - George Black

P. 353 Eid Nicklass Ammich
[Oath (of)] Nicholas Amy

P. 354 Michael Braun – Michael Brown
P. 354 Anna Magd. Braun – Anna Magd. Brown

P. 354 Johann Martin Stehle
        John Martin Stalley

P. 354 Johannes Notz – John Knotts

P. 355 Conrath Stehle – Conrad Staley

P. 357 Ludwig Klap – Ludwig Clap

P. 368 Lonhardt Meyers – Leonard Miner

P. 368 Henrich Lintenmann – Henry Linderman

P. 370 Johann Just Schafer – John Shepperd

P. 372 Johann Just Schafer – John Shepperd

P. 505 Re....achlin – ? ?

ABBREVIATIONS

Br.	Branch
ch.	chains
Cr.	Creek
E	east
lk.	links
N	north
p.	poles
R.	River
S	south
sd.	said
W	west

All other abbreviations in the abstracts are those to be found in the original record.

GUILFORD COUNTY
DEED BOOK ONE

P.1, 18 May 1771, William Wallace of Guilford to William Smith of same, sixty pounds, 413 acres, in Orange County on a branch of Reedy Fork of Haw R., half a tract made over by an original deed to Hugh Porter & conveyed from the orignial deed to Robert Gwinn & from him to Wallace & William Smith, begin at a red oak on Bazel Brashear's line, N 44 ch. to a red oak, E 94 ch. to a post oak, S 44 ch. to a gum, W 94 ch. with Basher's (sic) line to first station; signed: William Wallace; witness: Robert Gwinn, David Herrons, Samuel McIlroy; proved Augt. 1771 Term by Gwinn.

P. 3, 19 Aug. 1771, Robert Gwinn & wife Isbell and Rebekah Boyd admin. of estate of John Boyd of Rowan decd. widow of Guilford to George Rowland of same, Thomas Lovelatty sold Gwinn and Boyd (decd.) a tract on Haw River Guilford County and Gwinn & Boyd sold same to George Rowland for one hundred and thirty pounds and gave their bond to make a deed for same which has not been done, one hundred and eighty pounds, in possession of Rowland, on both sides North Fork of Haw R., begin at a white oak on W side of Kennedys Br., N across the North Fork 73 ch. to a black oak, W 80 ch. to a hicory sapling, S across the Fork 73 ch. to a white oak, E to first station, surveyed 9 October 1754, 584 acres; signed: Robert Gwinn, Isbell Gwinn, Rebekah (O) Boyd; witness: David ( ) Fulton, William Campbell; acknowledged August 1771 Term.

P. 6, 3 April 1771, William Stringfellow & wife Mary of Orange to David Low of same, three pounds, 3/4 acres, Lot # 15 in town layed out by Thomas Low, Thomas Low to Stringfellow 23 July 1770, David Low agrees to pay Thomas Low two shillings Sterling per year as quit rents; signed: Willm. Stringfellow, Mary (X) Stringfellow; witness: Peter Julian, Thomas Swift; proved August 1771 Term by Julian.

P. 7, 23 July 1770, Thomas Low & Lydia his wife of Orange to William Stringfellow of same, one pound ten shillings, 3/4 acres, Lot # 22 in town laid out by Thomas Lowe, part of a larger tract from Henry McCulloh to Low in Orange County on waters of Stinking Quarter Cr., Stringfellow to pay two shillings quit rents annually payments to begin 29 Aug. next; signed: Thos. Low (wife did not sign); witness: John Hawkins, Daolin Lau; proved Aug. 1771 Term by Lau.

P. 9, 3 Apr. 1771, William Stringfellow & wife Mary of Orange to David Low of same, five pounds, 3/4 acres, Lot # 22 in town laid out by Thomas Lowe, David Low to pay five shillings quit rents annually; signed: William Stringfellow, Mary (X) Stringfellow; witness: Peter Julian, Thomas Swift; proved August 1771 Term by

Julian.

P. 11, 29 September 1770, Samuel Brown, farmer, & Elizabeth his wife of Rowan to James Wilson, farmer, of same, sixty pounds, 300 acres, part of a 640 acres from Granville to Brown 22 August 1759 recorded in Book N:4 page 259, original tract described as in Parish of St. Luke in Rowan County lying on both sides of Buffillo adjoins Robert Thompson begin at a white oak & black oak, E 80 ch. to a hicory, N 80 ch. to a black oak, W 80 ch. to white oak, S 80 ch. to first station, tract sold begins at beginning cor. of original tract, E 126 perches to a post a cor. of another part of original tract now the property of John Kennedy, with same S 131 perches to a post, E 40.8 perches to a marked ash, by a line dividing this from the residue of sd. Samuel Brown's land N 189 perches to a post in the line of the original tract, with same W 106.8 perches to marked white oak, S 320 perches to beginning; signed: Samuel Brown, Elizabeth (E) Brown; witness: David Edwards, William Ramfield; proved by Ramfield August 1771 Term.

P. 14, 15 May 1770, John Bailles & wife Sarah of Rowan to Abraham Powel of same, twenty one pounds, 40 acres, in Rowan County, on waters of Powlcat [Polecat], begin at a hicory, N44E 119 p. to a stake, W 132 p. to a post oak, S4E 119 p. to beginning, part of tract Bailes lives on, laying to NW of Bailes; signed: John Beals, Sarah Beles; witness: John Powell, Wm. Millikan; proved August 1771 Term by Millikan.

P. 15, 2 March 1763, Robert Thompson of Rowan to William Patrick of same, thirty pounds, 360 acres, in Rowan on both sides Haw R. including mill & improvements made by John Davis, begin at a white oak standing on North Br. of Haw R., W 50 ch. to a W. oak, S 12 ch 25 lk crossing a branch to a hicory,, W 25 ch. to a B oak, S crossing river 40 ch. to a BO, E 33 ch. 50 lk. to a BO, S 15 ch. to a WO on N branch of the Mill, down creek N45E 39 ch. to a poplar by the mill pond, E 17 ch. 50 lk. to a BO, & WO to first station; signed: Robt. Thompson; witness: James M. Cayton Junr., Robert Rankin; proved August 1771 Term by Rankin.

P. 17, 22 day 6th month 1771, Thomas Jessop & Ann his wife of Guilford to Timothy Jessop of same, one hundred pounds, 198 acres, begin at a black oak saplin on E side of Horsepen Cr., W 320 p. to a chesnut, S 70 p. to a black oak saplin, E 101 p. to a white oak, S 40 p. to a hicory, E 40 p. to a white oak, S 12 p. to a sassafras, E 99 p. to a post, to first station; signed: Thomas Jessop, Ann Jessop; witness: Zach. Dicks, Rebekah Griffeth, William Jessop; proved August 1771 Term by Dicks.

P. 19, 22 day 6th month 1771, Thomas Jessop & wife Ann of Guilford to Joseph Jessop his son of same, one hundred pounds, 246 acres, whereon Joseph Jessop now lives, Thomas Hargrove to Thomas Jessop, [no description given]; signed: Thomas Jessop, Ann Jessop; witness: Zach. Dicks, Timothy Jessop, William Jessop; proved August 1771 Term by Dicks.

P. 20, 6 April 1771, Joseph Tate of Rowan to William Campbell of same, fifty pounds, 125 acres, on Dan R., begin on Dan R. bank at a spreading white oak near the Cross Rock Shoal, N 160 p. to a white oak on bank of Rocky Cr. near John Glenn's fence, E 156 p. to a gum on river bank, up river to beginning; signed: Joseph Tate; witness: Edward Hunter, Joseph Tate, Junr., John Hunter; acknowledged August 1771 Term.

P. 21, 26 July 1771, Martin Staley [Stealy] & Elizabeth his wife of Guilford to Jacob Stealy of same, farmer, eleven pounds, 40 acres, on waters of Stinking Quarter, part of tract to Staley from William Barten, part of a tract John Bartan to William Bartan, McCulloh to John Barton, original tract from McCulloh consisted of 1,000 acres, this part begins at a hicory saplin the third cor. tree of the original tract, W 82 p. to a branch, down branch N27W 90 p. to a marked ash, S80E 127 p. to original line, S on same to beginning; signed: Martin (M) Haley, Elizabeth (A) Haley; witness: Conzoyt Morgh, Riley Barnes; proved August 1771 Term by Morgh.

P. 23, 31 January 1771, Robert Doak to William Doak both of Rowan, twenty pounds, 320 acres, on a branch of Great Allamance, begin at a red oak, N 42 1/2 ch. to a white oak, W 37 1/2 ch. 15 lk. to a red oak saplin, S cross the main branch of the Allamance 42 1/2 ch. to a persimmon, E cross Allamance to first station; signed: Robert Doak; witness: Mes. Campbell, John Doak; proved August 1771 Term by John Doak.

P. 25, 10 August 1770, John Robinson of Rowan to William Robinson of same, one hundred pounds, 264 acres, on Reedy Fork, Granville to John Robyson, begin at a red oak, E 176 p. to a red oak, N 240 p. to a post oak, W 176 p., N 240 p. to first station; signed: John Robinson; witness: Joshua ( ) Edwards, George ( ) Rayl, Zacharias Dicks; acknowledged August 1771 Term.

P. 26, 15 August 1771, Henry Work to John Work, blacksmith, both of Guilford, one hundred and fifty pounds, 255 acres, on North Fork of Haw R., begin at a white oak on S side of Haw R., to the end of the original line, S to a red oak saplin, W to a red oak on the West line beyond Mistoney Rige [Ridge], five perches to a red oak, to a white oak on the river, along to the river to the beginning, Granville to William Curten 19 March 1755, Curtain to Henry Work; signed: Henry Work; witness: Robert Gwinn, John Corry; aclnowledged August 1771 Term.

P. 28, 14 August 1771, John Nilson & Levina his wife of Guilford to Francis Young of same, eighty five pounds, 125 acres, on East Fork of Jacobs Creek, begin at a black oak, E 50 ch. to a post oak, S 25 ch. to a hicory, W 50 ch. to a white oak, N 25 ch. to first station; signed: John Nilson, Levina Nilson; witness: [none listed]; acknowledged August 1771 Term.

P. 29, 3 March 1763, Robert Thomson & Latice his wife of Rowan to William Patrick of same, thirty pounds, 350 acres, on both sides of Haw R. including mill & improvements of John Davis, begin at a white on N bank of Haw R., W 50 ch. to a wt. oak, S 12 ch. 25

1k. crossing a branch to a hicory, W 25 ch. to a B. oak, S crossing river 40 ch. to a BO, E 33 ch. 50 1k. to a BO, S 15 ch. to a WO on N branch of Mill Cr., down creek N45E 34 ch. to a poplar by the Mill Pond, E 17 ch. 50 1k. to a BO & WO, to first station; signed: Robt. Thompson [no signature of wife]; witness: James McCuiston, Robert Rankin; proved August 1771 Term by Rankin.

P. 32, 20 October 1770, David Jackson & wife Elizabeth of Orange, blacksmith, to Levi McCollum of same, blacksmith, fifty pounds, 275 acres, on Sandy Cr., part of a tract from Granville to James Nicholson, Nicholson to John Athen Paulk, Paulk to Jesse Jackson, Jesse Jackson to David Jackson, begin at 3 marked hicory &s cor. of Herman Husband's land, E 76 ch., S 7 1/2 ch., W 103 ch. to a black jack oak, N 81 ch. to an oak, E 27 ch. to a white oak & black jack oak, S to original line to beginning; signed: David Jackson, Elizabeth Jackson; witness: Moses Hammond, Jabse (T) Jackson, Flower Swift; proved August 1771 Term by Swift.

P. 34, 15 March 1769, Herman Husband of Orange, farmer, to Conrad Staly of same, farmer, fifteen pounds, 450 acres, Granville to Husband 10 December 1762, begin at a hicory the beginning tree of the original survey, N 32 ch. to a post oak, W 25 ch. to a red oak, N 45 ch. to a hicory, W 48 chains to a red oak, S 14 1/4 ch. to William Hinshaw's cor., S along his line to a marked saplin, SE with Hinshaw's line to a marked white oak by a spring to the original line, E along original line to beginning; signed: Herman Husband, E[torn] Husband; witness: Jacob (+) Staly, Thomas (I) Green; proved August 1771 Term by Staley.

P. 35, 24 July 1771, Aaron Frazier & Sarah his wife of Guilford to Robert Green, one hundred twenty pounds, 301 acres, on SW side of Deep R. on Fraizers Fork, part of a larger tract from Granville to Fraizer 30 July 1760, begin at a white oak, E 46 ch. 20 1k. to a post a cor. between Nathaniel Kiser, N 65 ch. along a dividing line to a post, W 46 ch. 25 1k. to beginning; signed: Aaron Frazier, Sarah (S) Frazier; witness: William Draper, Edward Thornbrough, Absalom Tatum; proved August 1771 Term by Tatum.

P. 36, 15 October 1770, John Mills & wife Sarah of Rowan to Abraham Powell of same, fifty pounds, 100 acres, on waters of Powlcat [Polecat], begin at a black oak, E 96 p. to a post, S 75 p. to a post, S 75 p. to a post, W 187 p. to a post oak, N 150 p. to beginning, part of tract Mills lives on and lying to the W end; signed: John Mills, Sarah Mills; witness: John Powell, Wm. Millikan; proved August 1771 Term by Millikan.

P. 37, 14 May 1771, John Hunter of Guilford to George Jude of Cumberland County, Virginia, one hundred and fifty pounds, 500 acres, on both sides Dan R., begin at a white oak on S side of r., N320 p. to a maple, W 250 p. to a stake at pointers a double poplar, a black oak, & white oak, S crossing river to S line, down line 250 p. to beginning; signed: John Hunter; witness: Robert Boilstone, Joseph Tate Junr., Nathl. Hoggatt.

P. 38, Memorandum: That the within tract or parcel is a tract formerly sold to Nathl. Hoggatt for ywo hundred and fifty pounds which will & by the consent & desire of Nathaniel Hoggatt the sd. John Hunter hath received one hundred and fifty pounds from John Jude of Cumberland County, Virginia, & with consent of John Jude, John Hunter hath made a deed to George Jude & taken with sd. Hoggatt for the remainder of the above money; acknowledged; [no date].

P. 38, 17 August 1771, William Reynolds & Rachel his wife of Guilford or Rowan to William Field of same, five shillings Sterling, 209 acres, to Reynolds from Timothy Terril & Mary his wife of Orange now decd. 3 May 1753, on North Fork of Polecat Cr, begin at a white oak David Lewis' cor., N 78 p. to a hicory, W 240 p. to a post oak, S 120 p. to a black oak Jeremiah Reynolds Cr., E 60 p. to a stake, 80 p. to a stake, E by land of Jeremiah Reynolds & John Lewis 142 p. to fork of North Fork, up creek to first station; signed: William (M) Reynolds, Rachel Reynolds; witness: Will. Milliken, John Lewis; proved August 1771 Term by Lewis. [This is a lease, see release recorded on page 45.]

P. 40, 10 August 1767, William Trousdale of Orange & Ann his wife to David Allison of same, one hundred and ten pounds, 290 acres, in Rowan on waters of South Buffalo, joins Thomas Doneld & Thomas McQuiston, begin at a black oak, N 70 ch. to center between two white oaks, W 76 ch. to a black oak, S 36 ch. to a spanish oak, E 15 ch. to center between two black oaks McQuiston's cor., S along the same 32 ch. to a post oak, E to beginning; signed: William Trousdale, Agness (X) Trousdale; witness: [none listed]; acknowledged August 1771 Term.

P. 41, 13 October 1768, Isaac Jackson & Mary his wife of Orange, blacksmith, to David Jackson of same, blacksmith, fifty pounds, 275 acres, Granville to James Nicholson 22 December 1762 for 692 acres, Nicholson to Johnathan Paulk, Paulk to Isaac Jackson, begin for this part at three marked hicories the cor. of Harmon Husband's land, E 76 ch., S 7 1/2 ch., W 103 ch.to a B. J. O. a cor. of the original tract, N 81 ch. on original line to an oak, E 27 ch. to a WO & black jack oak, on original line to first station; signed: Isaac Jackson, Mary (M) Jackson; wit: Thomas Reece, William Aldredg, Jobe (S) Jackson; proved August 1771 Term by William Aldridge.

P. 43, 23 July 1770, Thomas Lowe of Orange and wife Lydia to William Stringfellow of same, one pound ten shillings, 3/4 acres, Lot # 15 in town laid out by Lowe, part of a larger tract from McCulloh to Thomas Lowe, on waters of Stinking Quarter Cr.; signed: Thom Lowe; wit.: John Hawkins, Danl. Lau; proved August 1771 Term by Daniel Lau.

P. 45, 18 May 1771, William Reynolds of Guilford (or Rowan), planter, & Rachel his wife to William Field of same, planter, two hundred pounds, & also five shillings Sterling, 209 acres, on waters of North Fork of Polecat Cr., part of 639 acres from Timothy Terrel & wife Mary 3 May 1755 & recorded in Orange County, land lies in Guilford (or Rowan) County on waters of North Fork of Polecat Cr., begin at a white oak standing by North Fork David Lewis' cor., N 78 p. to a hicory, W 240 p. to a post oak, S 120 p. to a black oak Jeremiah Reynolds' cor., E (by land of Jeremiah Reynolds & John Lewis) 142 p. to fork of North Fork, up creek to first station; signed: William (N) Raynolds, Rachel Raynols; wit.: Will: Millikan, John Lewis; proved August 1771 Term by Lewis.

P. 49, 26 July 1771, John Barton & Elisabeth his wife of Guilford, farmer, to Jacob Stealy of same, twenty two pounds ten shillings, 45 acres, on waters of Stinking Quarter Cr., part of a tract from Henry McCulloh 9 January 2nd year of George III [1762], for 1,000 acres, begin for this part on original E & W line in the branch 82 p. W from the third cor. hicory, down branch N27W 90 p. to a marked ash, S60W 157 p. to original E & W line, E on line 178 p. to beginning; signed: John Barton, Elizabeth Barton; wit.: Constext Brylo, Jumrb Jobl [names in German]; proved August 1771 Term by Brylo.

P. 51, 13 November 1771, Thomas Jessop & wife Ann of Guilford to John Hussey of same, one hundred pounds, 300 acres, on both sides of a branch of Deep River, a certain plantation or right of an improvement, adjoins Thomas Mills' line northward; signed: Thomas Jessup, Ann Jessup; wit.: Isaac White, Tomothy Jessup; proved November 1771 Term by Timothy Jessup.

P. 52, 16 July 1771, William Cox & Juliatha his wife of Guilford to John Pickrell of same, sixty one pounds, 100 acres, on E side of Deep R., Granville to Peter Youngblood 26 October 1759, Youngblood to Cox 8 May 1761, begin at mouth of Broad Mouth Cr., up creek to a white oak saplin notched on the E bank of the creek, E by a line of marked trees to a black jack & a stone at the original line of the tract, N 60 perches to a black oak, W 268 perches to a spanish oak by the river, down river to Broad Mouth Cr.; signed: William Cox, Juliathas Cox; wit.: Moses Hammond, Daniel Brown, Absolom ( ) Hanshato; proved November 1771 Term by Hammond.

P. 53, 11 November 1771, David Caldwell of Guilford to Alexander Caldwell of same, five shillings Sterling, 275 acres, begin at a white oak, W 75 ch. along Thornberry & Edwards line to a black oak, N 50 ch. to a black oak, E 40 ch. to a black oak, S 28 1/2 ch. to a post oak, E 35 ch. to Thomas McCuiston's line, S 21 1/2 ch. to beginning; signed: David Caldwell; witness: Jos. Kerr, Robert Cather (?); proved November 1771 Term by Kerr.

P. 55, 12 November 1771, David Caldwell of Guilford to Alexander Caldwell of same, forty two pounds, begin at a white oak, [this is the release for the lease described in the preceeding deed; signed: David Caldwell; wit.: Jos. Kerr, Robert Ceepy (?); proved November 1771 Term by Kerr.

P. 57, 7 October 1771, Robert Hudgins & Theodet [Theodate] his wife of Guilford, planter, to Sarah [Sarea] Duskins of Weak [sic]

County, eighty pounds, 140 acres, on Mill Cr. waters of Deep R., part of tract where Hudgins now lives, joins James Brown on E. & Cristofer Kersey on W, David Jenkins to Hudgens 26 January 1763, [no metes and bounds description]; signed: Robert Hodgen, Theodeat (H) Hodgen; witness: John Hussey, Thomas ( ) Habkns[?]; proved November 1771 Term by Hussey.

P. 58, 12 August 1771, Soloman Allred of Guilford & Mary his wife to John Lewis of same, planter, one hundred and twenty five pounds, 400 acres, on both sides the mouth of Sandy Cr., begin at a hicory by Deep R. on Hopkins line, his line N 30 ch. to his cor. black oak, N 25 ch. to a hicory, E cross Sandy Cr. 60 ch. to a white oak, S 80 ch. to a red oak, mulberry, & elm by Deep R., up river to beginning, Granville to Allred 1 August 1760, registered in Orange County Book F page 53 ; signed: Soloman (S) Allred, Mary (Me) Allred; witness: Isaac West, Jeremiah Reynolds; proved Novermber 1771 Term by West.

P. 61, 10 October 1770, John Owen & Ann his wife of Orange, farmer, to John Overby of same, one hundred pounds, 208 1/2 acres, on Sandy Cr., part of a tract from Granville to James Nicholson, Nicholson to John Owen, begin for this part at a persimon on the original line & cor. of John Lewis, E 35 ch. to a post oak, S 62 1/2 ch. to a stake, W 35 ch. to a stake, N to first station; signed: John Owens, Ann (A) Owens; witness: Henry Linderman [in German], Francis (F) York; proved November 1771 Term by Linderman.

P. 62, 5 November 1771, James Brown of Guilford, planter, to Robert Brown of same, forty pounds, 160 acres, on Mill Creek waters of Deep R., where James Brown now lives, Granville to David Jenkins 13 June 1762, Robert Hodges to Robert Brown, David Jenklins to Robert Hodges, begin at a black jack cor. on original line, N crossing a small run & creek 200 perches to a white oak cor. of Robert Hodgin, W along sd. line & cross creek twice 128 perches to a post by a small white oak, S cross Hodgin's land & twice crossing creek 200 perches to a small black oak, E along Hodgin's line to beginning; signed: James Brown; witness: John Hussey, Abreham Stroud; proved November 1771 Term by John Hussey.

P. 64, 12 8th month 1767, Zachariah Stanley of Rowan to John Mendenhall of same, sixty pounds, 233 acres, on Hicory Cr. waters of Deep R., begin at a hicory on John Osbun's line, N 55 ch. to a white oak, E crossing creek 42 1/2 ch. to a white oak, S 83 ch. to a hicory, W 5 ch. to Osburn's cor. white oak, his line W to a hicory, W 5 ch. to Osburn's cor. white oak, his line W to first station, Isaac Cox to Standley 6 April 1767; signed: Zachariah Stanley; witness: Moses Mendenhall, John Mendenhall; proved November 1771 Term by Moses Mendenhall.

P. 66, 8 November 1771, Thomas Cox & Sarah his wife of Guilford to Moses Hammond of same, twenty pounds, 50 acres, on W side Deep R., part of a tract willed by William Cox Senr. to Thomas Cox, begin at original line at a black oak, W 150 perches, N 54 perches to a stone, 150 perches to a hicory, S 54 perches along original line to first station, Granville to William Cox 13 May 1755; signed: Thomas Cox, Sarah Cox; witness: John Pickrell, William Moffet, Joseph Brown; proved November 1771 Term [jurat name not given].

P. 67, 15 July 1771, William Patrick of Guilford to William Mackey of Philadelphia, Pennsylvania, two hundred pounds, 350 acres, in possession of Mackey, on both sides of Haw R., includes mills & improvements made by John Davis, begin at a white oak on N bank of Haw R., W 50 ch. to a white oak, S 12 ch. 25 lk. crossing a branch to a hicory, W 25 ch. to a black oak, S crossing r. 40 ch. to a black oak, E 33 ch. 50 lk. to a black oak, S 15 ch. to a white oak on N branch of Mill Cr., down creek as it may appear in Robert Tompkins original deed; signed: William Patrick; witness: Sam Buchanan, John Work; proved November 1771 Term by Work.

P. 70, 4 8th month 1767, Zachariah Standley of Rowan to John Mendenhall of same, one hundred pounds, 214 1/2 acres, below mouth of Long Br. on North Fork of Deep R., begin at a hicory Anthony Nogget's W cor. & beginning of the wole [whole] tract, S along line of whole tract 139 1/2 perches to 2 black oaks, E 246 perches to a post on the line, N 139 1/2 perches to a post, W 246 perches to beginning, Robert Lamb to Zachariah Stanley 5 5th month 1764; signed: Zachariah Stanley; witness: Moses Mendenhall, John Mendenhall Junr.; proved November 1771 Term by Moses Mendenhall.

P. 72, 28 October 1771, John Stubbs of Wrightsboro Twp. St. Pauls Parish, Georgia, to Enoch Davis of Orange, sixty pounds, 350 acres, in Guilford, on both sides East Fork of Brush Cr. waters of Deep R., near Crafords path that goes to Pee Dee, begin at 3 black oaks on head of a bottom, S 70 ch. to a red oakk, W 50 ch. to a white oak, N ch. to a black oak, E 50 ch. to first station, Granville to Stubbs 6 November 1756; signed: John Stubbs, Esther Stubbs; witness: Joseph Maddock, Joel Cloud; relinquishment of dower by Esther Stubbs acknowledged before Joseph Maddock, J. P.; proved November 1771 Term by Cloud.

P. 74, 5 January 1771, Joseph Tate Senr. of Orange to Robert Ralstone Junr., love & affection for my son-in-law, 650 acres, both sides of Jacobs Cr. waters of Dan R., begin at a post oak, W 65 ch. to a black oak, N 100 ch. to a black oak, E 65 ch. to a poplar, to beginning; signed: Joseph Tate; witness: Edward Hunter, George Peay, Isham Browder, Phil Deatherage; proved February 1772 Term by Hunter.

P. 75, 20 August 1771, John Crabtree Senr. of Guilford to John Crabtree Junr. of same, twenty pounds, 100 acres, on E side of Sandy Cr., begin at Sandy Cr. on John Crabtree Senr.'s original line, E along line to cor. white oak saplin 34 1/2 ch., N along original line 30 ch. to a post oak, E along original line 6 1/2 ch. to a stake with stones about it, N along original line 14 1/2 ch. to a beach on bank of creek, down Sandy Cr. to first station, Granville to Edward Welborn 3 June 1762, Welborn to Crabtree;

signed: John (I) Crabtree; witness: Semore York, Jeremiah York; proved February 1772 Term by Semore York.

P. 76, 11 February 1772, John McDaniel Senr. of Guilford to John McDaniel Junr. of same, for love good will and affection for son and five shillings, 320 acres, on South Buffalo Cr., begin at a white oak on N side of creek on SW cor. of land belonging to McDaniel Senr., N 80 ch. to a stake, E to the creek, along creek to beginning, part of tract from Granville to John McDaniel Senr. 1 December 1761, registered in Rowan Book 4, page 816; signed: John McDaniel; witness: Jno. Campbell, John Butler; acknowledged February 1772 Term. [Ed. note: Deed from Granville to McDaniel recorded as Daniel to McDonald.]

P. 78, 1 January 1772, Nathaniel Kerr of Guilford, tanner, to Edward Sharp of same, farmer, five shillings, 301 acres, in Parish of St. Luke county of Guilford, on Fraziers Fork, begin at a white oak, W 25 ch. to a hicory, S 27 ch. to a white oak, 18 ch. 75 lk. to a post, S 65 ch. to a post, E 43 ch. 75 lk. to a white oak, N cross Fraziers Fork 72 ch. to beginning, Granville to Aaron Frazier 13 July 1760; signed: Nathaniel Kerr; witness: John McGee, John Collier; proved February 1772 Term by McGee.

P. 79, 1 January 1772, Nathaniel Kerr of Guilford, tanner, to Edward Sharp of same, farmer, two hundred pounds, [release of preceding lease, same signature, witnesses, and probate].

P. 81, 7 September 11th year of George III [1771], John Creson & Hannah his wife of Guilford to Christian Fouse of Orange, one hundred and seven pounds, 200 acres, on Great Allamance Cr. part of a large tract belonging to Henry Eustace McCulloh called No. 11, on branches of Haw R., Henry Eustace McCulloh to John Creson 10 September 1760, begin at a red oak on Great Allamance Cr., N45W 160 p. to a red oak, N45E 200 p. to a stake, S45E 68 p. crossing Alamance in all 160 p. to a stake, S45W 180 p. crossing Allamance in all 200 p. to beginning; signed: [John Creson in German], Hanah (H) Greson; witness: John Hawkins, [John House in German]; proved February 1772 Term by House.

P. 83, 8 February 1772, Anthony Goble & Mary his wife of Guilford to Nicholas Goble of same, forty three pounds, 194 acres, on waters of Stinkinfg Quarter, Henry McCulloh to Andrew Rudolph 8 June 3rd year of George III [1763], Rudolph to Coble, begiun at a black oak the 3rd cor. of original tract, N45W 22 p. to a cor. hicory, S45W 220 p. to a black oak, N 32 p., N45W 76 p., S 92 p., E 48 p., S till it intersects a line of marked trees between him & John Coble, E along line of trees to original N & S line, N to beginning; signed: Anthony (A) Goble, Mary (X) Goble; witness: [two witnesses sign in German]; proved February 1772 Term by Conran Staley.

P. 85, 8 February 1772, Anthony Coble & wife Mary of Guilford, farmer, to John Coble of same, farmer, forty three pounds, 194 acres, on waters of Stinking Quarter Cr., part of a tract from McCulloh to Andrew Rudolph 8 June 3rd year of George III [1763],

Rudolph to Anthony Coble, begin at the first bewginning white oak, N 188 p. to a line of marked trees, W along line of trees to the original line, S to beginning; signed: Anthony (A) Coble, Mary (M) Coble; witness: [two witness signed in German]; proved February 1772 Term by [in German].

P. 86, 31 August 1771, Roger Murphy of Guilford, farmer, & Mary his wife to Peter Mock of same, fifty pounds, 200 acres, on a branch of Sandy Cr., part of tract from Granville to Harmon Husband 5 August 1758 for 644 acres, called the Level, begin at original NE cor., S 184 p. to a marked black oak, W 174 p. to a stake, N 184 p. to a stake, E to beginning; signed: Roger Murphy, Mary (O) Murphy; witness: William Ward, Samuel Owings; proved February 1772 Term by Ward.

P. 87, 31 January 1772, William Carlin of Guilford, farmer, to William Hindman of same, cooper, fourteen pounds, on S side of North Buffalo, on which I at present live, opposite land of Adam Mitchell, [no metes and bounds description]; signed: William Carlon; witness: Thos. Black, Samuel Hindman; proved February 1772 Term by Samuel Hindman.

P. 88, 15 January 1772, William Mackey, yeoman, of Guilford to Mary Patrick, two hundred pounds, 550 acres, Granville to Robert Thomson 2 August 1760, Thomson to William Patrick 2 March 1763, Patrick to Mackey 15 July 1771, on both sides of Haw R., begin at a white oak on the North bank of Haw R., W 50 ch. to a white oak, S 12 ch. 25 lk. S cross branch to a hicory, W 25 ch. to a black oak, S cross river 40 ch. to a black oak, E 33 ch. 50 lk. to a black oak, S 15 ch. to a white oak on N bank of Mill Cr., down creek NE 34 ch. to a poplar by the Mill Pond, E 17 ch. 50 lk. to a black oak & white oak, to first station; signed: William Mackey; witness: Henry Work, Sam Buchanan, Thomas Willson; proved February 1772 Term by Henry Work.

P. 90, 25 December 1771, Ralph Gorrell of Guilford, storekeeper, to Martin Boon of same, planter, one hundred and sixty pounds, 251 acres, begin at Christian Funkhowser's cor. stone, his line N65E cross Cedar Cr. 205 p. to a stake, S45E 207 p. to a Lodiwick Isely's cor., his line S45W 180 p. his other cor. in all 200 p. to a stake a cor. of a small tract called number 38 of the McCulloch tracts, along line of same crossing Cedar Cr. N45W 256 p. to beginning; signed: Ralph Gorrell, Mary (M) Gorrell; witness: none listed; acknowledged February 1772 Term.

P. 92, 5 March 1770, Joseph Hinds & Susannah Hinds of Rowan to Simon Hinds of same, five pounds, 30 acres, on a branch of Polecat Cr, quit claim deed, begin at a white oak on the Old Trading Path, W cross the Trading Path 24 ch., S to a branch of Polecat Cr., up branch to mouth of a small branch coming from the E up large branch 6 1/2 ch., easterly a straight line to beginning; signed: Joseph Hinds, Susannah (X) Hinds; witness: William Norton, John Wood; proved February 1772 Term by John Wood.

P. 93, 10 December 1771, William Cox late of Guilford & Isaac Cox of Guilford Executors of William Cox decd., farmer, to John Cox [no county given], fourty five pounds, 240 acres, on both sides Cox Mill Cr., begin at a hock stone it being a cor. Phebe Allen's tract, S 240 p. till it crosses the original south line, W 158 p. to the original cor. black oak, N 240 p. to the original cor. hicory, E 158 p. to beginning, one half of a tract from Granville to William McFarson, McFarson to Joshua Gregg, Gregg to William Cox; signed: William Cox, Isaac Cox; witness: John Allen, Isaac Cox Junr.; proved [term not given] by John Allen.

P. 94, 14 November 1771, John Overby of Guilford, planter, to Jacob Little of same, fifty pounds, 11 1/2 acres, on Sandy Cr., Granville to James Nicholson, Nicholson to John Owen, Owen to Overby, begin at a post oak, S 120 p. to a WO, W 140 p. to a post oak, S 34 p. to creek, up creek E5N 23 p. to a white oak, N to ye 2nd line; signed: John Overby; witness: Daniel ( ) McDaniel, Thos. Hill, [another name in German]; proved February 1772 Term by McDaniel.

P. 96, 22 March 1772, John Reagan & Mary his wife to John & Samuel Henderson [no county given for either], one hundred and fifty pounds, 200 acres, on S side of Dann R., begin at a haw tree on river, up river 180 p. to an ash at mouth of a gut below the Lone Island Ford, S 240 p. by a new dividing line between Reagan & George Oliver to Oliver's beach, E 180 p. to a post oak, N 240 p. to beginning; signed: John Reagan, Mary H. Reagan; witness: Thos. Henderson, Alexander McClaran; acknowledged and Mary Reagan examined 23 March 1772.

P. 97, 14 March 1772, Joseph Buffington of Guilford, iron master, to John Phifer of Mecklenburgh, five hundred and eleven pounds, premises, blumery & iron works now erected & built on Big Troublesome with all lands sold by John Nicks to Buffington, also all mine & ore that is opened or to be opened or may be operated for the business of the iron works together with the Mine Hill which is conveyed by Henry Work to Buffington adjoining Works' line whereon he now lives, also one horse, two cows, 4 feather beds, 28 blankets, 12 sheets, 4 rugs, a case of drawers, 3 chests of drawers, 12 chairs & tables, & all other household furniture with the carts, sadles, tools and all other implements of husbandry on the premises or unto me belonging which are remaining or being in John Phifer's possession; signed: Joseph Buffington; witness: John Lewis Beard, Martin Phifer, Paul Barringer; proved 14 March 1772 before Richard Henderson by Beard

P. 99, 29 February 1772, William Millikan & Jane his wife of Guilford to Robert Grey of same, one hundred pounds, twenty five pounds in hand paid, 168 acres, lying on a ridge between the waters of Deep R. & Carraway, joins William Thornborough, begin at a black oak, N 29 ch. to a post oak on Thornborough's line, along his line W 58 ch. to a white oak Thornborough's cor., S along Samuel Millikan's line 29 ch., 58 ch. to the beginning; signed: William Millikan, Jane Millikan; witness: Saml. Millikan, Edward Sharp; proved May 1772 Term by Sharp.

P. 100, 12 May 1772, Mordicai Mendenhall of Guilford, planter, & Charity his wife to Stephen Mendenhall of same, planter, twenty shillings, 200 acres, land in possession of Stephen Mendenhall, begin at a red oak saplin, S20E 136 p. to a hicory, N70E 282 p. to a red oak, N20W 186 p. to a hicory, N70E 282 p. to first station, part of a tract from Granville to Thomas Ridge 25 March 1752; signed: Mordicai Mendenhall, Charity Mendenhall; witness: Jno. Odeneal, Sam. Martin; acknowledged May 1772 Term.

P. 103, 12 May 1772, Mordicai Mendenhall & Charity his wife of Guilford, planter, to Stephen Mendenhall of same, planter, five shillings, 200 acres, [this and preceding deed are a lease & release of same tract].

P. 105, 12 May 1772, William Kennedy of Guilford, farmer, to Samuel Kennedy, for love goodwill and affection toward my son, 300 acres, one half of the plantation where I now live, N 50 ch., W 60 ch. S 50 ch., E 60 ch. to first station, formerly Jas. McGown's place, known by name of Kennedy Cr., one half the plantation, William Kennedy and Judith his wife to have their maintenace of the whole of the plantation during their life; signed: William (+) Kennedy; witness: James Buchanan, Henry Read; acknowledged May 1772 Term.

P. 106, 12 May 1772, William Kennedy of Guilford, farmer, to William Kennedy Junr. of same, for love goodwill & affection to my son, 300 acres, one half the plantation he now posses, N 50 ch., W 60 ch., S 50 ch., E 60 ch. to first station, known by name of Kennedys Cr., Willm. & Judith Kennedy his wife to have their maintenance of the whole during life; signed: William Kennedy; witness: James Duff, William Russell; acknowledged May 1772 Term.

P. 107, 18 September 1770, John Fruit of Orange, farmer, to John Husband son of Herman Husband of same, 200 pounds, 434 acres, in Orange County, on Sandy Cr., from Granville 13 May 1757 for 634 acres, begin at a clift of Rocks the beginning of the original survey, S 42 ch. to a black oak, E 100ch. to William Ward's line, N 42 ch., W 100 ch. to first station; signed: John Fruit; witness: James Pugh, Samuel Frazier, George Lewis; proved May 1772 Term by Pugh.

P. 108, 18 September 1770, John Fruit of Orange, farmer, to William Husband his cousin & son of Hermon Husband of same, two hundred pounds paid by Thomas Pugh grandfather of William Husband, and for natural love & affection for William, and for better maintenance & livelihood of William Husband, 640 acres, on Sandy Cr., Granville to Herman Husband 14 November 1755, begin at original beginning white oak, W 20 ch. 25 lk. to ahicory, N 38 ch. 50 lk. to a hicory, white oak, & black oak, E 29 ch. 25 lk. to a stake, S 95 ch. 50 lk. to a stake, W 59 ch. to 2 white oaks & a hicory, N cross Sandy Cr. 6 times to first station; signed: John Fruit; witness: James Few, James Pugh, George Lewis, Samuel Frazier; proved May 1772 Term by James Pugh.

P. 110, 13 May 1772, Thomas Donneal of Guilford to John Donneal of same, fifty pounds, 347 acres, begin at a hicory on North Buffalo, E crossing creek 3 times 47 ch. to a post oak, N 47 ch. to a hicory, W 20 ch. to a post, N 47 ch. to a post, W 27 ch. to a post, S 94 ch. to beginning; signed: Thos. Donnel; witness: William Spruiel [or Shruiel], Jas. McCuiston; acknowledged May 1772 Term.

P. 112, 8 May 1772, Daniel McCollum of Guilford to John Odeneal of same, fifty four pounds, 60 acres, on S side of Hogans Cr., begin at an oak on the creek, E 207 p. to a white oak, N 14 p. to Orange Courthouse Old Road, along road to creek, up creek to beginning, part of a tract from Willm. Wymie [?] to Daniel McCullom; signed: Danel (X) McCullom; witness: none listed; acknowledged May 1772 Term.

P. 113, 3 April 1770, Samuel Parks of Orange to Benjamin Ellis of same, twenty five pounds, 50 acres, on W side of Hogans Cr., begin at a red oak on the creek, W 106 p. to a red oak on Parkes' W line, S 104 p. to a spanish oak on the creek, down creek to beginning, part of tract Parkes bought of Benajah King the upper end; signed: Samuel Parks; witness: Jno. Odeneal, Natt Harken; proved May 1772 Term by Odeneal.

P. 115, 9 February 1772, William Millikan & Jane his wife of Guilford to Robert Gray, of same, one hundred pounds, seventy five pounds in hand paid, 252 acres, on the ridge between waters of Deep R. & Carraway, begin at a post oak, N 61 ch. to a post oak, E 50 ch. to a post Samuel Millikan's cor., his line S14 67 ch. to a post, W81 58 ch. along his line to a post, S45 86 ch. along Samuel Millikan's line , W 41 ch. to beginning; signed: William Millikan, Jane Millikan; witness: Samuel Millikan, Edward Sharp; proved May 1772 Term by Sharp.

P. 116, 8 May 1772, Samuel Lowe of Guilford to Edward Moore Junr. of Anson, one hundred pounds, 250 acres, on waters of Carraway, on E side, part of a larger tract from Granville to Lowe 27 August 1762, begin at a post oak to the E of Grogin's improvement, W 45 ch. 46 lk. to a red oak, S 55 ch. to small post oak, E 45 ch 46 lk. to a black jack, S 55 ch. to beginning; signed: Samuel Lowe, Tabitha (X) Lowe; witness: William Millikan, Ab. Tatom; proved May 1772 Term by Tatom.

P. 118, 20 October 1771, William Savage of Guilford to Samuel Watt of same, forty one pounds, 103 acres, on S side of Pine Br. & Cabin Br., begin at a small hicory on Pyney Br., S 57 p. to a white oak, E 200 p. to another white oak, N 20 p. to a small burch saplin on Cabbin Br., N80W 220 p. to beginning; signed: William Savage, Elizabeth Savage; witness: John Long, Charles Lashley, Thomson (+) Noris, Jeremiah Farguson; acknowledged May 1772 Term.

P. 119, 12 March 1772, James Mathews of Guilford to James Duff of same, one hundred pounds, 307 acres, on both sides of South Buffalo, begin at a white oak Hall's cor., his line N 20 ch. to a hicory, W 26 ch. to a black oak, S 43 1/2 ch. to a black oak on

John McAdoo's line, his line E 5 ch. 25 lk. to a white oak saplin, his line S 36 ch. 50 lk. to a hicory, E 39 ch. to a post oak saplin, N 60 ch. to a black oak on Watt's line, his line to the beginning; signed: James Matthews, Mary (M) Matthews; witness: Ralph Gorrell, Daniel Gillespie; proved May 1772 Term by Ralph Gorrell Esq.

P. 121, 21 December 1770, Robert Meteer of Orange, farmer, to Robert Gwin, John Robertson, & Thomas Flack of same, Trustees of the Presbyterian Congregation belonging to the United Synod of New York & Philadelphia Adopting the Discipline of the Church of Scotland as far as the circumstances of that Church being an Establishedment & this will agree, five pounds, 2 acres, on S side Haw R., begin at N cor. of the Meeting House at a black oak, S 17 perches to a black oak, 41 perches to the spring, E 1 perche, N 41 perches to a stake, E 15 perches to a post oak, N 17 perches to a hicory, W 16 perches to beginning; signed: Robert Mateer; witness: James Nesbitt, William Denny, John Coory; acknowledged May 1772 Term.

P. 123, 11 May 1772, John Mullins of Guilford to Thomas Mullins of same, ten pounds, 140 acres, on the Lick Fork of Hogans Cr., begin at a red oak on S side of creek, 140 p. crossing creek to a white oak, E 29 p. to a white oak, N 86 p. to a red oak, S40E 266 p. to a white oak, S 44 p. to a red oak bush, W 140 p. to beginning, Granville to Mullins 6 December 1761; signed: John Mullins; witness: William Chambers Senr., William Odell; acknowledged May 1772 Term.

P. 124, 2 May 1772, John Mullins of Guilford to William Chambers of same, forty five pounds, 140 acres, on both side of Lick Fork of Hogans Cr., begin at a red oak in Mullin's line, W 30 ch. to a post oak, S 35 ch. across creek to a white oak, E 49 ch. to a red oak on a branch, down branch N25W 35 ch. to creek, N25W to first station, part of a larger tract from Granville to Mullins 6 December 1761; signed: John Mullin; witness: Thomas (+) Tilswort, Jonathon Williams; acknowledged May 1772 Term.

P. 125, 13 September 1771, William Chambers of Guilford to Thomas Titsworth of same, thirty two pounds, 141 acres, on both sides of Lick Fork of Hogans Cr., begin at a white oak on bank of creek, W 72 p. to a hicory, S 200 p. cross creek to a red oak, E 120 p. to pointers, N 143 p. to a poplar, N37W to a beach on bank of creek, down creek to beginning, John Lea to Chambers 26 February 1767; signed: Willm. Chambers; witness: Patrick ( ) Mullins, Abraham Cantrell; acknowledged May 1772 Term.

P. 126, 30 November 1771, Robert Mitchel & Margaret his wife of Guilford to John Foster of same, five pounds, 50 acres, on waters of Horsepen Cr., begin at a black oak on Foster's N line, S 45 ch. to a black oak, E 45 ch. to a black oak, N 45 ch. to a black oak, W 45 ch. to first station; signed Robert Mitchel, Margaret (+) Mitchel; witness: Jno. Campbell, David Walker; proved May 1772 Term by Campbell. "Be it remembered that the measure of chains as mentioned above are only half chains that is to say 33 feet to the chain instead of 66 ft."

P. 127, 10 April 1772, John Lewis & Priscilla his wife of Guilford, farmer, to Josiah Lamb of same, forty five pounds, 96 acres 53 poles, begin at the North Fork on Beniamin Beeson's line, N with line 19 p. to Beeson's cor., W 132 p. to a stake in Beeson's line, N 75 p. 9 ft. to a black oak, E 252 p. to a spanish oak by the creek, down creek to first station, part of 291 acres from Thomas Lamb & Sarah his wife to John Lewis & Hercules Ogls 21 March 1765, Ogle & wife Mary to Lewis 5 July 1766, registered in Rowan; signed: John Lewis, Priscilla Lewis; witness: Thomas Wilson, Thomas Lamb; proved May 1772 Term by affirmation of Wilson.

P. 129, 12 May 1772, Jeremiah Reynolds of Guilford, farmer, & Susanna his wife to William Field of same, farmer, ten pounds, 15 acres on waters of North Fork of Polecat, begin at a small hicory Reynold's cor., N by land of Fields 40 p. to a stake, W by sd. land 60 p. to a black oak, S 40 p. to a stake, E to first station, part of 200 acres from William Reynolds & wife Rachel to Jeremiah Reynolds 27 August 1753, registered in Rowan; signed: Jeremiah Reynolds, Susanna Reynolds; witness: John Lewis, Joseph Field; proved May 1772 Term by Field.

P. 130, 12 February 1772, William Wiley of Guilford to Thomas Cummings of same, one hundred pounds, 250 acres, in Guilford formerly Orange, begin at a black jack [torn], W 49 p. to a white oak, S45W 236 p. to a black jack, S45E 144 p. to Nicholas Puntricks [Patricks ?] cor. a stone, N65E 140 p. crossing Cedar Cr. in all 240 p. to beginning, part of a larger tract from McCulloh to Christian Funkhousen; signed: William Wiley, Mary (X) Wyley; witness: Arthur Forbis, John Smith; proved February 1772 Term by Smith.

P. 132, 18 August 1772, Thomas Morgan of Guilford, constable, to David Russell of same, thirteen pounds, acres unknown, to satisfy lien of Ralph Gorrel against John Hannon for four pounds sixteen shillings, land and improvements sold; signed: Thos. Morgan; witness: William Flemming; acknowledged before Thos. Henderson, CC [no date of probate].

P. 134, 11 August 1772, Thomas Thornburgh of Guilford to Joseph Thornburgh of same, eighty pounds, 100 acres, joins Brush Cr. waters of Haw R., begin at a sweet gum nigh creek, E 157 rods to a stake, N 112 rods to a stake, W 117 rods to a stake adjoining creek, along creek to first station, part of a tract from Granville to Thornburgh 1761; signed: Thos. Thornburgh; witness: Enoch Macy, Zachr. Dicks, David Macy; acknowledged before Thos. Henderson CC [no date of probate].

P. 136, 11 August 1772, Thomas Thornburgh Senr. of Guilford to James Thornburgh of same, eighty pounds, 100 acres, joins Brush Cr. waters of Haw R., begin at a sweet gum nigh creek, E 22 rods to a black oak, S45E 30 rods to a black oak, E 167 rods to a post oak, N 100 rods to a stake, W 167 rods to a sweet gum by creek, by creek to first station, part of a tract from Granville to

Thornburgh 1761; signed: Thos. Thornburgh; witness: Enoch Macy, Zach. Dicks, David Macy; acknowledged before Thos. Henderson CC [no date of probate].

P. 138, 29 July 1772, Zacharias Dicks of Guilford to David Macky [no county given], forty pounds, 46 acres, part of a tract willed to Zacharias Dicks by his brother Nathan Dicks, NW part of a tract from Granville to Mordicai Mendenhall recorded in Rowan County, begin at a large white oak on Zacharias Dicks' & David Macy's E & W line, N70E 76 rods to a large white oak to the Little Br. being the line between Zacharias Dicks & heirs of Nathan Dicks, up a straight fork of the branch until it intersects with line of the whole at a white oak saplin, W to cor. post oak, to beginning; signed: Zacharias Dicks; witness: Enoch Macy, Anna Macy, Abijah Macy; acknowledgwed before Thos. Henderson CC [no date of probate].

P. 139, 12 March 1772, John Nix of Guilford to James Denny of same, five shillings Sterling, 230 acres, on N side of Buffalo, begin at a white oak on Robert Donnel's line, N 15 ch. to a black oak, W 30 ch. to a hicory, N 22 ch. to a white oak, S70W 41 3/4 ch. to a black jack, S67W 18 ch. to a white oak, S81W 104 ch. to a black oak, S73W 7 1/2 ch. to a white oak, S76W 19 1/2 ch. to a stake, S 11 ch. to William Anderson's line, E his line to first station; signed: John (J) Nix; witness: Jno. Anderson, Wm. Anderson; proved by John Anderson [no date of probate].

P. 141, 7 August 1772, William Ingleson of Guilford, planter, & Sarah his wife to Simor York of same, thirty six pounds seven shillings, 120 acres, part of a tract on Sandy Cr., begin at the N cor. of Simor York's land at a white oak, S 40 ch. to a black oak, W 30 ch. to center between a white oak & black oak, N 40 ch. to a black oak, E 30 ch. to first station, part of a tract from Granville to York 5 August 1758, York to Ingleson 20 January 1759; signed: William (X) Ingleson, Sara (!) Ingleson; witness: John McGee, Peter Julian, Junr.; proved by John Gee [no probate date given].

P. 142, 7 March 1772, Nicholas Cuntz & Mary his wife of Guilford to Thos. McCollok of Orange, tanner, ninety five pounds, 250 acres, in counties of Guilford & Orange, mostly in Guilford, on Stinking Quarter Cr., part of a Tract No. 11 from McCulloh to Cuntz 14 September in second year of George III, begin at a white oak between 2 rocks on a hill, N45W at 54 p. crossing Stinking Quarter in all 200 p. to a stake on a hill, N45E 90 p. to the Spring Br. in all 200 p. to a black jack grub, S45E at 130 p. crossing creek in all 200 p. to a stake between 2 white oaks, S45W 200 p. to beginning; signed: Nicholas Cuntz [in German], Mary (_) Cuntz; witness: Lancelot Johnston, James McCarroll; proved by James McCarrel [no date of probate].

P. 144, 16 March 1772, Richard Right of Guilford, farmer, & Ann his wife to Robert Field of same, farmer, sixty seven pounds ten shillings, 218 acres, on a branch of Sandy Cr., part of a tract from Granville to Harman Husband 29 July 1764 [?] for 641 acres, begin at a red oak the south-easternmost cor. of the original tract, N 134 p. to a hicory, the NE original cor., W 274 p. to a marked hicory on the original line & on Nathan Maddocks line, S on Maddock's line 92 p. to an ash by Sandy Cr., E 40 p. to a maple in a branch, S 42 p. to the original line, to beginning; signed: Richard Right, Ann (A) Right; witness: John McGee, Joseph Field; proved by Joseph Field [no date of probate].

P. 146, 13 March 1772, John Nix & Margaret his wife of Guilford, planter, to James Denny of same, planter, one hundred pounds, 230 acres, on N side of North Buffalo, begin at a white oak on Robert Donnel's line, N his line 15 ch. to a black oak, W 30 ch. to a hicory, N 22 ch. to a white oak, S70W 41 3/4 ch. to a black jack, S67W 18 ch. to a white oak, 81W 10 1/4 ch. to a black oak, S73W 7 1/2 ch. to a white oak, S76W 9 1/2 ch. to a post, S 11 ch. to William Anderson's line, E his line to first station; signed: John Nix, Margaret (_) Nix; witness: Jno. Anderson, William Anderson; proved by John Anderson [no probate date].

P. 149, 29 May 1772, William Garrott & Sarah his wife of Guilford to Lawrence Bankston of same, sixty two pounds, 134 acres, on N side of Wolf Island Cr., begin at a white oak on Mill Cr. the west side, W 52 ch. crossing the North Fork called Thrashers Fork to a chesnut tree, S 45 ch. to a white oak saplin, E to South Fork of Wolf Island Cr., down creek to the old N line, N to beginning; signed: William (+) Garrott, Sarah (R) Garrot; witness: Isham Browder, Sampson Bell, Tabitha Browder; proved by Isham Browder [no probate date].

P. 151, 28 June 1772, Henry Linterman of Guilford, farmer, & Margaret his wife to Lenard Mier of same, farmer, thirty one pounds, 300 acres, on waters of Rocky R., part of a tract from Granville to Moses Nelson 28 June 1762, Nelson to Linterman 11 September 1767, begin at a marked white oak on the original N & S line 18 p. S from the original cor., S along line 289 p. to the original cor. black oak, W 45 ch. to a stake, N 40 ch. to cor. of original survey, N on original line 129 p., E 45 ch. to first station; signed: [Henry Linterman in German], Margaret (+) Linterman; witness: John McGee, William Harris; proved by McGee [no probate date].

P. 153, 5 August 1772, Simon Taylor Sr. of Guilford to David Macy of same, seventy five pounds, 150 acres, William Perry to Taylor 1764, on Reedy Fork a branch of Haw R., begin at at a stake in the bottom of Bever Cr. being a branch of Ready Fork, E 83 rods to a black oak, S 288 rods to a white oak saplin, W 83 rods to a stake, N 288 rods to the beginning, part of tract from Granville to Perry 1759; signed: Simeon Taylor; witness: Zachr. Dicks, Enoch Davis, Thomas Taylor; proved by Dicks [no probate date].

P. 155, 11 January 1772, Thomas Jessop & Ann his wife of Guilford to Calep Jessop [no county given], one hundred and forty pounds, 81 3/4 acres, begin on Horsepen Cr. on James Johnston's line, along line S 130 p. to a marked saplin, E 110 p. to 3 marked saplins, N to a black haw at the fork of sd. creek, along creek to beginning; signed: Thomas Jessop, Ann Jessop; witness: Gayer Strabuck, Wm. Braselten, Henry Thornburgh; proved by Gayer Straybuck [no probate date].

P. 156, 8 August 1772, Mordicai Mendenhall Senr. of Guilford to Mordicai Mendenhall Junr. of same, one hundred pounds sterling, 480 acres, begin at a white oak standing on E side of Brush Cr waters of Haw R., E 60 ch. to a white oak saplin, N 80 ch. to a white oak, W 60 ch. to a white oak, S 80 ch. to beginning; signed: Mordicai Mendenhall, Charity Mendenhall; witness: Richard Haworth, Daniel Britain; proved by Britain [no probate date].

P. 160, 11 August 1772, Richard Moon Sr. of Guilford to Simon Moon of same, eighty pounds, 100 acres, on Moons Cr., begin at a white, W 120 rods to a black oak, N 160 rods to a black, E 80 rods to a white oak, to first station, part of tract from Granville to Moon 1762; signed: Richard Moon; witness: Zachar. Dicks, Enoch Macy, Thos. Thornburgh; acknowledged [no probate date].

P. 161, 9 March 1772, John Pickrell & Catherine his wife of Guilford to Jacob Hollingsworth of same, sixty pounds, 100 acres, on E side of Deep R., begin at the mouth of Broad Mouth line, up creek to a white oak saplin notched on the E bank of creek, E by line of marked trees to a black jack and a stone at the original line, N 60 perches to a black oak, W 268 perches to a spanish oak by the river, down river to Broad Mouth Cr., part of a tract from Granville to Peter Youngblood 20 October 1759, Youngblood to William Cox 8 May 1771, Cox to Pickrell 16 July 1771; signed: John Pickrell, Catherine Pickrell; witness: Enoch Davis, Samuel Barker; proved by Davis [no probate date].

P. 163, 5 August 1772, Thomas Eldreg [Eldredge] of Guilford to David Macy of same, sixty five pounds, 135 acres, on waters of Reedy Fork of Haw R., begin at a black oak on S side of Bever Cr., S52W 164 rods to a black oak, S 112 rods to a hicory & black oak, E 131 rods to a stake, N to first station, to Eldridge from his father-in-law Simon Taylor, see records of Rowan Court; signed: Thomas Eldridg; witness: Enoch Macy, Zach. Dicks; proved by Zacharias Dicks [no probate date].

P. 165, 8 May 1772, James Aldridge of Guilford to Simone York of same, forty seven pounds, 50 acres, on both sides of Mount Pleasant Cr. a branch of Sandy Cr., begin at a cor. post in Absalom McDaniel's line, S 25 ch. to a black oak, W 20 ch. to a white oak, N cross Mount Pleasant Cr. to Absalom McDaniel's back line, E his line crossing creek to first station, part of a tract from James Aldridge to Simon York, Absalom McDaniel to James Aldridge, William Aldridge to Absalom McDaniel, Daniel McDaniel to William Aldridge, Absalom McDaniel to Daniel McDaniel, James Mickelroy to Absalom McDaniel, Granville to Mickleroy 30 June 1762; James (A) Aldridge; witness: William Willbourn, Jeremiah York; proved by Willbourn [no probate date].

P. 167, 1 November 1771, Hezekiah Sanders & Martha his wife of Guilford to James Johnston of same, forty five pounds, 120 acres, part of tract from Granville to Hen. Mills 28 2nd month 1759, Mills to Sanders 2nd month 1759, begin at Henry Mills old cor. at a white oak, his line E 20 ch. to a stake still E 22 ch. to a stake on Willm. Hyat's line, his line N 192 ch. to a black jack, his line E 130 ch. to a black jack, following line of tract 12 p. & cor. W to the back line being 72 ch. , follows sd. line S to first station; signed: Hezekiah Sanders, Martha Sanders; witness: Rubin Mills, Richard Mills, Hugh Morris ; acknowledged [no probate date].

P. 170, 29 July 1772, John Hanna [Hannah] & Martha his wife of Guilfrod to Robert Hanna [Hannah] his son of same, ten pounds Sterling, on both sides of Beaver Cr., 211 acres, begin at a hicory on S side of creek, W 3 outs & 12 rods to John Harris' line to a red oak, S his line 10 outs & 4 rods to a black oak [illegible], N 6 outs to a black oak, W 6 outs & 8 rods to a black oak, N 2 outs & 8 rods to a hicory, W 1 out to a black oak, N 2 outs to first station, part of tract John Hanna now lives on; signed: John Hanna, Martha Hanna; witness: James Matthews, William Matthews; proved by James Matthews [no probate date].

P. 173, 7 November 1767, Patrick Mullin of Orange to John Odeneal of same, 30 pounds, 80 acres, Daniel McCullom to Mullins 2 August 1766, on S side of Hogans Cr., begin at a sycamore on the creek, E 50 p. to 2 hicorys, S 170 p. to a spanish oak on the Court House Road, by Road 112 p. to a birch on creek, down creek to beginning; signed: Patrick (S) Mullins; witness: Daniel D. McCollum, James McCollum, William Odell; proved by Odell [no probate date], check affidavit of John Oneal at end.

P. 175, 11 August 1772, Adam Mitchel of Guilford to Samuel Hunter of same, eighty four pounds, 280 acres, on both sides Beaver Island Cr., begin at pointers in the old line on W side of creek joining James Hunter, S 123 p. to pointers joining Charles Perkins, E 320 p. to pointers in old line, N 150 p. to pointers joining Jas. Hunter, W 180 p. to a sycamore on E side of creek, down & crossing creek 27 p. to a sycamore on bank of creek, W 140 p. to first station; signed: Adam Mitchel; witness: none listed; acknowledged; wife Agness Mitchell relinquished dower.

P. 176, 11 August 1772, Adam Mitchel & Agness his wife & Isabel Mitchel of Surry to Jas. Hunter of Guilford, eighty four pounds, 284 acres, in Guilford, on both sides Beaver Island Cr., part of a tract taken by Robt. Jones Junior on the upper end, begin at a white oak on E side of creek an old cor., W 320 p. to a stake in Neels Field, S crossing creek 159 p. to pointers near a branch, E a new line 140 p. to a sycamore on bank of creek, N crossing creek 27 p. to sycamore on E side of creek, E 180 to pointers in Old Line, N 132 p. to first station; signed: Adam Mitchel, Agness (X) Mitchel, Isabel (+) Mitchel; witness: none listed; acknowledged [no date given].

P. 177, August term 1772 - William Coltrane who intermarried with Rachel Worthington proves birth of children begotten on body of wife Rachel Coltrane since their intermarriage;

David Coltrane born 8 May 1762
Abigal Coltrane born 26 June 1764
Jacob Coltrane born 15 December 1766
Mary Coltrane born 22 May 1769
James Coltrane born 11 October 1771.

P. 178, 5 August 1772, Thos. Neal, Sarah Neal, & Judith Neal of Guilford to Archibald Hughs & John Wimbish of Pittsylvania County, Virginia, one hundred twenty pounds, 630 acres, on both sides Beaver Island Cr., joins Joseph Tate on upper end, begin at a white oak on Tate's line on E end of tract, his line W 70 ch. to a chestnut, N 90 ch. to a white oak, E 70 ch. to a black oak, S to beginning, Granville to William Neal 10 May 1762, recorded in Rowan; signed: Thomas Neal, Sarah (O) Neal, Judith (+) Neal; witness: Mervil Stone, Adam Mitchel; acknowledged [no date]; Judith Neal examined apart from her husband & relinquished dower.

P. 179, 1 August 1772, John Rankin of Guilford to William Rankin of same, twenty eight pounds, 218 acres, begin at center of a white oak & black oak saplin on N side Buffaloe Cr. & on bank of same, N 22 1/2 ch. to a hicory saplin, W 5 ch. to a white oak saplin, N 59 1/2 ch. to a hicory saplin, E 38 ch. to a hicory, S 10 ch. to William Blackwood'sd line at a white oak, his line S 52 1/2 ch. to a black oak saplin by Buffaloe, up Buffaloe to first station, part of 511 acres from Granville to Jno. McNight 2 February 1759, Jno. McvNight to Alexander McNight, Alexander McNight to Jno. Rankin 19 April 1765; signed: John Rankin; witness: Robt. Breden, William Dannal; acknowledged [no date].

P. 180, 28 September 1771, John Butler of Orange, Sheriff, to Abner Nash of Halifax Gounty, three hundred seventy pounds, 720 acres, Nash obtained a judgment of three hundred twenty five pounds against Harmon Husband, land valued at five hundred fifty five pounds, at sale no one bid sufficiently, Nash agrees to take land at 2/3 value (three hundred seventy pounds), "in Orange formerly in County of Guilford" [?], begin at a white oak the NE cor. of a tract called Bottom, W 280 p. to a N & S boundary line, along line S 92 p. to a black oak, W 16 p. to a black jack & 2 white oaks, S 292 p. to 3 hicorys, E 304 p. to a white oak, N 384 p. to beginning; signed: Jno. Butler; witness: G. Sothberry, Thomas Person; proved 25 September 1772 before M. Howard, C.J., by George Sothberry.

P. 182, 25 September 1772, Abner Nash of Halifax County to James Young, Andrew Miller, John Alston, James Marton, Alexander Grinley, William Littlejohn, & George Alston merchants in partnership by the name of Young Miller & Company, five shillings, 720 acres, Nash had given Young Miller & Co. 2 notes on Harmon Husband, one for three hundred pounds and the other for twenty five pounds, this sale was to reimburse Young Miller & Co., same description as deed on page 180 above; signed: A: Nash; witness: Thos. Burke, J. Kinchen; proved 28 September 1772 before M. Moore by John Kinchen.

P. 183, 20 August 1772, Richard Hargrave of Granville to Thomas Person of same, fifty pounds, 520 acres, on S side of North Fork of Haw R., begin at a hicory by the fork, S 85 ch. to a [torn], W cross a branch 85 ch. to a red oak on Peter Dillon's line, his line [torn] to his cor. red oak saplin, continued N 12 1/2 ch. to a gum by the North Fork of Haw R., down river to first station; signed: Richard Hargrave; witness: none listed; acknowledged 20 August 1772 before Richard Henderson.

P. 184, 17 September 1770, Samuel Scott of Twp. of Little Brittain, Lancaster County, Pennsylvania, formerly of Rowan, planter, to his son William Scott of Twp. of Little Brittain, natural love & affection & five shillings, 640 acres, Granville to Samuel Scott 3 December 1753, registered in Rowan Book 3 page 275, begin at a white oak on to number 13, S that line [torn] chains to a small white oak & black oak, W 80 ch. [torn] oak, N a straight line to Reedy Fork crossing mouth of Rich Fork; signed: Samuel Scott; witness: Alexr. Caldwell, Francis Cummings; acknowledged 17 September 1770 before Isaac Sanders, J.P., of Lancaster County, Pennsylvania; proved May 1771 Term in Guilford by Alexr. Caldwell.

P. 186, 14 August 1772, William Denny of Guilford to John Maxwell of same, three pounds, 5 acres, piece of land containing an improvement in possession of Maxwell, begin on W line of William Dennys Br. at a white oak, to include Maxwell's improvements; signed: William Denny; witness: William Thomas, William Donnall; acknowledged November 1772 Term.

P. 188, 2 November 1772, Josiah Carr of Guilford & Jane his wife to Jennings Thompson of same, one hundred pounds, 200 acres, in fork of Flat Cr. of Deep R., begin at a cor. of Carr's land that he obtained from James Graves on the including line called the Back Line, N along line to the N cor., another line of plan including the plantation, along sd. line to another cor., to cor. of Graves" land, along Carr's line cross Flat Cr. at a gut to first station; signed: Joseph (O) Carr, Jean Carr; witness: Willm. Searcy, Windsor Pearce; proved November 1772 Term by Searcy.

P. 189, 11 November 1772, Robert Hannah of Guilford to John Forbush of North Carolina, waggonmaker, one hundred thirty pounds, 211 acres, on both sides Beaver Cr., begin at a hicory tree on S side of creek, W 3 outs & 12 rods to John Hanna's line to a post oak, S that line 10 outs & 8 rods to a black oak, E 11 outs to a black oak, N 6 outs to a black oak, W 6 outs & 8 rods to a black oak, N 2 outs & 8 rods to a hicory, W 1 out to a black oak, N 2 outs to first station; signed: Robt. Hanna; witness: Samuel Duff, Benjn. Starratt, proved November 1772 Term by Starratt.

P. 190, 18 August 1772, David Morrow of Guilford & Martha his wife to Thomas Cummings of same, one hundred twenty pounds, 440 acres, on Buffaloe Cr. waters of Haw R., part ofd a tract from

Granville to Robt. Brashears 6 December 1761, Brashears to Harmon Husband, Husband to Morrow, begin at a white oak the cor. tree of original survey, E 72 1/2 ch. to a hicory, S 40 ch. to a white oak saplin, W 107 1/2 ch. to a black oak saplin, N 40 ch. to Archibald Mickleroy's cor., E 35 ch., S to beginning; signed: David Morrow, Martha (O) Morrow; witness: [name in German], Adam Starr; acknowledged November 1772 Term.

P. 191, 11 November 1772, Arthur Forbish & Lydia his wife of Guilford to Robert Rankin Junr. of same, one hundred fifty pounds, 620 acres, on both siders Nixes Cr. near headwaters of North Buffaloe Cr., begin at a post oak Adam Mitchel's cor., his line S 55 ch. to a white oak, W 80 ch. to a white oak, N 55 ch. to 2 maples & a white oak, E 40 ch. to a white oak, N 45 ch. to a white oak, E 40 ch. to a poplar, S 45 ch. to first station, surveyed for George Rankin, decd., Granville to Lydia Rankin widow 13 January 1761, excepting what Adam Mitchell justly claims by deed from Granville 13 January 1761; signed: Arthur Forbis, Lydia ( ) Forbush; witness: Hugh Braly, Andrew Finly; acknowledged November 1772 Term.

P. 193, 11 11th month 1772, Henry Ballenger of Guilford to Joseph Jessop of same, twenty five pounds, 25 acres, part of a tract from Granville to Ballenger 1753, on Horsepen Cr., begin on N line of the whole tract where it crosses Horsepen, E along line to a post oak saplin, S 80 p. to Timothy Jessop's line, W to creek, down creek to first station, signed: Henry Ballenger; witness: Eleazer Hunt, Enoch Macy, Zacharias Dicks; proved November 1772 Term by affirmation of Hunt.

P. 194, 9 November 1772, Thomas Cummins & Marian his wife of Guilford to Peter Sallinger of Chatham, one hundred fifty pounds, 251 acres, where Cummins now dwells, begin at a black jack, N45W 194 p. to a white oak, S45W 236 p. to a black jack, S45E 144 p. to Nicholas Puntrick's cor. a stone, N65E at 140 p. crossing Cedar Cr. in all 2142 p. to beginning, part of a larger tract from McCulloch to Christian Funkhausen; signed: Thomas Cuming, Maryan (X) Cumin; witness: Jas. Powell, Robert Cimmons; acknowledged November 1772 Term.

P. 196, 10 November 1772, Robert Smith of Guilford to Samuel Smith of same, one hundred pounds, 190 1/2 acres, on waters of North & South Buffaloe, begin at a hicory in Jno. Rankin's line, W 24 3/4 ch. to a hicory grub, S 10 ch. to a hicory, E 5 ch. to a black oak, S 48 ch. to a post, W 14 1/2 ch. to a white oak bush, S 16 1/2 ch. to a post, E 48 1/4 ch. cross South Buffaloe to a red oak, N 30 ch. to a white oak by mouth of South Buffaloe, up Rankin's line to a hicory, white oak, & poplar on North Buffaloe, N 24 ch. to first station; signed: Robert (O) Smith; witness: Francis Alexander, William Rankin; proved November 1772 Term by Rankin.

P. 197, 3 September 1772, Samuel Watt of Guilford to Nicholas major of same, eighty pounds, 103 acres, on S side Penny Br. &

Cabbin Br., begin at a small hicory on Penny Br., S 57 perches to a white oak, E 200 perches to a white oak, N 20 perches to a small burch saplin on Cabbin Br., N 80 perches, W 220 perches to beginning, William Savage to Watt 20 October 1771; signed: Samuel ( ) Watt; witness: Hugh McAdam, Kenneth McCallum, William Clark; acknowledged November 1772 Term.

P. 198, 20 August 1772, Ephriam Potter of Guilford to Thomas Lovelatty of same, fifty pounds, 100 acres, on N side Woolf Island Cr., part of a tract to Enoch Lewis, Lewis to Ephriam Potter Senr., at death of Ephriam Potter Senr. descended to son Ephriam Potter as heir at law, [no metes and bounds description]; signed: Ephriam (+) Potter; witness: Seth Stubblefield, Isham Browder, L. Pierpoint; proved November 1772 Term by Larkin Pierpoint.

P. 199, 12 October 1772, Thomas Jessop Senr. & wife Ann of Guilford to David Macy of same, one hundred fifty pounds, 222 acres, 200 acres bought of Jas. Brittain Senr., decd., 1768, it being part of a tract from Granville to Jas. brittain Senr. 1760, and the other 22 acres bought of Zacharias Dicks 1768, on Horsepen Cr., begin at a small white oak near a large poplar on Balesses Br. on Zacharias Dicks line, N79W 70 p. to a white oak, N60W 70 p. to a stake to end of James Brittain's lane, N26W 22 p. to mouth of Saw Pitt Br., up branch to fountain head, same general course of branch until it joins with line of whole tract, E 232 p. to a black oak, S 83 p. to a black oak, S36E 148 p. to an elm, S 44 p. to first station; signed: Thos. Jessop, Ann Jessop; witness: Eleazer Hunt, Enoch Macy, Zacharias Dicks; proved November 1772 Term by affirmation of Hunt.

P. 200, 5 October 1772, Conrad Stally of Guilford, planter, to Michael Brown of North Carolina, one hundred fifty pounds, 450 acres, on branches of Sandy Cr., part of tract to Herman Husband 10 December 1762, begin at a hicory the beginning tree of the original survey, N 32 ch. to a post oak, W 25 ch. to a red oak, N 45 ch. to a hicory, W 48 ch. to a red oak, S 14 1/4 ch. to William Hinshaw's cor., S his line to a marked saplin, south easterly with Hinshaw's line by a marked white oak by a spring to the original line, E along original line to beginning; signed: [Stally and wife sign in German; witness: Frederick (f) Brown, Adam (X) Smith; proved November 1772 Term by Brown.

P. 201, 7 January 1773, Aquila Jones of Guilford, farmer, to Ninian Hamilton of same, seventy pounds, 100 acres, on a branch of Sandy Cr., part of 2 tracts from Granville to Harmon Husband 13 November 1755 for 640 acres called the Thicket & 5 August 1758 for 644 acres called the Level, begin at a red oak saplin the original beginning tree of the Level, E 103 p. to a stake, N 160 p. to a marked spanish oak, W 51 p. to a stone, S 8 p. to a marked walnut, W 52 p. to a stone, S to beginning by a black oak the 2nd cor. tree of the Level standing 62 p. from the last cor. stone & 15 1/2 p. W from & in the original cor. white oak of the Thicket, 6 acres is out of the Thicket; signed: Aquila (AI) Jones, Elizabeth (E) Jones; witness: James Hunter, James (I)

Davidson, William (+) Marley; proved February 1773 Term by Hunter.

P. 202, 9 January 1773, Victor Thompson of Guilford, yeoman, to John Johnston of same, farmer, one hundred eighty pounds, 200 acres, on Carraway the waters of Hewwarry, begin at a B:G, N 55 ch. to a white oak, E 47 ch. crossing Carraway Cr. fork to a stake, S 20 ch., W 60 ch. to a stake, W to beginning; signed: Victor Thompson; witness: Jno. Collier, Robt. Gray; proved February 1773 Term by Collier.

P. 203, 17 November 1772, John Bryan of Guilford to Nathaniel Kerr of same, thirty seven pounds, 200 acres, joins John Bryan on W & Emas Williams on E, [no metes and bounds description]; signed: Jno. Bryan, Anna (X) Bryan; witness: Jno. Collier, Edward Sharp; proved February 1773 Term by Collier.

P. 204, 10 February 1773, Henry Whitsel of Guilford to George Nees of same, one hundred fifteen pounds, 238 acres, on S side of Great Allamance, part of a tract from Henry Eustace McCulloh to Whitsell, begin at a black oak, S25E 60 p. to a hicory, S20E 82 p. to a red oak, S45E 160 p. to a spanish oak, N35E 36 p. to a black oak, N10E 142 p. to beginning; signed: [Henry Whitsel in German], Mary (+) Whitsel; witness: James Morgan, Samuel Duff; acknowledged February 1773 Term.

P. 205, 2 January 1773, William Denny & Margaret his wife of Guilford to Thomas Hays of same, sixty five pounds, 230 acres, on N side of Reedy Fork of Haw R., begin at a white oak cor. of Denny, S 50 ch. 1 perch, 12 1/2 lk. to a black oak, W 80 ch. to a white oak, N 20 ch. 1 perch 12 1/2 lk. to a hicory, E 55 ch. to a red oak saplin, N 30 ch. to a white oak, E 25 ch. to first station; signed: WM. Denny, Margaret Denny; witness: George Finley, John Maxwell; acknowledged February 1773 Term.

P. 206, [Blank] day of [blank]] 1772, James Brown & Jane his wife of Surry to William Jackson of Guilford, sixty pounds, 220 acres, part of a tract from Granville to William Brown 11 May 1757, recorded in Rowan, begin on S side of North Buffaloe Cr. at a red oak on bank of creek, S 160 p. to a post oak, E 210 p. to a red oak, N 247 p. to a hicory on the creek, up creek to beginning; signed: James Brown, Jane Brown; witness: Rees Porter, William Hall; proved February 1773 Term by Hall.

P. 207, 9 February 1773, James Coleman of Guilford to John Leak of same, one hundred sixty pounds, 125 acres, on N side of Dan R., begin at an oak on river, N 90 p. to a cor. white oak, W 180 p. to a red oak, 132 p. to a hicory on the river, down river to beginning; signed: James Coleman; witness: Samuel Henderson, Isham Browder, William Henderson; acknowledged February 1773 Term.

P. 207, 27 November 1772, George Parks of Guilford to William Wiley of same, planter, forty pounds, 600 acres, begin at a red oak cor. of James Russell on N side of Buffaloe, N 240 p. to 2 white oaks & a hicory, W 400 p. to a red oak, S 240 p. to a white oak & hicory, E to beginning; signed: George Parks, Anna ( ) Parks; witness: James Wilson, Ralph Gorrell; proved February 1773 Term by Gorrell.

P. 209, 18 January 1773, Samuel Brown of Rowan to David Macy of Guilford, sixty five pounds, 240 acres, on both sides of South Buffaloe, begin at a stake on N side of South Buffaloe, E 148 p. to a black jack, S 325 p. cross Buffaloe to a hicory, W 69 p. to a post oak, N 127 p. cross Buffaloe to 3 black jacks, W 88 p. to an ash, N 193 p. to first station, part of a tract from Granville to Brown 1759, recorded in Rowan; signed: Samuel Brown; witness: Enoch Macy, Isaac (+) Edwards, James (I) Armfield; proved February 1773 Term by Enoch Macy.

P. 209, 29 Janaury 1773, Jacob Hinshaw of Guilford, weaver, to Joseph Hinshaw of same, farmer, twenty pounds, 200 acres, on waters of Sandy Cr., part of 2 tracts from Harmon Husband to Jacob Hinshaw 19 August 1768, begin at a stake at W end of a conditional line between John Fruit & Jacob Hinshaw, N 43 p. to a stake, W 140 p. to a white oak, N 98 p. to a stake, E 153 p. to a stake, SE 174 p. to the conditional line between Fruit & Hinshaw, SW 154 p. to beginning; signed: Jacob Hinshaw, Rebecca (R) Hinshaw; witness: Jno. McGee, Saml. McGee; proved February 1773 Term by Saml. McGee.

P. 210, 25 August 1772, John Buis & Martha his wife of Guilford to John Baldwin of same, sixty five pounds, 130 acres, on Deep R., begin at a white oak Buis' SW cor., E 80 p. to a hicory Buis' 2nd cor., N30E along original line 92 p. to a maple, N18W 38 p. to a persimon on S bank of Deep R. being a dividing line, N37W along river bank to a persimon at the mouth of a branch 6 p., N25W 50 p. to a small post oak, N52W to a stake on original line, S along line to beginning, part of a tract from Granville to William Buis, decd., William Buis willed to John Buis, part of tract John Buis lives on, on W side of Deep R.; signed: Jno. Buis, Martha Buis; w: Thos. Dudley, Isaac Beeson, William Baldwin; acknowledged February 1773 Term.

P. 211, 15 September 1772, Jane Field of Guilford, planter, to John Hawkins of Orange, one hundred sixty pounds, 286 acres, on both sides Quaker Fork waters of Allamance, begin at Capt. Nation's cor. gum & black oak, S along his line cross a branch 15 ch. to a white oak, E cross a Spring Br. 55 ch. to a black oak, N 52 ch. to a hicory, W cross Quaker Fork 55 ch. to a white oak saplin, S cross the fork to first station, Granville to Jane Field 25 July 1760; signed: Jane ( ) Field; witness: [name in German], Peter Julien Junr.; proved February 1773 Term by [name in German].

P. 212, 8 2nd month 1773, Henry Sigfret of Guilford to Eleazer Hunt of same, forty seven pounds, 125 acres, part of a tract from Robert Thompson to Sigfret 1765, on waters of South Buffaloe, begin at David Edwards' N cor. the E end of his land, N 132 p. to a white oak saplin, W 152 p. to a black oak saplin, S 132 p. to a black oak & sassafras on David Edwards' line, E his line 152 p. to first station; signed: [Henry Sigfret in German]; witness: Enoch Macy, Zach. Dicks, Thomas Jessop; proved February 1773 Term by affirmation of Macy & Dicks.

P. 213, 3 August 1772, William Reynolds of Guilford, farmer, & Rachel his wife to Jeremiah Reynolds of same, farmer, ten pounds, 15 acres, on both sides North Fork of Polecat Cr., begin at a white oak & hicory, E 60 p. by land of John Lewis to a stake, N by land of Jeremiah Reynolds 40 p. to a hicory, W 60 p. by sd. Reynolds to a stake, S to first station, part of a survey for 639 acres, Timothy Terrel & wife Mary of Orange, decd. to William Reynolds 3 May 1753, registered in Orange; signed: William ( ) Reynolds, Rachel Reynolds; witness: William Field, Henry Reynolds; proved February 1773 Term by Field.

P. 214, [Blank] February 1773, Thomas Flack & Jane his wife of Guilford to John Chambers of same, one hundred twenty five pounds, 181 acres, on both sides Walnut Br. of Reedy Fork waters of Haw R., begin at a black oak in James Denny's line (formerly William Denny), N along line 49 ch. to a white oak James Denny's cor. & William Scott's cor., E 37 ch. to a black, S 49 ch. to a black oak, W to beginning, Granville to Flack 21 December 1761; signed: Thomas Flack, Jean Flack; witness: Daniel England; proved February 1773 Term by England.

P. 215, 25 November 1770, Robert Bell of Rowan to Samuel Bell of Guilford, seventy two pounds, 360 acres, on waters of Sugar Tree waters of Haw R., joins John Nix & John McNight, begin at a forked black oak on Nix's cor., E 80 ch. to a post oak on Nix's cor., N 45 ch. to 2 post oaks, W 80 ch. to a white oak, to beginning, Granville to Robert Bell 10 May 1762; signed: Robert Bell; witness: William Hamilton, Francis Bell, John Walker; proved February 1773 by Hamilton.

P. 216, 18 January 1773, Peter Julien Senr. of Guilford, miller, & Ann his wife to John Emack of same, farmer, one hundred ninety five pounds, 247 acres, on South Fork of Allamance, begin at a black jack, S45W at 200 p. cross Allamance Cr. in all 220 p. to a white oak, N45W at 180 p. cross a branch several times to a stake, N45E at 180 p. cross creek in all 220 p. to a white oak on Thomas Kimman's line, S45E at 100 p. his cor. in all 180 p. to beginning, part of a tract from Henry McCulloh to Julien 18 January 11 yr. of George III [1771]; signed: Peter Julian, Ann (+) Julian; witness: John McGee, James Kinman, Anthony ( ) Coabel; proved February 1773 Term by Coabel.

P. 217, 6 February 1773, Thomas Lowe of Guilford to William Dent of same, three hundred thirty pounds, 320 acres, formerly in Orange now in Guilford, on a branch of Reedy Fork & both sides of the Trading Path, begin at a red oak, S45E 220 perches cross the Trading Path & Reedy Fork to a white oak on the brow of a hill, S45W 233 perches to a stake in a slash, N45W 220 perches to a stake between pointers crossing Reedy Fork & the Trading Path, N45E 253 perches to beginning, McCulloh to Lowe; signed: Thos.

lowe; witness: James Hunter, Ninian Hamilton, Jeremiah (I) Field; proved February 1773 Term by Hunter.

P. 218, 4 February 1772, Thomas Lamb of Guilford, farmer, to Josiah Lamb of same, farmer, fifty pounds, 3 feather beds & furniture, 1 chaff bed & furnioture, 1 desk, 1 case of bottles, 2 trunks, 1 looking glass, 2 linnen wheels, 1 woolen wheel, 1 dozen pewter plates, 2 pewter dishes, 4 pewter basins, 1 arm chair, 3 common chairs, 3 iron pots, 1 skillet, 1 black walnut table, 4 cows & calves, 2 heifers, this deed is null & void if Josiah Lamb is paid twenty five pounds before 1 May next; signed: Thomas Lamb; witness: William Norton, Reuben (R) Lamb; proved February 1773 Term by Norton.

P. 219, 8 February 1773, John McCuiston of Guilford to Francis McNairy of same, sixteen pounds due McNairy by McCuiston, 20 acres, begin at James McCuiston's SW cor. white oak on a branch of Richland Cr., E 80 roods, then begin again at the beginning white oak, N 80 roods to a red oak, SE to 2nd. cor., James McCuiston to John McCuiston 5 October 1769, registered in Rowan Book 7 page 171, also a claim to a survey on which John now lives bought of James McCuiston, 329 acres, begin at James McCuiston's white oak, W 40 ch. to a white oak on head of Richland Cr., S 20 ch. to a white oak, W 40 ch. to a white oak on head of Richland Cr., N 50 ch. to a black oak, E 22 ch. to a red oak, S 32 ch. to a white oak, W 30 ch. N 15 ch. to Arthur Forbis' line, E 40 ch. to a stake, to beginning, property to be sold after 10 February 1774 to repay McNairy sixteen pounds plus interest; signed: John McCuiston; witness: Alexr. Moody, Jno. Campbell; proved February 1773 Term by Campbell.

P. 220, 27 September 1771, John Butler Esq. of Orange, Sheriff, to James Milner of Halifax County, counselor at law, sixty seven pounds four shillings eight pence, 200 acres, Milner recovered a judgment against Harmon Husband for fifty pounds, land sold is property of Harmon Husband, on both sides Sandy Cr., now Guilford County, begin at a clift of rocks at an old mill dam where a cor. marked hicory formerly stood, E 50 p. to a red oak saplin, S cross Sandy Cr. 160 p. to an E & W line of Harmon husband, W 50 p. to Jacob hinshaw's line, N 60 p. to Hinshaw's cor., W 100 p. to a line called Mill-falls, N 240 p. along sd. line to Stephen Jones' line, E 100 p. to Richard Wright's land, S 140 p. to first station; signed: John Butler; witness: Henry Skipworth; proved 28 September 1771 before Richard Henderson by Skipworth.

P. 221, Timothy Jessop enters his mark: a half crop in the left ear, an under & over keel & a crop in the right ear, 20 January 1774.

P. 222, 15 November 1773, John Underhill & Hannah his wife of Guilford, blacksmith, to Benjamin Coffin of Nantucket County, Massachusetts Bay in New England, taylor, now residing in Guilford, eighty pounds, 140 acres, on waters of Pole Cat, begin at a hicory, N44E to a stake 199 p., W 35 p. to a stake, N 75 p. to a stake, W 21 p. to a stake, N 75 p. to a stake, W 96 p. to a black jack, S 150 p. to a post oak, SE 110 p. to beginning, part conveyed by Jno. Bates Junr. & part by Jno. Mills to Abraham [?]; signed: Jno. Underhill, Hannah Underhill; witness: Daniel Worth, Wm. Reynolds; proved May 1774 Term by Worth.

P. 223, 18 10th month 1773, Moses Mendenhall of Guilford to William Coffin of same, one hundred twenty pounds, 231 1/2 acres, on a branch of Deep R., the North Fork, begin at a white oak, W 20 ch. to a black oak, N 10 ch. to a white oak, W 4 ch. 40 lk. to a black oak, N 1 ch. 50 lk. to a black oak, W 13 ch. 40 lk. to a hicory, N 2 ch. to a white oak, W 11 ch. to a white oak, N 5 ch. to a white oak, W 5 ch. to a white oak, N 5 ch. to a white oak, W 15 ch. to a black oak, N 20 ch. to a hicory, E 80 ch. to Thos. Mills' cor., S 50 ch. to beginning; signed: Moses Mendenhall; witness: David Brooks, Jas. Mendenhall; proved May 1774 Term by Brooks.

P. 224, 10 10th month 1773, Moses Mendenhall of Guilford to William Coffin of same, one hundred twenty pounds, 231 1/2 acres, on a branch of North Fork of Deep R., begin at a white oak, W 20 ch. to a black oak, N 10 ch. to a white oak, W 4 ch. 40 lk. to a black oak, N 1 ch. 50 lk. to a black oak, W 13 ch. 40 lk. to a hicory, N 2 ch. to a white oak, W 11 ch. to a white oak, N 5 ch. to a white oak, W 5 ch. to a white oak, N 5 ch. to a white oak, W 5 ch. to a black oak, N 5 ch. to a white oak, W 15 ch. to a black oak, N 20 ch. to a hicory, E 80 ch. to Thos. Mills' cor., S 50 ch. to beginning, Jno. Mendenhall to Moses Mendenhall 11 2nd month 1771; signed: Moses Mendenhall; witness: David Brooks, Jas. Mendenhall; proved May 1774 Term by Brooks.

P. 225, 4 March 1773, Jennings Thompson of Guilford & Elizabeth his wife to Joseph Carr of same, one hundred pounds, 200 acres, on N side of Deep R., 'begin at a stake or marked tree near Flatt Cr. on the Back Line, cross creek at a marked tree at a gut a N course to the other line, along line to a cor., to first station; signed: Jennings ( ) Thompson, Elizabeth ( ) Thompson; witness: William Searcy Senr., Wm. Searcy Junr., Windsor Pearce; proved May 1774 term by Willm. Searcy Esq.

P. 226, 5 February 1773, Abner Hunt, planter, & Mary his wife of Guilford to George Starbuck of same, planter, seventy five pounds, five pounds in hand paid, 158 acres, begin at a stake on Eleazer Hunt's line, W 167 roods to Henry Ballenger's line, S 127 1/2 roods to a post oak, E 233 roods to a gum, N27W along Eleazer Hunt's line 145 roods to first station, divided to Abner Hunt by his father's will 13 October 1763, Granville to Abner's father Thos. Hunt 5 December 1753; signed: Abner Hunt, Mary Hunt; witness: Jacob Hunt, Willm. Jessop; proved May 1774 Term by affirmation of Jessop.

P. 227, 7 December 1773, Willm. Triplette of Guilford to Samuel Cobaen of York County, Pennsylvania, one hundred pounds one shilling, 100 acres, begin on N cor. of a tract entered by Southwell & by him sold to Richard Simpson Esq., the cor. being at a large white oak, along line W 127 p. to a white oak saplin on side of a branch, S 127 p. to a post, E 127 p. to a post in line of Simpson's tract but now property of Wm. Nunn Esq., N 127 p. to beginning, deed from Carteret to Southwell; signed: Willm. (X) Triplett, Eleanor (X) Triplett; witness: Jno. Robertson, Wm. Smith, James Warnock, Wm. Clark; proved May 1774 Term by Clark.

P. 229, 15 November 1773, John Nation of Guilford, planter, & Elizabeth his wife to Joseph Lamb of same, planter, one hundred twenty pounds, 174 1/2 acres, on Pole Catt Cr., begin at 2 black oaks the cor. of Henry Lamb, N 10 ch. to a black oak, W cross creek 34 ch. to a post, S 45 ch. to a white oak, E 40 ch. to a black oak saplin, N 35 ch. to a hicory, W 6 ch. to first station, Granville to John Nation, John Nation to Christopher Nation, Christopher Nation to John Nation Junr. 8 June 1769, registered in Rowan; signed: Jno. (I) Nation; witness: Isaac Beeson, Jacob Elliot; proved May 1774 Term by affirmation of Beeson.

P. 230, 16 July 1773, Jno. Odeneal, sheriff, of Guilford to Ralph Gorrell Esq. of same, sixty pounds, 250 acres, John McGee obtained a judgment of twenty eight pounds plus costs against Ralph Gorrell administrator of the estate of John Kerr decd., land of Kerr being sold, begin at a black oak saplin, E along Isaac Matthews' 45 1/2 ch. to a stake, 55 ch. to a stake, W 45 1/2 ch. to a black oak, N 55 ch. to beginning, on waters of Allamance; signed: Jno. Odeneal; witness: Alex. Martin, Jno. Mitchel; proved May 1774 Term by Martin.

P. 232, 14 April 1774, Robert Field & wife Ann of Guilford to Daniel England of same, one hundred eighty pounds, 200 acres, on South Fork of Allamance, in McCulloh Tract # 11, McCulloh to England [?] 25 June 1763, begin at a post oak on N side of South Fork of Allamance Cr., N25E 136 p. to a spanish oak, S50E cross fork 200 p. to a white oak, S45W 200 p. to a stake, to beginning; signed: Robt. Field, Ann (A) Field; witness: Jeremiah (j) Field; proved May 1774 Term by Jeremiah Field.

P. 233, 21 August 1770, Abraham Powell & Jane his wife of Guilford to Jno. Underhill of same, one hundred pounds, 140 acres, on waters of Poll-Catt [Polecat], begin at a hicory, N44E to a stake 119 p., W 35 p. to a stake, N 75 p. to a stake, W 21 p. to a stake, N 75 p. to a stake, W 96 p. to a black oak, S 150 p. to a post oak SE 100 p. to beginning, part from Jno. Bates & part from Jno. Mills to Abraham Powell; signed: Abraham Powell, jane (X) Powell; witness: Moses Mendenhall, John (X) Stanly; proved May 1774 Term by Mendenhall.

P. 234, 13 5th month 1774, Samuel Curry & Jane his wife of Guilford to David Macy of same, two hundred sixty five pounds, 246 1/4 acres, on both sides Horse Pen Cr., begin at a white oak, on N side the cor. tree of Willm. Forster's & Nathan Dicks' heirs land, S 179 p. to a white oak saplin Christopher Hiatt's cor., E 220 p. to a post, N 179 p. to a post, W 220 p. to beginning, Oliver Matthews to Curry 1764, registered in Rowan; signed: Saml. Curry, Jane (I) Curry; witness: Timothy Russell, Jno. Smalley; proved May 1774 Term by Russell.

P. 235, 18 5th month 1774, Joseph Nation of Surry to Willm. Barden of Carteret, five shillings Sterling, 235 acres, by virtue of his father's will & a deed of gift for 100 acres recorded in Guilford, part of the same tract, both the 100 acres & the other that fell to him by his father's will begin at a black oak on Hearman Cox's line, W 54 ch. to a black, S 39 to a black oak, E 20 ch. to a hicory, S to Joseph Lamb's line, E with Lamb's line to Cox's, N on Cox's line to beginning; signed: Joseph (IN) Nation, Beththyyuk (B) Nation, Eleanor (E) Nation; witness: Timothy Jessop, Willm. Jessop; affirmed May 1774 Term by Timothy Jessop.

P. 236, 16 September 1773, Robt. Millsaps & Ellender his wife of Rowan to Thos. Millsaps of Guilford, eighty pounds, 153 acres, on waters of Uwarry, begin at a black oak, N15E 105 perches to the old line, E 132:15 to a hicory, S20E 120 perches to a stake at the creek, W 40 perches to a walnut, S 20 perches to a walnut, 75W 120 perches to a black oak, W 66 perches to beginning; signed: Robt. Millsaps, Ellender (E) Millsaps; witness: Wm. Draper Esq., Henry Wade; proved May 1774 Term by Draper.

P. 237, 1 January 1773, Henry Eustace McCulloh of North Carolina to Ludowick Isley of Guilford, sixty pounds, 250 acres, begin at a cor. of tract Christopher Founkhauser lived upon, 45W 172 p. to black jack on Granville's line, along his line S45W 193 p. to a poplar in a bent of a branch of Cedar Cr., down branch S45E 162 p. cross Cedar Cr. to Funkhauser's other cor., his line N45E 193 p. cross Cedar Cr. beginning; signed: Henry E. McCulloh; witness: Robt. Rear, Michael Hoots; proved May 1774 by Michael Hotsz.

P. 239, 19 5th month 1774, Joseph Nation of Surry to William Borden of Carteret, two hundred seventy pounds, 235 acres, this is release of lease recorded on page 235.

P. 240, 4 December 1773, Arthur Read & Martha his wife of Guilford, planter, to Ransom Southerland of same, twelve pounds ten shillings, lot or acre of land to Arthur & Martha Read by will of Enoch Spinks decd., surveyed out of Manor Plantation of Spinks, on Fork Cr. a branch of Deep R., begin at a stake near the cor of the Stonehouse on S side, S65W 10 p. to a stake, N12W 16 p., N65E 10 p., S12E 166 p. to beginning; signed: Arthur Read, Martha (X) Read; witness: Wm. Searcy Junr., Wm. Searcy, Thos. Cox; proved May 1774 Term by Willm. Searcy Esq.; Martha Read relinquished dower August 1774 Term.

P. 241, 11 October 1773, William Reade Senr. of Guilford to Arthur Read of same, paternal love & affection to son, 150 acres, on N side of Deep R., begin at the mouth of a certain cut opposite against Winsor Pearce's plantation, up cut to fork, from fork a straight line to the including line, down line to a white oak a cor. tree, W course along Searcy's line to Deep R., up river to first station; signed: William (R) Reade; witness: Wm. Searcy, Windsor Pearce; proved May 1774 Term by Searcy.

P. 242, 8 December 1770, Jacob Gregg of Orange, millwright, to John Husband 2nd cousin to Jacob Gregg & son of Harmon Husband of Orange, natural love & affection & better maintenance, 750 acres, 2 tracts, on Sandy Cr waters, begin at the beginning tree of tract originally granted to Thos. Branson at the clift of rock below an old Mill Dam on Sandy Cr., N 35 ch. to Stephen Jones, W 30 ch., S 60 ch. to Jacob Hinshaw, E 30 ch., N to beginning, 200 acres, second tract begins on NE cor. of tract from Granville to Harmon Husband 14 November 1755 called the Cabbin, E 66 ch. to cor. of Roger Murphey, S 40 ch. with Murphey to cor. of Thomas Pugh, W along Pugh to his other cor., S along Pugh to his other cor., W to SE cor. of aforesd. tract called Cabbin, N95 1/2 ch. to beginning, 550 acres; signed: Jacob Gregg; witness: Isaac Cox, Jno. Cox; affirmed May 1774 Term by Isaac Cox.

P. 243, 9 May 1774, David Lowe & Mary his wife of Guilford to William Plunkett of same, one hundred pounds, 255 acres, Henry Eustace McCulloh to Lowe 23 February 1765 for 355 acres, begin at a post oak on North Fork of Stinking Quarter Cr. on S side of creek, N10W 80 perches to a white oak saplin, N65 160 perches to a white oak in Samuel Lowe's line, S45W 16 perches to his cor. hicory, N45W 16 perches to Hugh Smith's cor., with Smith's line S45W 240 perches, S45E 40 perches with sd. line to the end thereof, with given line to beginning, that part of land under waters of Mill Pond on creek excepted out of conveyance to David Lowe; [David Lowe in german], Mary (N) Lowe; witness: Wm. Dent, Willm. Dent Junr., proved May 1774 Term by William Dent.

P. 244, 29 3rd month 1754 [1774 ?], Boater Bales of Surry to William Coffin Senr. of Guilford, two hundred twenty five pounds, 200 acres, begin at a hicory saplin, N 100 p. to a persimon saplin, N30W 8 p. to a spanish oak, N 40 p. to a hicory saplin, W 123 p. to a stake, S 210 p. to a black oak, E 163 p. to first station, part of 300 acres Richard Williams to Boater Bales 5 5th month 1756; signed: Boater Bales; witness: Richard Williams, Jesse Williams; affirmed May 1774 Term by Richd. Williams.

P. 245, 24 September 1772, Jno. Cheedle of Goochland County, Virginia, to John Stewart of Guilford, one hundred pounds, 440 acres, on Wolf Br. in fork of Deep R., part of a survey Obadiah Harris to Cheedle, begin at the N cor. the tract, the W line 256 p. to a cor. hicory, S 278 p. to a cor. hicory, E 256 p. to a post, N to beginning; signed: Jno. Cheedle; witness: Zachariah Stanley, Moses Mendenhall, Joseph Stanley, William Lane; affirmed May 1774 Term by Moses Mendenhall.

P. 246, 20 April 1773, Bryan Roark of Guilford to William Quail of same, one hundred eighty six pounds, 640 acres, on North Fork of Allamance, begin at a maple on Mebane's cor., his line E 64 ch. to a post oak Mebane's cor., S 100 ch. to a post oak, W 64 ch. to a black jack, to beginning, Granville to Roark; signed: Bryan ( ) Roark; witness: Ralph Gorrell, Andw. Hall; proved May 1774 Term by Gorrell.

P. 248, 14 December 1773, Soloman Morgan & Mehetabel his wife of

Chatham to Lombard Reade of Guilford, seventy pounds, 100 acres, Granville to William Searcy 7 January 1761, on N side Deep R., begin at a stake at S cor. of Richeson's line, S to a white oak on Granville's line, W along line for compliment of 100 acres, N to a stake, if joining river not to cross it, E to Richeson's line, along line to first station; signed: Soloman Morgan, Mahetabel (M) Morgan; witness: William Searcy, Windsor Pearce; proved May 1774 Term by Searcy.

P. 249, 10 February 1773, John Doak Junr. of Guilford to Jas. Alexander & George Alexander Junr. of same, one hundred pounds, 291 acres, in their possession, begin at a white oak in Jno. McGee's line, W 56 ch. to a black oak, S 52 ch. to a hicory grub, E 56 ch. to a red oak, N 52 ch. to first station, signed: John Doak; witness: Jas. Mathies, Jno. (I) Alexander; proved May 1774 Term by John Alexander.

P. 251, 19 May 1773, George Valentine Clap & Barbery his wife of Guilford to George Tobias Clap of same, two hundred fifty pounds, 320 acres, whereon Tobias Clap now lives, begin at a white oak, N45W 221 p. to a white oak, S45W 232 p. cross 3 branch to a red oak, S45E 221 p. to a stake by a small hicory bush, N45E 232 p. crossing 3 branch to beginning; signed: [George Clap in German], Barbery (X) Clap; witness: Philip (FK) Clap, [Barnaby Clap in German]; proved May 1774 Term by Barnaby Clap.

P. 252, 21 1st month 1774, David Macy of Guilford to Enoch Macy of same, sixty five pounds, 240 acres, on both sides South Buffaloe, begin at a stake on N side of South Buffaloe, E 143 p. to a black jack, S 520 p. cross Buffaloe to a hicory, W 69 p. to a post oak, N 127 p. across Buffaloe to 3 black jacks, W 88 p. to an ash, N 193 p. to first station, Samuel Brown to David Macy 1773; signed: David Macy; witness: Timothy Russell, Deborah (X) Davis, Zach. Dicks; proved May 1774 Term by Russell.

P. 252, 8 July 1773, Conrad Low & Rosannah his wife of Guilford, miller, to David Low son of Conrad of same, one hundred fifty pounds, 302 acres, on both sides of Little Allamance Cr., begin at a white oak on Adam Lawrence's line, N45W 220 p. to a stake, N45E 220 p. cross creek to a stake, S45E 220 p. to a stake, S45W 220 p. along with Adam Lawrence's line to beginning; signed: Conrad (O) Low, Rosannah (+) Low; witness: Adam Starr, [Henry Whitsel in German]; proved May 1774 Term by Whitsel.

P. 253, 6 April 1774, Stephen Jones of Guilford, farmer, to Zebedee Wood of same, farmer, eighty pounds, 100 acres, on Sandy Cr., part of a tractfrom Granville to Harmon Husband 10 December 1762 for 700 acres, Husband to Jones 19 October 1768, begin at a black oak, E 70 p., N 17 p. to a black oak, N 43 p. to a hicory, N60W 200 p. to original line on Main Road, S on original line 154 p. to original stake, E to cor. white oak, S to branch down branch to Sandy Cr., a straight line to first station; signed: Stephen (-) Jones, Agnes ( ) Jones; witness: James Hunter, Samuel (S) Deviney, Elizabeth ( ) Jones; proved May 1774 Term by Hunter.

P. 254, 27 January 1772, William Matthews of Guilford, planter, to Ralph Gorrell of same, planter, eighty seven pounds, 200 acres, begin at a post on line of Gorrell's land he lives on & on S side of South Buffaloe, S 60 ch. to a black oak, W 33 1/2 ch. to a stake, N 60 ch. to a black oak, E 33 1/2 ch. to beginning, part of Benjamin Starrett's tract on both sides of South Buffaloe to Matthews April 1765; signed: William Matthews, Moothman ( ) Matthews; witness: John Hall, Ann Hall, Benja Starret; proved May 1774 Term by Starret.

P. 256, 12 February 1774, William Jackson & Margaret his wife of Guilford to Abraham Mucklehatton of same, one hundred ten pounds, 220 acres, begin on S side of North Buffaloe Cr. at a red oak on bank of creek, S 160 p. to a post oak, E 210 p. to a red oak, N 247 p. to a hicory on the creek, up creek to beginning, Granville to William Brown 11 May 1757, recorded in Rowan; signed: William (H) Jackson, Margaret (X) Jackson; witness: Thomas Black, Jas. McCuiston, William Anderson; acknowledged May 1774 Term.

P. 256, 22 May 1773, Joseph Scales Sr. & Mary his wife of Guilford to John Davis of same, twenty shillings, 200 acres, part of a tract on both sides the North & South Forks of Beaver Island Cr., begin at pointers on old line, S 110 p. to a white oak old cor., E 292 p. to a white oak, N 110 p. to a stake, W 292 p. to first station; signed: Joseph Scales, Mary (X) Scales; witness: Jno. Morgan, Jas. Scales, Joseph Scales Junr., Thomas Walker; proved May 1774 Term [jurat not given].

P. 257, 2 April 1774, James Duff & Agness his wife of Guilford to Robert Donnell of same, one hundred fifty three pounds fifteen shillings, 307 acres, on both sides South Buffaloe, begin at a white oak Hall's cor., his line N 20 ch. to a hicory, W 26 ch. to a black oak, S 43 1/2 ch. to a black oak on John McAdoo's line, his line E 5 ch. 25 lk. to a white oak saplin, his line S 36 ch. 50 lk. to a hicory, E 39 ch. to a post oak saplin, N 60 ch. to a black oak on Hall's line, his line to beginning; signed: James Duff, Agness (A) Duff; witness: Thos. Donnell, Ralph Gorrell; proved May 1774 Term by Donnell.

P. 258, 1 January 1774, James Nickoll of Guilford, planter, to John Hays of same, planter, one hundred forty pounds, 130 acres, on both sides Haw R., part of a tract from Granville to Nickoll 17 September 1744, [no metes and bounds description]; signed: James Nickell, Ealsie Nickell; witness: Joseph Pritchett, Jeremiah McCarthy, Jno. Coory; acknowledged May 1774 Term.

P. 259, 16 July 1773, Henry Whaitsell & Mary his wife of Guilford to Adam Starr of same, taylor, one hundred fifteen pounds 238 acres, on both sides Great Allamance Cr., begin at a black oak, S48E 248 p., N10E 86 p. to a spanish oak, N60E 100 p. to a white oak on Adam Lawrence's line, his line N45W cross creek 120 p. to a black oak, to beginning crossing creek again; signed: [Henry Whaitsell in German], Mary Whaitsell; witness: [two names in German]; acknowledged May 1774 Term.

P. 260, John Odeneal Esq. married Sarah Tate 13 August 1774; Death & Deceased 23 February one negro boy 1 August & 28th one negro boy named Guilford.

P. 260, 16 November 1772, James Matthews Junr. of Guilford to John Doak Junr. of same, one hundred eighty pounds, 300 acres, in his possession, on North Fork of Allamance, begin at a white oak & black oak cor., W 55 ch. to a stake, S 55 ch. to a stake, E 55 ch. cross North Fork of Allamance to a stake, N 55 ch. to first station; signed: James Matthews, Mary (M) Matthews; witness: Robert Doak, Robert Hanna; proved May 1774 Term by Robt. Doak.

P. 261, 24 February 1773, Phillip Gates of Halifax County, Virginia, to Benjamin Gates of Guilford, eighteen pounds four shillings, 30 acres, on S side Dann R., begin at a spanish oak on the river, down river to a white oak, S to a white oak, to beginning; signed: Phillip Gates; witness: Samuel Henderson, Alexander McClarran; proved May 1774 Term by Henderson.

P. 262, 1 July 1773, Daniel Winters of Guilford, miller, to Benjamin Cox of same, one hundred pounds, 70 acres, on Richland Cr., begin at a white oak in the Back Line being a fore & aft tree standing on the side of a branch or run, down branch to Richland Cr., down creek to lower line, round with line to first station, part of a survey for 422 acres, Granville to John Tracks 1 May 1752; signed: Daniel Winter; witness: Ransom Southerland, Charles Dixon; proved May 1774 Term by Southerland.

P. 263, 27 December 1773, David Macy of Guilford to Paul Starbuck of same, one hundred sixty pounds, 285 acres, on both sides Ready Fork a branch of Haw R., begin at a stake in Low Grounds of Beaver Cr. a branch of Ready Fork, E 83 roods to a black oak, S 288 roods to a white oak saplin, W 214 roods to a black oak & hicory, N 112 roods to a black oak, N52E 164 roods to a black oak, N to first station, Simeon Taylor to Macy 150 acrez, Thomas Eldridge to macy 135 acres, part of a tract from Granville to William Perry 1759; signed: David Macy; witness: Timothy Russell, William Starbuck; proved May 1774 Term by William Starbuck.

P. 264, 18 August 1774, James Denny of Guilford, farmer, to William Anderson of same one hundred pounds, 298 acres, on N side of North Buffaloe Cr., begin at a red oak on the bank of the creek, N 300 p. to a stake, E 172 1/2 p. to a hicory, S to a black oak on bank of creek, up creek to first station, Granville to John Nix 4 December 1753; signed: James Denny; witness: George Denny, James Denny; acknowledged August 1774 Term.

P. 265, 4 November 1773, Ebenezer Starns & Anne his wife of South Carolina to Aquila Jones of Guilford, ninety pounds, 244 acres, on a branch of Sandy Cr., part of a tract from Granville to Harmon Husband 11 December 1762 for 660 acres, begin at a marked hicory Jno. Field's cor., N 124 p. to one of the original cor., E 60 p. on original line to original cor. red oak, N 14 p. to a stake James Davis' cor., E 228 p. cross original tract to original line, S 143 p. to John Field's line, W to first station; signed: Ebenezer Starns, Anne ( ) Starns; witness: James Hunter, Stephen (I) Jones; proved August 1774 Term by Hunter.

P. 265, 16 September 1773, John Buis & Martha his wife of Guilford to Robert Lindsey of same, two hundred eighty seven pounds, 354 acres, on Deep R., begin at a white oak about 70 ch. from the South Fork of Deep R. on the N side, S30W 76 ch. to a maple John Baldwin's cor., N18W 38 p. to a persimon on the S bank of Deep R. Baldwin's dividing line, N37W along the river bank to a persimmon at mouth of a branch 6 p., N25W 50 p. to a small post oak, N52W to a stake on the original line, N along line to a white oak, S 22 ch. to first station, part of tract from Granville to Willm. Buis 5 November 1756, Willm. Buis willed to John Buis; signed: Jno. Buis, Martha Buis; witness: William Bostick, Benjamin (B) Redock; acknowledged August 1774 Term.

P. 266, 12 February 1774, Robert Doak of Guilford to Lewis Hutton of same, one hundred fifty two pounds ten shillings, 201 1/2 acres, on the Bleating Br. waters of Allamance, begin at post oak, N 35 ch. 3 rods to a post oak, W 56 ch. to a white oak, 35 ch. 3 rods to a red oak, E 56 ch. to the beginning, part of land he lives on called Bleating-house Land; signed: Robt. Doak, Hannah Doak; witness: Wm. Reynolds, James Matthews; proved August 1774 Term by Reynolds.

P. 268, 7 April 1774, Mary Patrick of Guilford to James Patrick of same, fifty pounds, 175 acres, on S side of Haw R., part of land from Granville to Robt. Thompson 2 August 1760, begin on river adjoining the conveyance of the other part to Hugh Patrick's line, from end of his line on W side of tract at river to first cor. mentioned on the tract which is a black oak, E 33 ch. 50 lk. to a black oak, S 15 ch. to a white oak on the N bank of Mill Cr., down creek NE 34 ch. to a poplar by the Mill Pond, E 17 ch. to a black oak & white oak, to first station, Thompson to William Patrick 2 March 1763, Willm. Patrick to William Mackie 15 July 1771, Mackie to Mary Patrick 15 January 1772, James Patrick is to pay his brother Ebenezer Patrick or his chosen guardian thirty pounds on 1 April 1788, James Patrick is not to be in full possession of land until he is 21, Mary Patrick reserves 1/3 of all profits during her life; signed: Mary Patrick; witness: Henry Work, William Buchannan, William Mackey; acknowledged August 1774 Term.

P. 269, 11 April 1774, Mary Patrick of Guilford to Hugh Patrick of same, one hundred fifty pounds, 175 acres, on N side of Haw R., begin at a white oak on N bank of Haw R., W 50 ch. to a white oak, S 12 ch. 25 lk. crossing branch to a hicory, W 25 ch. to a black oak, S to Haw R. down river to first station, part of land from Granville to Robt. Thompson 2 August 1760, Thompson to William Patrick 2 March 1763, Patrick to William Mackie 15 July 1771, Mackie to Mary Patrick 15 January 1772, Hugh Patrick to pay William Armstrong Patrick or his chosen guardian thirty pounds 1 April 1786, Hugh Patrick not to be in full possession until he reaches aged 21 except on death of Mary Patrick, in case Mary should live longer than the term of 21 years she excepts 1/3 of profits from same to her use; signed: Mary Patrick; witness: Henry Work, William Buchannan, William Mackie; acknowledged August 1774 Term.

P. 270, 25 3rd month 1774, Anthony Hoggat & Mary his wife of Guilford to Edward Bond of same, thirty five pounds, 100 acres, on Long Br. the E side of the East Fork of Deep R., part of a tract from Granville to Hoggat 7 February 1755, begin at a spanish oak the NW cor. of the tract, S along the old line 100 p. to a stake, E 160 p. to a hicory, N 100 p. to a black oak standing in the old line, the old line W 160 p. to beginning; signed: Anthony Hoggat, Mary Hoggat; witness: Abraham Powel, Jesse (O) Lane, Samuel Hoggat, proved August 1774 Term by Samuel Hoggat.

P. 271, 6 February 1773, Jacob Lienbarger & Catherine his wife of Chatham, farmer, to Francis Lienbarger of Guilford, eighteen pounds, 121 acres, part of a tract from Henry McCulloh 9 June 3rd year of George III [1763] for 242 acres, begin at a hicory the 2nd cor. tree of original tract, N75E 130 p. to a stake in George Lienbarger's line, N till it intersects the given line of the tract, W to beginning; signed: [Jacob Liebarger in German], Catherine (O) Lienbarger; witness: [Jacob Greeson in German], [another Lienbarger in German]; proved August 1774 Term by Greeson.

P. 272, 22 July 1774, Thomas Lamb of Guilford, miller, to son Josiah Lamb of same, love & affection, all estate both real & personal, Josiah Lamb had been given a complete inventory which is not recorded; signed: Thomas Lamb; witness: Abraham Elliot, Joseph Elliot; proved August 1774 Term by Joseph Elliot.

P. 273, 17 June 1774, Robert Greer of Guilford to Martha McGee of same, [amount of consideration not given], 301 acres, on S side of Deep R. on Frazier's tract, 1/2 of a larger tract from Granville to Aaron Frazier 30 July 1760, Frazier to Robert Greer 24 July 1774, begin at a white oak, S 65 ch. to a white oak, E 46 ch. 20 lk. to a post a cor. between sd. land & Nathaniel Kerr, N65 65 ch. along dividing line to another post, W 46 ch. 25 lk. to beginning; signed: Robert (R) Greer; witness: John Clark, James Hunter, Stephen (I) Jones; proved august 1774 Term by Hunter.

P. 274, 29 November 1773, Nicholas Major of Guilford to Nathaniel Williams of same, eighty pounds, 103 acres, on both sides Hogans Cr., begin at a small hicory on Piney Br., S 57 p. to a white oak, E 200 p. to another white oak, N 20 p. to a small burch saplin on Cabbin Br., N 80 p., W 220 p. to beginning on Piney Br., William Savage to Samuel Watt, Watt to Major; signed: Nicholas Major; witness: Jere Williamson, Josiah Mann, George (+) Allen; proved August 1774 by Allen.

P. 274, 16 December 1772, William Anderson of Enoe Settlement in Orange, taylor, to James Brown of Surry, farmer, ninety seven pounds ten shillings, 282 acres, on a branch of Reedy Fork of Haw

R., on S side of fork & both sides of the County Line between Orange & Rowan (now Guilford), begin at a black oak, S 56 1/2 ch. to 2 hicorys, E 50 ch. to a black jack, N 56 1/2 ch. to a black oak saplin, W crossing branch near the Old County Line 50 ch. to first station, Granville to William Anderson 23 May 1758; signed: Wm. Anderson; witness: Lawrence Thompson, Samuel Thompson, Ralph Gorrel, George Park; proved August 1774 Term by Gorrel.

P. 275, 11 8th month 1774, Joseph Jessop & Priscilla his wife of Surry to William Jessop his brother of Guilford, three hundred thirty pounds, 271 acres, money to be paid as follows: one hundred pounds in hand, one hundred thirty pounds 1 7th month next, one hundred pounds in 6 months after that, where William Jessop now lives, 246 acres of which Joseph Jessop purchased of Thomas Jessop his father, remaining 25 acres is part of a tract from Granville to Henry Ballenger 1753, on Horse Pen Cr., begin on N line of whole tract where it crosses Horse Pen Cr., E along line to a post oak saplin, S 80 p. to Timothy Jessop's line, W to creek, down creek to first station; signed: Joseph (J) Jessop, Priscilla (P) Jessop; witness: Caleb Jessop, Timothy Jessop, Joshua Sumner; affirmed August 1774 Term by Caleb Jessop.

P. 276, 18 10th month 1772, Simeon Taylor & Esther his wife of Guilford, planter, to William Rees of same, planter, five shillings, 208 acres, on both sides of Reedy Fork, begin at a white oak saplin, S 21 ch. to a hicory, W 45 1/2 ch. to a white oak bush on Forster's line, his line N cross Reedy Fork 50 1/2 ch. to a white oak, E 25 ch. to the center of 3 black oaks, N 17 1/2 ch. to a white oak bush, E 12 1/2 ch. to a hicory, S12E 14 1/2 ch. to a black oak David Macy's cor., S on Macy's line cross Reedy Fork 34 ch. to a black oak, E 4 ch. to a white oak saplin the first station; signed: Simeon Taylor, Esther Taylor; witness: Daniel Dillion, Joseph Perkins; proved August 1774 Term by Dillion.

P. 277, 8 12th month 1772, Simeon Taylor & Esther his wife of Guilford, planter, to William Rees of same, planter, two hundred pounds, 208 acres, [release of preceding deed, same signatures, witnesses, and probate].

P. 279, 10 8th month 1774, Thomas Bales & Sarah his wife of Surry to Thomas Jessop of Guilford, two hundred seventy four pounds, 274 acres, on a branch of Horse Pen Cr., begin at a black oak, W 200 p. to a red oak, N 228 p. to a white oak, E 112 p. to a stake, S 20 p. to a stake, E 88 p. to a stake, S 208 p. to first station, part of a tract from Granville to Bales 22 December 1753, recorded in Rowan Book B page 225; signed: Thomas Bales, Sarah Bales; witness: Henry Worley, Caleb Jessop; affirmed August 1774 Term by Worley. [Ed. note: The deed from Granville to Bales is recorded in Deed Book 2:225 in the name of Thomas Beals.]

P. 280, 11 July 1767, James McCain of Rowan to James Coleman of same, one hundred pounds, 125 acres, on N side of Dann R., begin at an oak on the river, N 90 p. to a cor. white oak, W 180 p. to a red oak, S 132 p. to a hicory on the river, down river to beginning; signed: James McCain; witness: Edwd. Hunter, James

Conway, Henry Conway, Jas. Roberts Junr.; proved August 1774 Term by Edward Hunter.

P. 281, 27 April 1774, Adam Mitchel & Mary his wife of Guilford to John Mitchel of same, twenty pounds, 400 acres, begin at a hicory on N side of North Buffaloe, W 30 ch. to a white oak, N 50 ch. to a stake, E 75 ch. to a stake on William Anderson's line (formerly John Nickolls), S 39 ch. his line to Buffaloe Cr., up creek to first station, part of tract from Granville to A. Mitchel 4 December 1753; signed: Adam ( ) Mitchel, Mary (D) Mitchel; witness: Robert Rankin, Wm. Anderson; proved November 1774 Term by Rankin.

P. 282, 2 November 1774, Michael Ricter late of Rowan now of Guilford, planter, to James Hendricks of Guilford, two hundred pounds, 200 acres, on both sides of Uharee Cr., includes improvements known as Salley's Place, begin at a white oak saplin, N 70 p. to a pine, W 160 p. to a pine, S at 20 p. cross Richland Fork of Uharee in all 200 p. to a stake, E 160 p. to a stake, N cross creek 130 p. to beginning, Henry Eustace McCulloh to Rictor 5 May 1767; signed: [signed in German]; witness: Jno. Braley, George Smith; acknowledged November 1774 Term.

P. 284, 13 November 1774, Robert Mitchel & Margaret his wife of Guilford to Henry Ross of same, fifty five pounds, 150 acres, on Horse Pen Cr. & on S side of Main Road, begin at a post & a marked chesnut bush on Robert Mitchel's line, N 33 ch. to a post on Mitchel's line, W 45 1/2 ch. to a white oak saplin on Robert Sumner's line, S 33 ch. to a post oak saplin on Sumner's line, E to beginning; signed: Robt. Mitchel, Margaret Mitchell; witness: Alexr. Moody, James Ross; acknowledged November 1774 Term.

P. 285, 14 November 1774, Robert Mitchel & Margaret his wife of Guilford to James Ross of same, seventy five pounds, 150 acres, on Horsepen Cr. & both sides of the Main Road, begin at a white oak saplin cor. to Henry Ross, N 22 ch. to a post oak on Hugh Forster's line, E 13 1/2 ch. on Forster's line to a white oak, N 16 ch. on Forster's line to a hicory, E to a white oak 32 ch. to Robert Mitchel's line, S 38 ch. on Mitchel's line to a post cor. to Henry Ross, Henry Ross' line to beginning; signed: Robt. Mitchell, Margaret Mitchell; witness: Alexr. Moody, Henry Ross; acknowledged November 1774 Term.

P. 286, 10 November 1774, John Thrasher of Guilford to Isaac Thrasher of same, fifty pounds, 218 acres, on both sides of Lick Fork of Hogans Cr., part of a survey & land granted to John Thrasher December 1761 for 693 acres, begin at a white oak on W side of creek, S 272 p. to a cor. white oak, E 128 p. to a cor. white oak, N 201 p. to a red oak, W 50 p. to a dogwood, N 64 p. to a cor. white oak, W 78 p. to beginning; signed: John (IT) Thrasher; witness: Aaron Fletcher, Joseph Cloud Thrasher, John Thrasher; proved November 1774 Term by Joseph Cloud Thrasher.

P. 287, 8 November 1774, John Thrasher of Guilford to Joseph Cloud Thrasher of same, fifty pounds, 255 acres, on both sides of

Lick Fork of Hogans Cr., part of 693 acres granted to John Thrasher December 1761, begin at a red oak on E side of the creek, W 140 p. to a hicory, same course 76 p. to a cor. white oak, S23E 64 p. to a blazed dogwood on the creek, S118E 50 p. to a red oak, S 201 p. to John Thrasher's back line, E 140 p. to a white oak, N 272 p. to beginning; signed: John (IT) Thrasher; witness: Aaron Fletcher, Isaac Thrasher, John Thrasher; proved November 1774 Term by Isaac Thrasher.

P. 288, 13 February 1773, William Forster & Martha his wife of Guilford to John Forster & Samuel Forster of same, two hundred pounds, 257 acres, on both sides Horse Pen Cr. waters of Haw R., begin at a black oak, N 200 p. to a stake, W 205 p. to a stake, S 200 p. to 2 black oak saplins marked, E 205 p. to beginning, joins southerly on Robert Mitchell, Granville to Hugh Forster 3 December 1753; signed: William Forster, Martha ( ) Forster; witness: Wi. Avery, Thomas Lindsey, Benjamin Piggot; acknowwledged November 1774 Term.

P. 289, 9 October 1772, James McCuiston & Catherine his wife of Guilford to John Clark of same, one hundred fifty pounds, 200 acres, on James McCuiston's line & Samuel Scott's line at a black 70 rods from the cor., N 130 perches across Richland Cr. to a white oak & black oak, W 250 perches to James McCuiston's line, S 130 perches to his cor., E to the beginning, includes mill place, land conveyed out of a tract of 640 acres, Granville to James Mccuiston 22 February 1759; signed: James McCuiston, Catherine (m) McCuiston; witness: James (I) Johnston, John McCuiston; proved November 1774 Term by Johnston.

P. 291, 15 November 1774, John Lewis of Guilford, planter, & Priscilla his wife to Jacob Lewis of same, planter, natural love & affection & better maintenance [no relationship given], 200 acres, on a branch of Polecat Cr., begin at 2 ash saplins, 245 p. by lands of late John McGee to a hicory, N 80 p. to a black oak, E by Jeremiah Reynolds 185 p. to a white oak bush, N 80 p. to a stake, E 140 p. to a hicory, S 160 p. to first station, part of 2 tracts, Mary Terrel to John Lewis & David Reynolds to John Lewis, registered in Rowan; signed: John Lewis, Priscilla Lewis; witness: Jeremiah Reynolds, David Lewis; acknowledged November 1774 Term.

Page numbers 292 through 299 missing.

P. 300, 17 February 1775, Edward Cowen of Guilford, planter, & Mary his wife to Martha McGee of same, twelve pounds, 43 acres 16 rods, on Sandy Cr., begin at a mulberry tree on the S side of Henry York's survey, S10E 46 perches to a poplar, W 17 perches to a poplar, S10E 48 perches to a gum tree, E 77 perches to a hicory, n 93 perches to a hicory, W to first station, part of Edward Cowen's land and part of Edward Wilbourn's from Granville 1769 [?]; signed: Edward (EC) Cowen, Mary ( ) Cowen; witness: Thomas Cowen, William Wellbourn Junr.; proved February 1775 Term by Wellbourn.

P. 301, 20 10th month 1774, Joseph Unthank of Guilford to Allen Unthank of same, two hundred pounds, 421 acres, begin at a post oak on George Rankin's SE cor., N 247 p. to an ash saplin, E 180 p. to a post oak, S 225 p. to a black gum, E 77 p. to a cor. stone, S45E 180 p. to 2 post oak saplins on S side of Salisbury Road, along road S45W 88 p. to a black oak saplin, W 108 p. to a hicory saplin, N29W 168 p. to a cor. stone, W 10 p. to another cor. stone, S 21 p. to a spanish oak saplin, N49W 168 p. to 3 post oak saplins, W 71 p. to beginning, part of a tract from Granville to Joseph Unthank 4 November 1757 for 912 acres, on branches of Horse Pen & Brush Cr; signed: Joseph Unthank; witness: William Gray, David Brooks; proved February 1775 Term by William Gray Esq. & Brooks.

P. 302, 20 10th month 1774, Joseph Unthank of Guilford to John Unthank of same, thirty pounds, 78 acres 151 poles, begin at a post oak George Rankin's SE cor., S 120 p. to a hicory, E 116 p. to a stake, N 76 p. to a spanish oak saplin, N49W 65 p. to 3 post oak saplins, W 71 p. to beginning, on branches of Horsepen & Brush Cr.; signed: Joseph Unthank; witness: William Gray, David Brooks; proved February 1775 Term by William Gray Esq. & Brooks.

P. 303, 20 10th month 1774, John Unthank of Guilford to Allen Unthank of same, five pounds, 7 acres 110 poles, begin at a white oak saplin on the N side of Horsepen Cr., N49W 82 p. to a spanish oak saplin, N 21 p. to a cor. stone, E 10 p. to another cor. stone, S29E 88 p. to beginning, part of a tract from Granville to Joseph Unthank 4 November 1757 for 912 acres, on branches of Horsepen & Brush Cr., Joseph Unthank to Richard Williams 10 May 1759 for 110 acres, Williams to John Unthank 3 5th month 1769 for 55 acres; signed: John Unthank; witness: William Gray, David Brooks; proved February 1775 Term by William Gray Esq. & Brooks.

P. 304, 22 February 1775, Hugh Wiley Sr. of Guilford to Hugh Wiley Junr. of same, six pounds, 97 acres, part of a tract from Granville to Hugh Wiley Sr. for 696 acres, on the S side of Beaver Cr., begin at the beginning of the original tract at a black jack in a glade, N 184 p. along the old line to a cor. on a poplar, E 44 p. to a post oak, N 13 p., W to the creek 45 p., S38W 252 p. running & bounding by various turns of the creek 151 p. E to beginning; signed: Hugh (H) Wiley; witness: William Hamilton, Andrew Finley; acknowledged February 1775 Term.

P. 304, 8 February 1775, William Wiley of Guilford to Robert Wiley his son of same, two hundred pounds, 300 acres, on both sides Beaver Cr., begin at a black oak, E 224 p. to a stake, S to original cor., W 224 p., along original line to beginning; signed: William Wiley; witness: Robt. Agnew, Wm. Peasly; acknowledged February 1775 Term.

P. 306, 22 February 1775, Rebecca Boyd of Guilford to Robert Bell of same, twenty shillings, 320 acres, on North Fork of Belews Cr., begin at a red oak, S 80 ch. to a red oak, E 40 ch. to a white oak, N 40 ch. to the center of 3 white oaks, W 40 ch. to first station, Granville to Patrick Hays of Rowan 18 July 1760,

Hays to Boyd 13 April 1767; signed: Rebecca (O) Boyd; witnerss: [none listed]; acknowledged February 1775 Term.

P. 307, 2[blank] August 17[blank], Jacob Gregg of Orange, millwright, to Herman Husband Junr. second cousin to Jacob Gregg & son of Herman Husband the elder of same, two hundred pounds, paid by Phebe Cox grandmother of Herman Husband Junr., 1090 acres, on Deep R., begin at a white oak a beginning tree of a tract called Barber which was granted Herman Husband 5 November 1757, N 40 ch. to a persimmon tree, E 661 ch. to a forked pine, N 74 1/2 ch. to a pine, E 75 ch. to a pine, S 50 ch. to a white oak, W 25 ch. to a pine, S to the line of a tract granted Jesse Hollingsworth, E to Hollingsworth's cor. pine, S 75 ch. to a white oak, W 60 ch. to a mulberry tree on the bank of Deep R., up river leaving 10 acres to John Wilcocks & William Thompson as by their deed to first station; signed: Jacob Gregg; witness: James Pugh, Samuel Frazier, Herman Husband; proved February 1775 Term by Frazier.

P. 308, 20 August 1774, Jacob Gregg of Orange, millwright, to Mary Husband second cousin to Jacob Gregg & daughter of Harmon Husband of Orange, one hundred pounds paid by Phebe Cox grandmother of Mary Husband & natural love & affection & for better maintenance, 640 acres, in Orange County, on Sandy Cr., begin at 2 white oaks & a hicory the beginning tree of the original survey, S across creek in Samuel Walker's mill dam 22ch. 50 lk. to a black oak, W crossing creek below mill 40 ch. to 2 white oaks & a black jack, S 73 ch. 50 lk. to 3 hicorys, E 76 ch. to a white oak, N 96 ch. to a white oak, W 36 ch. to first station; signed: Jacob Gregg; witness: James Pugh, Samuel Frazier, Herman Husband; proved February 1775 Term by Frazier.

P. 309, 27 January 1775, Thomas Mills of Guilford to John Wheeler of same, one hundred seven pounds, 150 acres, on both sides of the uppermost North Fork of Deep R., part of a tract from Granville to Thomas Mills, begin at a large post oak cor., S 231 p. to a stake, E 75 p. to a white oak, N 142 p. to a post oak, E 75 p. to a stake, N 89 p. to a hicory, W 150 p. to first station; signed: Thomas Mills; witness: William Gray, Aaron Mills; proved February 1775 Term by W. Gray Esq. & A. Mills.

P. 310, 16 December 1774, Henry Ross & Margaret his wife of Guilford to Thomas White of same, one hundred fifty pounds, 150 acres, on waters of Horsepen Cr. & the S side of Main Road, begin at a post & a marked chesnut bush on Robert Mitchell's line, N 33 ch. on Mitchell's line to a post a cor. to James Ross, W 45 1/2 ch. on James Ross' line to a white oak saplin on Robert Sumner's line, S 33 ch [torn] oak saplin, E to beginning; signed: Henry Ross, Margaret Ross; witness: James Ross, Jno. Stanton; proved February 1775 Term by James Ross.

P. 311, 20 February 1775, Thomas Davis & Elizabeth his wife of Guilford, farmer, to Levi Branson of Chatham, one hundred twelve pounds, 205 acres, on both sides of Deep R., begin at a cor. of the Mill tract by the river, along that W line 20 ch. to a hicory, S 60 1/2 ch. along William Cox's line to a white oak, E

38 1/2 ch. along Wm. Cox's line of the Thicket to a spanish oak by the river, up river N5E 8 ch. to Peter Youngblood's cor. white oak, his line E 30 ch. to a white oak saplin, N 16 1/2 ch. to Harmon Cox's line cornered between 2 white oaks & a hicory, his line W 24 ch. to a cor. black oak saplin, W 8 1/2 ch. to a black oak by Deep R., up r. to first station, Granville to William Cox 5 November 1757, Cox to Frederick Syfrert 4 February 1764, Syfrert to Davis 12 June 1767; signed: Thos. Davis, Elizabeth (X) Davis; witness: Hugh Patten, Jacob Hollingsworth, Jno. (+) Rease; proved February 1775 Term by Patten.

P. 312, 6 January 1775, Francis Cummins of Guilford to Thomas Cummins of same, seventy five pounds, 400 acres, on a branch of South Buffaloe on the S side, begin at a post, N 200 perches to a post, W 230 perches to a post by a marked white oak saplin, S 200 perches to a post by a marked black oak, E to the beginning; signed: Francis Cummins; witness: Alexr. Caldwell, Robert Rogers; proved February 1775 Term by Caldwell.

P. 314, 22 December 1774, Andrew Hall of Guilford, planter, to Daniel Gillespie of same, planter, one hundred eleven pounds, 240 acres, on both sides of South Buffaloe where Hall now lives, begin at a hicory, E to a sugar maple 160 p., N 82 p. to an ash, E 160 p. to a white oak, to a white oak & black oak saplin 82 ch, 320 p. to a white oak, 150 p. to a hicory thew beginning cor.; signed: Andrew Hall; witness: Isabellah (H) Hall, Ralph Gorrel; proved February 1775 Term by Ralph Gorrel esq.

P. 315, 24 February 1775, Micajah Mills of Guilford to Joseph Stanly of same, fifty pounds, 50 acres, on Piney Br. of North Fork of Deep R., part of a tract given Micajah Mills by his father Hus Mills, Granville to Hus Mills 28 February 1759, begin at a white oak tree the NW cor. of the entire tract, S 29 ch. to a stake, E 17 ch. 25 lk. to a stake, N 29 ch. to a stake, W 17 ch. 25 lk. to beginning; signed: Micajah Mills; witness: Wi Strangman Stanley, Thomas Mills Junr.; proved February 1775 Term by Strangman Stanley.

P. 316, 20 February 1775, Thomas Mills of Guilford to Reuben Mills of same, five pounds, 170 acres, on both sides of the uppermost North Fork of Deep R., begin at a white oak, W 42 ch. 2 poles to a hicory, S 40 ch. to a black oak, E 42 ch. 2 poles to a hicory, N 40 ch. to first station; signed: Thomas Mills; witness: William Gray, George Stalker; proved February 1775 by William Gray esq. & Stalker.

P. 317, 12 February 1775, Simeon Hinds & Sarah his wife and Levi Hinds & Sarah his wife of Guilford to Joseph Hinds of same, five shillings, one parcel containinfg two equal thirds of 220 acres, on Old Trading Road & one of the SE forks of Polecat Cr.; begin at a black oak standing a small distance from the creek on the E side & on the NW side of a small hill, S 67 ch. crossing the creek & Trading Road to a black jack, cross branch E 41 ch. 25 lk. to a black jack, N 52 ch. to a red oak, W 17 ch. 25 lk. to a spanish oak, N 15 ch. to a white oak by the side of the Old

Trading Road, along road SW as road runs & agreeable to the deed from Joseph Hinds decd. to Simeon Hinds untill it comes to a branch, down branch to first line, Granville to Zachariah Cox 6 December 1761, Cox & wife to Joseph Hinds 1 March 1763, Joseph Hinds willed to Simeon Hinds & Levi Hinds by will dated 14 April 1772; signed: Simeon Hinds, Sarah (H) Hinds, Levi Hinds, Sarah (S) Hinds; witness: Richard Norton, Elias Cowen; proved February 1775 Term by Norton.

P. 318, 13 February 1775, Simeon Hinds & Sarah his wife and Levi Hinds & Sarah his wife of Guilford to Joseph Hinds of same, one hundred pounds, [this is the release of the preceding lease, signatures, witnesses, and probate are the same].

P. 321, These are to certify to all to whom it may concern that on Tuesday the 28th day of April in the year of our Lord 1761 Francis McNairy & Mary Boyd were lawfully married by Thos. Barton, Missionary at Lancaster;
    John McNairy son of Francis & Mary was born 20 March 1762;
    Mary McNairy daughter of Francis & Mary was born 15 January 1764;
    Andrew McNairy son of Francis & Mary was born 10 January 1766;
    Robert McNairy son of Francis & Mary born 21 June 1768;
    Mary McNairy daughter of Francis & Mary born 5 January 1771;
    James McNairy son of Francis & Mary born 20 January 1773;
    Catherine McNairy daughter of Francis & Mary born 30 January 1775.

P. 321, 1 September 1774, James Thompson & Dorithy his wife & William Boddington & Sarah his wife of Middlesex County in the Island of Great Britain to Colonel Edmund Fanning L.L.D. late of North Carolina, three hundred pounds, 640 acres in Orange County in possession of Hugh Woods & all houses & lots in hillsborough & all estate of William Churton Esq. decd., real or personal, which grantors may have a right as legatees, [no description of the land]; signed: James Thompson, Dorothy Thompson, William Boddington, Sarah Boddington; witness: C. Williams, Nicholas (X) Conner; acknowledged 2 September 1774 before Fred. Bull, Mayor of London.

P. 322, 2 September 1774, Charles Williams proved the following affidavit before Frederick Bull Esq. Lord Mayor of London.

P. 323, Affidavit of Charles Williams of St. James Place in city of Wesminster County of Middlesex Esq. that he and Nicholas Conner of New Bond Street of same city & county witnessed signatures of James & Dorothy Thompson & William & Sarah Boddington which was signed to the indenture, letters of attorney, and general release, 1 September 1774.

P. 323, 1 September 1774, Letter of Attorny, James & Dorothy Thompson and William & Sarah Boddington constitute Col. Edmund Fanning LLD late of North Carolina attorney to receive property belonging to estate of William Churton Esq. decd. to which they have claim as legatees, this is a full power of attorney; signed: James Thompson, Dorothy Thompson, William Boddington, Sarah Boddington; witness: Charles Williams, Nicholas Conner; acknowledged before Fred. Bull 2 September 1774.

P. 324, General Release, a quit claim deed to Col. Fanning from James & Dorothy Thompson and William & Sarah Boddington for the assets of William Churton decd., signed: James Thompson, Dorothy Thompson, William Boddington, Sarah Boddington; witness: Charles Williams, Nicholas Conner; acknowledged 2 September 1774 before Frederick Bull Mayor of London.

P. 324, 10 February 1775, William Lowther & Edmund Fanning of New York surviving executors of William Churton Esq. decd. to John Blagge of New York Esq., three hundred pounds Sterling, assets of Churton; signed: Edmd. Fanning, Wm. Lowther; witness: William Deane, Isaac (X) Dupues, Jno. Knapp; proved 16 May 1775 in New Bern before M. Howard, CJ, by Dupues.

P. 328, 11 February 1775, John Blagge of City of New York to Edmund Fanning of same, three hundred pounds Sterling, all assets of William Churton decd.; signed: John Blagge; witness: William Deane, Isaac (X) Dupues, Jno. C. Knapps; proved 16 May 1775 in New Bern before M. Howard, CJ, by Dupues.

P. 330, 4 February 1774, John Mendenhall of Guilford, farmer, & Mary his wife to William Field of same, one hundred twenty five pounds, 233 acres, on Hickory Cr. waters of Deep R., begin at a hicory on John Ozbun's line, N 55 ch. to a white oak, E crossing creek 42 1/2 ch. to a white oak, S 55 ch. to a hicory, W 5 ch. to Ozbourn's white oak, his line W to first station, Zachariah Stanly to John Mendenhall 12 8th month 1767, registered in Guilford; signed: Jno. Mendenhall, Mary Mendenhall; witness: James Wilson, Moses Mendenhall; proved May 1775 Term by Moses Mendenhall.

P. 331, 13 November 1779, North Carolina to William Dick, 240 acres, on waters of Hunting & Richland Cr., begin at a spanish oak in Arthur Forbess' line, E cross 3 branches 230 p. to a spanish oak in Samuel Scott's line, his line S to James McCuiston's line, his line same course crossing 2 branches in all 167 p. to a black oak, W 230 p. to a chesnut in the line of the Court House Tract, N that line 167 p. to first station, Grant #238; signed: J. Glasgow; no probate record.

P. 332, 20 October 1775, Baker Degraffenreitt of Guilford to Francis Degraffenreitt of Chatham & William Degraffenreitt of Lunenburg County, Virginia, three hundred pounds which Baker owes Francis & William and five shillings, nine negroes: Cato, Judah, Winny, Abraham, Silva, Esther, Julias, Cremy, & Absalom with future increase of the females, all stock of hogs & cattle, 1 dark bay mare, 1 ditto coloured horse colt, 1 sorrel mare, & all household furniture, to be sold 1 Janaury 1776 if three hundred pounds is not repaid; signed: Baker Degraffenriadt; witness: Christopher Billups, William Cowan, Mary Cowan; acknowledged

November 1775 Term.

P. 336, 14 February 1775, Windsor Pearce & Mary his wife of Guilford to Ransom Southerland of same, ninety pounds, 100 acres, on S side of Deep R., begin at the center or channel of the river at a stake 3 p. from a spanish oak on the river bank, W 129 p. to a pine near a path called the Road, N 77 p. to a red oak saplin on S side of Pearces Cr., N81W 84 p. to a pine, S57W 8 p. to a stake among 4 red oak pointers, N 30 p., N61E 175 p. to a hicory on the bank of river, the course continued 3 p. to a stake near the lower end of Reads Island, down center or channel of river to first station, part of 2 tracts of 640 acres from Granville to William Searcy 9 June 1761, Searcy to Mary Pearce; signed: Windsor Pearce, Mary (M) Pearce; witness: John Lawrence, Jacob Shepherd; proved February 1775 Term by Lawrence.

P. 337, 25 April 1775, Relinquishment of dower in previous deed by Mary Pearce.

P. 338, 14 February 1774, William Searcy Senr. of guilford to Ransom Southerland of same, twenty seven pounds fifteen shillings, 37 1/4 acres, on S side of Deep R., begin at a hicory about the middle of Reads Island near the lower end 3 p. from a large hicory on the edge of the river bank one of Mary Pearce's cor. of her 100 acre tract, her line S61W 175 p., N 80 p., E 148 p. to first station, part of 640 acres from Granville to William Searcy Senr. 9 June 1761; signed: Wm. Searcy; witness: Jacob Shepherd, John Larrance; proved February 1775 Term by Larrance.

P. 339, 13 January 1775, Richard Lynam of Virginia son and heir of Andrew Lynam decd. to John Thompson of Guilford, one hundred pounds, 200 acres, known as Lynams Tract, on both sides of Hogans Cr., part of a survey of Robert Jones Esq. decd. of 400 acres, 200 acres of which Jones sold William Savage, recorded in Orange, [no metes and bounds description]; signed: Richard Lynam; witness: Jno. Williams, Nathl. Williams; proved May 1775 Term by John Williams Esq.

P. 340, 27 July 1774, Solomon Cox & Naomi his wife of Guilford to William Ashmore of same, three hundred pounds, 237 1/2 acres, on a fork of Richland Cr. waters of Deep R., joins Stephen Hussey & land that belonged to Thomas Cox decd., begin at a hicory, W 50 ch. to a black jack, S 47 1/2 ch. to a hicory on Stephen Hussey's line, sd. line 50 ch. to a spanish oak, N 47 1/2 ch. to beginning, part of a tract from Granville to Benjamin Ellis 21 December 1761, Ellis to Solomon Coxx 20 July 1765; signed: Solomon Cox, Naomi Cox; witness: Wm. Cole, Edmd. Williams Junr., John Conner; proved May 1775 Term by William Cole Esq.

P. 341, 4 June 1774, Robert Agnew of Guilford, merchant, to Wells Cowper of Nansemond County, Virginia, merchant, one hundred seventy nine pounds nineteen shillings ten & a half pence, 215 acres, on both sides of Rock Cr., bounded by Conrad Lowe on S, John Smith on NW side, on E by plantation where Robert Agnew now lives, [no metes and bounds description], deed void if Robert

Agnew repays one hundred seventy nine pounds nineteen shillings ten & a half pence plus six percent interest by 1 May 1775; signed: Robt. Agnew, Wells Cowper Company by William Johnston; witness: Matt: Keaughy; acknowledged May 1775 Term.

P. 343, 7 June 1774, Zebedee Wood of Guilford to Martha McGee of same, forty one pounds seven shillings, 100 acres, begin at a black oak, E 70 p., N 17 p. to a black oak, N 43 p. to a hicory, N60W 200 p. to the original line on the Main Road, S on original line 154 p. to the original cor. stake, E to a cor. white oak, S to a branch, down branch to Sandy Cr., a straight line to beginning, part of a tract from Granville to Herman Husband 10 December 1762 for 700 acres on Sandy Cr., Husband to Stephen Jones, Jones to Wood, deed void if Zebedee Wood repays forty one pounds seven shillings by 7 June 1776; signed: Zebedee Wood; witness: James Morgan, George Lewis, Stephen (I) Jones; proved May 1775 Term by Morgan.

P. 344, 7 July 1770, John Payne of Rowan, planter, to Thomas Jessop of same, planter, one hundred fifty pounds, 198 acres, where I formerly lived, part of 640 acres where Henry Ballenger now lives, Granville to Ballenger 20 December 20 December 1753, begin at a black oak saplin in Henry Ballenger's line on E side of Horsepen Cr., W 320 p. to a chesnut, S 70 p. to a black oak saplin, E 101 p. to a white oak, S 40 p. to a hicory, E 40 p. to a white oak, S 12 p. to a sassafras, E 99 p. to a post, to first station, 20 March 1768 John Payne had a clear title to the land, Payne confirms a former indenture from "me & Mary my wife" to Thomas Jessop 20 March 1768; signed: John Payne; witness: Eleazer Hunt, Walter (M) Matthews, Martha Stanley; proved February 1775 Term [jurat not named].

P. 345, 14 July 1775, William Searcy Senr. of Guilford, planter, to Ransom Southerland of same, thirty seven pounds seventeen shillings six pence, 75 3/4 acres, on SW side of Deep R., begin at a pine on the Great Road being the 2nd cor. of 100 acres bought of Windsor Pearce, W 110 p. 10 lk. to a hicory saplin, S77W 50 p. 29 lk. cross road to several pine pointers, N 52 p., N57E 84 p., S81E 84 p., S 77 p. to beginning; signed: Wm. Searcy; witness: Windsor Pearce; acknowledged August 1775 Term.

P. 346, 23 March 1775, Isaac Vernon of St. Pauls Parish, Georgia, to Samuel Allen of Guilford, farmer, thirty pounds, 100 acres, on W side of Coxes Cr. begin at a stone on bank of creek in original W line, W 108 p. to original cor. white oak, S 200 p. to original cor. 2 small black oaks, E 28 p. to a stone on bank of the creek, up creek to first station, part of a tract from Granville to Harmon Cox 5 August 1758, Cox to Vernon, recorded in Orange; signed: Isaac Vernon; witness: John Allen, David Cox, Isaac Cox; affirmed May 1775 Term by Allen.

P. 347, 14 August 1773, Samuel Hargrave of Caroline County, Virginia, to Thomas Jessop of Rowan, one hundred eighty pounds, 246 acres, on both sides Horsepenn Cr., begin at a cor. poplar & hicory adjoining Zachariah Dicks' land, along line Jessop bought of Daniel Britton, over Horsepen Cr., up Sawpit Br., cross ridge to William Britton, to land of Jessop bought of John Payne, to beginning; signed: Samuel Hargrave; witness: William Jessop, Joseph ( ) Jessop, John Payne; affirmed May 1775 by William Jessop.

P. 348, 12 November 1774, Nathan Pike of Surry, yeoman, to John Flanen of Chatham, sixty pounds, 175 acres, on waters of Brush Cr. waters of Rock [Rocky ?] R., begin at a marked post oak in the W line of Moses Nelson, W 160 p. to a red oak, N 172 p. 75 lk. to a post oak, E 110 p. to a red oak, S 172 p. 75 lk. to first station, part of a tract from Granville to Moses Nelson 28 June 1762, Nelson to Jeffry Beck 4 January 1764, Beck to John Johnston 27 July 1767, body of deed refers to grantors as Nathan Pike & Elizabeth his wife; signed: Nathan Pike, Elizabeth Pike; witness: John Pike, William Rhoades, William Green; acknowledged May 1775 Term.

P. 347(A), 6 March 1775, Peter Lawrence of Rowan to William Shaver of Guilford, eighty one pounds, 274 acres, on waters of Great Allamance a fork of Haw R., adjoins McCulloh's line, begin at a white oak saplin, E 45 ch. to a sweet gum, N45E 30 ch. to a red oak, N 33 ch. to a stake, W 67 ch. to a stake, S to beginning, part of a larger tract from Granville to Peter Lawrence Senr. decd.; signed: Peter (P) Lawrence; witness: John Butler, Thomas Hamilton; proved May 1775 Term by Butler.

P. 348(A), 3 May 1775, William Baldwin of Guilford to Peres Chapman of same, four hundred fifty pounds, 343 acres, part of a survey on waters of Deep R. from Granville to Baldwin 6 November 1756, begin at a white oak in the S line of the survey & cor. of land of the heirs of William Beuis decd., E 62 ch. to a black oak saplin marked for a cor. standing on the side of a run that comes through the plantation & enters Obidiah Harris' Mill Pond, N10E 21 ch. to a black oak saplin, N16E 9 ch. to a small black walnut, N31E 7 ch. 1 rod to a small ash saplin on the W side of the run, N 45 ch. 50 lk. to a post oak saplin marked for a cor. in the N line of the survey, W 34 ch. to a white oak, S 30 ch., S40W 61 ch. to first station, bounded on E by William Baldwin's other land; signed: William Baldwin; witness: William Gray, James Morphus; proved May 1775 Term by William Gray Esq.

P. 349, 3 May 1775, William Baldwin of Guilford to Peres Chapman of same, sixty five pounds, 297 acres, on waters of Deep R., Michael Farlow to William Baldwin, begin at a hicory in the W line of land Peres Chapman purchased this day of William Baldwin, N 46 ch. to a stake, W 69 ch. to last cor. of William Beuis' land where he lived last, S 22 ch. to Beuiss' beginning tree, S30W 18 ch. E to beginning; bounded on S by land Chapman purchased of Baldwin & part of land that did belong to Beuis & W by land of Beuis; signed: William Baldwin; witness: William Gray, James Morphew.

"Whereas it is supposed that James Morphew of Guilford County hath a right to the above described land that William Baldwin sold to Peres Chapman, these are to certify that for five shillings pd. to James Morphew by Peres Chapman, James Morphew doth discharge & acquit Peres Chapman from all right or claim James Morphew hath to any part of premises." 5 May 1775; signed: James Morphew; witness: William Gray, William Baldwin; proved May 1775 Term by William Gray Esq.

P. 350, 4 January 1775, Thomas Lovelatty of Guilford to Moss Armstead of Pittsylvania County, Virginia, one negroe boy slave & four pounds, 165 acres, land purchased of Ephriam Potter Senr. 15 March 1769, proved in Orange, [no metes and bounds description]; signed: Simeon (+) Lovelatty; witness: Isham Browder, Sampson Bethel, William Grizsel; proved May 1775 Term by Browder.

P. 351, 18 May 1775, John McAdoo Senr. of Guilford to John McAdoo Junr. of same, ten pounds, 160 acres, on South Buffaloe & Mebanes Mill Cr., part of a tract from Granville to John McAdoo Senr. 1759, begin at the beginning tree of the larger tract, E 23 ch., N 69 ch. 57 lk. cross tract, W 23 ch., a straight line to beginning; signed: Jno. McAdoo; witness: William Mebane, David Gillespie; proved May 1775 Term by Mebane.

P. 352, 14 March 1775, James Graves of Guilford to John Needham of same, one hundred twenty pounds, 300 acres, on both sides of Deep R., begin at a white oak saplin on William Searcy's line, N 25 ch. on Thomas Graves' line to a red oak & hicory, E along line to Joseph Carr's line, S along Carr's line to a red oak on the r., down river to Searcy's old line now John Spinks', W along line to beginning, land James Graves fell heir to by death of his father Thomas Graves, Granville to Thos. Graves 30 June 1762; signed: James Graves; witness: Ransom Southerland, John Moon; proved May 1775 Term by Southerland.

P. 352, 12 May 1775, Jacob Stalley & Barbara his wife of Guilford, farmer, to Martin Stally of same, farmer, sixty pounds, 85 acres, on waters of Stinking Quarter, part of tract to Martin Stally from William Barton, part of tract from John Burton to Wm. Barton, part of 1,000 acres to John Barton, begin at a post oak on McCulloh's original line, his line S to a hicory, W to an oak, SW on Barton's original line to the beginning; signed: Jacob (X) Stally, Barbara (\) Stally; witness: [two names in German]; proved May 1775 Term by Nicholas Amy.

P. 353, 13 May 1775, Michael Brown of Guilford, farmer, to Frederick Brown of same, seventy pounds, 225 acres, on a branch of Sandy Cr., part of a tract from Granville to Harmon Husband 10 December 1762, part of a tract from Conrad Staley to Michael Brown for 450 acres, begin at the end of 70 perches on the third line, N 110 perches to a hicory, W 192 perches to a red oak, S 57 perches to William Hinshaw's cor., S on Hinshaw's line 112 perches to a marked white oak, S25E 4 perches, S87E 60 perches, S43E 34 perches, S87E 40 perches, a straight line to beginning; [two names in German]; witness: [two names in German]; proved May 1775 by Martin Stalley.

P. 354, 2 April 1773, Bartholomew Dunn of Guilford, planter, & Elizabeth his wife to Jacob Staley of same, one hundred five pounds, 200 acres, on waters of Sandy Cr., begin at John McGee's in Barton's line a cor. also opposite McCulloh's tract of 1,000 acres, McGee's line W 60 p. to a bush, S45W 142 p. to an iron oak, S45E 180 p. to a black oak on Granville's line, along same N45E 170 p. to a turkey oak, to beginning, Henry Eustace McCulloh to Dunn 21 April 1764; signed: Bartholomew ( ) Dunn, Elizabeth (E) Dunn; witness: John McGee, Martin (M) Stalley, Henry Underwood, [a name in German]; proved May 1775 Term by Martin Staley.

P. 355, 12 May 1775, Hugh Wiley of Guilford to William Wiley of same, twenty shillings, 200 acres, part of 696 acres from Granville to Hugh Wiley, on the W end, begin at the beginning of the E line of the original tract, with line 146 perches, N 220 perches cross tract, W 146 perches with old line to cor., to first station; signed: Hugh (H) Wiley; witness: Alexander Ramage, John Wiley, Thomas Wiley; proved May 1775 by Ramage.

P. 356, 9 September 1774, Ludewick Irving & Eve his wife of Guilford, farmer, to George Cotner of same, farmer, twenty pounds, 190 acres, on waters of Stinking Quarter Cr., part of a tract from Henry McCulloh to Ludwick Irving in 3rd year of George III [1763], begin at a black oak, S44W on the original line 144 p. to cor. of original survey, NW 160 p. on original line to a marked hicory, NE 100 p. to a black oak, NW 20 p. to a black oak, NE 56 p., SE 2 p. to a white oak cor. of the original survey, NE to the original line 60 p., to the beginning; signed: Ludwick (X) Irving, Mary Eve (D) Irving; witness: Samuel Suther, Jacob (+) Engel, [Ludwig Clap in German]; proved May 1775 by Clap.

P. 357, 21 April 1765, Henry Eustace McCulloh [no residence given] to Bartholomew Dunn of Orange, planter, thirty pounds, 200 acres, includes improvements where he now lives, begin at John McGee's cor. in Barton's line a cor. also of McCulloh's tract of 1,300 acres, McGee's line W 60 p. to a bush, S45W 142 p. to an iron oak, S45E 180 p. to a black oak on Earl Granville's line, the same N45E 170 p. to a turkey oak, to beginning; signed: Henry E. McCulloh; witness: Jas. Campbell, B. McCulloh, Michael Holt; proved May 1775 by Holt.

P. 358, 16 August 1775, Edward Hunter & wife [not named] of Guilford to John Diques of same, fifty pounds, 250 acres, on E side of Dann R., begin at the mouth of Little Reed Cr. on sd. river, N a new dividing line 223 p. to a pine & white oak saplin the old line, E on line 164 p. to river, up river to beginning, includes Neal's Bent; signed: Edward Hunter; witness: [none listed]; acknowledged August term 1775.

P. 359, 29 July 1775, Baker Degraffenreidt of Guilford to Robert Donald, merchant, of Chesterfield County, Virginia, five hundred pounds, 300 acres, on N side of Dann R., begin at a persimmon on the river, N 204 p. to a red oak, W 212 p. to a saplin, S 250 p. to a hicory on the river, down river to beginning; signed: Baker

Degraffenreidt; witness: Saml. Burks, Chas. Galloway, Richd. Dickison; proved August 1775 Term by Galloway.

P. 360, 15 August 1775, Wyatt Stubblefield of Orange to John Stubblefield of Guilford, ninety pounds, 164 acres 137 perches, on N side of Hogans Cr., begin at a white oak, S75W 111 p. to a red oak, N 215 p. to a white oak, E 140 p. to a hicory in Wyatt's Spring Br., E70S down branch 30 p. to a maple, E down branch 21 p. to a plum tree on creek bank, up Hogans Cr. to beginning; signed: Wyatt (X) Stubblefield; witness: Jno. Odeneal, Sarah Odeneal, Henry Dixon Junr.; proved August 1775 Term [jurat not named].

P. 360, 4 January 1775, Thomas Lovelatty Jr. & Leah his wife of Guilford to Moses Armstead of Pittsylvania County, Virginia, merchant, one hundred fifty pounds, 300 acres, on both sides Woolf Island Cr. a branch of Dann R., part of a tract to Thomas Lovelatty from Ephriam Potter Senr. & Ephriam Potter Junr., Ephriam Potter Senr. to Thomas Lovelatty 15 March 1769, registered in Orange, Ephriam Potter Junr. to Thomas Lovelatty 20 August 1772 for 100 acres on Woolf Island Cr, proved in Guilford, [no metes and bounds description]; signed Thomas (T) Lovelatty, Leah ( ) Lovelatty; witness: Isham Browder, Sampson Bethel, William Grizsel; proved May 1775 Term by Browder; Leah Lovelatty relinquished dower August 1775 Term.

P. 362, 1 August 1775, John Sanders Senr. of Guilford to Hezekiah Sanders of same, seventy pounds, 81 acres, on North Fork of Deep R., part of a survey from Granville to Henry Mills for 585 acres, begin at the mouth of Piney Br., along by degrees to a white oak cor. of Mills, N 138 p. to a post a cor. of the Old Line, W along the Old Line to the river, 80 acres, another part below it & part of the land to Henry Mills. Mills to John Sanders, begin on the N side of the river above the mill at a black oak, NNE 4 p. to a white oak saplin, ESE 18 p. to a willow oak, S 20 p. to the Old Line, along the Old Line to below the mill, 1 acre, includes mill & mill seat; signed: John Sanders; witness: Joel Sanders, Cam Moore, John (+) McNair; acknowledged August 1775 Term.

P. 363, 10 August 1775, Darby Callahan of Guilford to Nathaniel Harris [no residence given], sixty seven pounds, 125 acres, on N side Dann R. on Matrimony Cr., where Harris now lives, 1/2 of the land Callahan obtained of Joseph Scales Senr., begin on Hopper's line at an ash tree, across line to a sycamore on the bank of Matrimony Cr., out to said line that is now open; signed: Darby Callahan; witness: Forster Callahan, Frank Wells; proved August 1775 Term by Wells.

P. 364, 13 March 1775, Jacob Little of Guilford & Hannah his wife to John Downing of same, sixty five pounds, 110 1/2 acres, on Sandy Cr., part of a tract from Granville to James Nicholson, Nicholson to John Owings, Owings to John Overby, Overby to Little, begin at a post oak, S 120 p. to a white oak, W 140 p. to a post oak, S 34 p. to the creek, up creek E5N 23 p. to a white oak, N to the second line; signed: Jacob [Little in German],

Hannah (X) Little; witness: Thomas Savage, John York, John Overby; proved August 1775 Term by Overby.

P. 364, 5 August 1775, William Wiley of Guilford to David Wiley of same, six pounds, 200 acres, part of a tract from Granville to William Wiley for 200 acres, on N side of Beaver Cr., begin of E 96 ch. of his father's tract, with the line 146 p., N 220 p. cross the tract, W 146 p. with the Old Line to the cor., to first station; signed: William Wiley; witness: Hugh Wiley Junr.; acknowledged August 1775 Term.

P. 365, 20 June 1775, James Denny of Guilford to George Denny of same, three hundred pounds, 136 1/2 acres, begin at a hicory on the N side of North Buffaloe, N along Robert Donnel's line 27 1/2 ch. to a black oak, W 30 ch. to a hicory, N 22 ch. to a white oak, S70W 32 3/4 ch. to a black jack, S45E 36 1/2 ch. to a stake, E 9 ch. to a black oak, S45E 21 1/4 ch. to a white oak on the bank of the creek, down the creek to the beginning; signed: James Denny; witness: Wm. Anderson, Alexr. Caldwell; acknowledged August 1775 Term.

P. 366, 15 8th month 1775, David Macy of Guilford to Timothy Russell of same, forty pounds, 46 acres, Zacharias Dicks to Macy 1772, recorded in Guilford, on waters of Horsepen Cr., begin at a large white oak on David Macy's E & W line & Zachariah Dicks' NW cor., N70E 76 rods to a large white oak to the Little Br., being a line between David Macy & the heirs of Nathan Dicks, up the Straight Fork of the branch till it intersects with a line of the whole ata white oak saplin, W to the cor. a large post oak, to the beginning, the NW part of a tract from Granville to Mordecia Mendenhall, recorded in Rowan; signed: David Macy; witness: Gayer Starbuck, William Starbuck; affirmed August 1775 Term by Gayer Starbuck.

P. 367, 9 August 1775, Leonard Miner of Guilford, farmer, & Mary Madeleena his wife to David Fox of same, farmer, sixty five pounds, 300 acres, on waters of Rocky R., part of a tract from Granville to Moses Nelson 28 June 1762, Nelson to Henry Linderman 11 September 1767, begin at a marked white oak on the original N & S line 118 p. S from the original cor., S along the original line 289 p. to the original cor. black oak, W 45 ch. to a stake, N 40 ch. to the cor. of the original survey, N on original line 129 p., E 45 ch. to first station; signed: [Leonard Miner in German], Mary Magdalene (O) Miner; witness: [German name], Henry Linderman; proved August 1775 Term by Linderman.

P. 368, 22 December 1774, Morris Birbeck late of Settle, York County, Great Brittain, now in Virginia, to Edward Stabler, merchant of Petersburg, Virginia & Thomas Thornbrugh the Younger of New Garden, Guilford Co., power of attorney, to administer land in North Carolina, John Fothergill of London Doctor of Physik to Birbeck 17 July 1773 for 1,280 acres, proved before Hon. James Townsend Lord Mayor of London by John Hughes; signed: Morris Birkbeck; witness: David Ross, William Douglass, James Jay, William White, Thos. Shore, Henry Morris, John Holloway;

proved August 1775 Term by Jay.

P. 369, 4 October 1775, John Shepperd of Guilford to Peter Shepperd son of John Shepperd of same, for natural love & affection, 100 acres, on waters of Carraway, begin at a stake, N60E 150 p. to Carraway Cr., creek is dividing line [no other description]; signed: [In German], witness: John (IL) Ledford, William Millikan; proved November 1775 Term by Millikan.

P. 371, 13 March 1773, William Campbell of Guilford to William Walker of same, two hundred pounds, 125 acres, on Dann R., begin on Dann R. bank at a spreading white oak near the Cross Rock Shoal, N 160 p. to a maple on the bank of Reed Cr. near John Glenn's field, E 156 p. to an elm on the river, up river to the beginning; signed: William Campbell, Sarah (+) Campbell; witness: James (+) Gallaway, Warren Walker; proved November 1775 Term by Warren Walker.

P. 372, 4 October 1775, John Shepperd of Guilford to Charles Skepperd son of John Shepperd of same, for natural love & affection, 100 acres, on waters of Carraway, begin at the creek, N60E 70 p. & all that part of the tract on the E side of Carraway, part of a tract from Henry Eustace McCulloh to John Shepperd; signed: [In German]; witness: John (IL) Ledford, Willi Millikan; proved November 1775 Term by William Millikan Esq.

P. 373, 7 August 1775, George Oliver of Guilford to James Roberts of Pittsylvania County, Virginia, twenty pounds, 80 acres, on the S side of Dan R. on Hogans Cr., on S side of the Salisbury Road, begin at sd. road where Henderson's line crosses, S along sd. line 123 p. to an oak saplin Henderson's cor., W 152 p. to a white oak near the Mill, N 52 p. to the road, down the road to the beginning; signed: George (U) Oliver; witness: Thos. Henderson, Alex McClaran; proved November 1775 Term by Henderson.

P. 374, 18 November 1775, James Gates of Guilford to Valentine Allen of same, fifty pounds, 100 acres, on the S side of Dann R., begin at a hicory Presnel's cor. on the river bank, Presnel's line to the cor. black oak, by Benjamin Gates' line to a white oak, by a line of marked trees to the river bank to a sycamore, down river to the first station; signed: James Gates; witness: Thos. Henderson, Alex. McClaran; proved November 1775 Term by Henderson.

P. 374, 22 August 1774, William Forster & Martha his wife of Guilford to James Forster of same, for brotherly love & natural affection, 50 acres, on both sides Horse Pen Cr. waters of Haw R., begin at a white oak & sourwood Francis McNairy's cor., W 205 p. to an ash by a branch, S 40 p. to a stake, E 205 p. to a stake in Francis McNairy's line, N 40 p. to the beginning, the NE part of 615 acres from Granville to Hugh Forster 3 December 1753; signed: William Forster, Martha (+) Forster; witness: Waightstill Avery, Hugh Forster; proved February 1775 Term by Waightstill Avery Esq.

P. 375, 26 November 1774, Samuel Buchanan of Guilford to Edward Stabler of Petersburg, Virginia, merchant, one hundred seventy one pounds fifteen shillings five pence which Buchanan owes Stabler & five shillings in hand paid, 500 acres, on Haw R., where Samuel Buchanan lives, part of the tract from Granville to William Patrick, Patrick to Samuel Buchanan, includes the Tannyard & Tann-house, the money is due 26 February 1776 with interest from 13 April 1768 until paid; signed: Saml. Buchanaan; witness: Mary Espey, Alexr. Martin; proved November 1775 Term by Col. Alexr. Martin.

P. 377, 6 January 1776, Richard Barton of Guilford & Martha his wife to George Hamilton Junr. of same, forty five pounds, 110 acres, on both sides of Mars [Mairs] Fork of Haw R., begin at a white oak on the S side of Mars Fork in John Hallum's cor., W 40 ch. to a red oak bush, S30E 22 1/2 ch. to a spanish oak near Mars Fork, S36E 44 ch. to John Hallum's line, N to the first station; signed: Richard Borton, Martha (M) Borton; witness: Charles Bruce, William Dickson; acknowledged February 1776 Term.

P. 378, 12 2nd month 1776, William Coffin of Guilford to Barnabas Coffin of same, twenty pounds, 115 acres, on North Fork of Deep R., begin at a stake, W11:15N 1 ch., S22:10W 7 ch. 50 lk., W1N 10 ch., N33:45W 3 ch., N5:6E 5 ch., W11:15N 5 ch. 20 lk. N22:30E 2 ch., WSW 3 ch., W11:15N 56 ch. S 10 ch., E 15 ch., S 5 ch., E 5 ch. S 5 ch., E 5 ch., S 5 ch., E 13 ch. 40 lk., S 1 ch. 50 lk. E 4 ch. 40 lk., S 10 ch., E 2 ch., N 25 to the beginning, part of 231 1/2 acres from Moses Mendenhall to William Coffin 19 10th month 1773; signed: William Coffin; witness: Eleazer Hunt, Richard Williams; proved February 1776 Term by Hunt.

P. 379, 2 April 1776, John Hallum & Elizabeth his wife of Guilford to Archibald & James Campbell sons of John & Mary Campbell [no residence given], one hundred sixty pounds, 220 acres, on both sides of Mairs Fork waters of Haw R., begin at a post oak on the N side of Mairs Fork, S 55 ch. to a white oak, E 60 ch. to a hicory, N36W 44 ch. to the creek, N30W 22 1/2 ch. to a red oak bush, W to the beginning, part of a tract from Granville to Hallum 27 August 1762, registered in Rowan; signed: Jno. Hallum, Elizabeth (/) Hallum; witness: James Hays, Richard Borton; acknowledged May 1776 Term.

P. 381, 25 April 1776, John Ward of Bedford County, Virginia, to Hugh Challes of Pittsylvania County, Virginia, one hundred fifty five pounds, 500 acres, on both sides of Wolf Island Cr., begin at a cor. white oak in William Buster's line on the S side of the creek, E 400 p. to pointers, a new line crossing the creek N45W 568 p. to pointers, S 400 p. to the beginning; signed: John Ward; witness: Peter Perkins, Theops. Lacey, Jno. Salmon, R. Williams, Jno. Wilson, Jno. Tate; proved May 1776 Term by Wilson.

P. 382, 19 2nd month 1776, William Coffin of Guilford to Samuel Coffin of same, fifty pounds, 116 acres, on North Fork of Deep R., begin at a stake, W by N 1 ch., SSW 7 ch. 56 lk., W1"N 10 ch., NW by N 3ch., N half E 5 ch., W by N 5 ch. 20 lk., NNE 2 ch., WSW 3 ch., W by N 56 ch. N 10 ch., E 80 ch., S 25 ch. to the beginning, part of 231 1/2 acres from Moses Mendenhall to William Coffin 14 10th month 1773; signed: William Coffin; witness: Jno. Tate, Thomas Jamison; acknowledged May 1776 Term.

P. 383, 2 May 1776, John Kimbrough & Mary his wife of Guilford to Samuel Parke of Chatham, nine hundred pounds, 325 acres, on the head of Huwary, begin at a locust on the side of a hill, S 260 p. to a locust, E 86 p. cross Mill Cr. in all 200 p. to a poplar in a branch, N 260 p. to a stake, W 154 p. cross the creek in all 200 p. to the beginning; signed: John Kimbrough, Mary Kimbrough; witness: Thomas Hutchins, John Woodleif, Saml. Thackstone; proved February 1777 Term by Woodleif.

P. 384, 11 January 1777, John Hall & Ann his wife of Guilford, planter, to James Duff of same, planter, sixty five pounds, 121 acres, on both sides of South Buffaloe where Duff now lives, begin at a stake, W to a black oak 121 p., N 160 p. to a hicory, E 121 p. to a white oak, 160 p. to the beginning; signed: John Hall, Ann Hall; witness: Daniel Gillespie, John Foster; acknowledged February 1777 Term.

P. 386, 22 July 1775, William Forster of Guilford, farmer, to William Johnston & Charles Bruce of same, sixty six pounds fifteen shillings, 307 acres, on both sides of Horsepen Cr., part of a tract where Forster now dwells, Granville to Hugh Forster 3 December 1753, begin at an ash on the W side of Horsepen Cr. in or near a branch, W 205 p. to a white oak (alias) a post oak, S 240 p. to a stake in the Low Grounds of the creek, E 205 p. to a black oak, N 200 p. to the first station, if Forster repays sixty six pounds fifteen shillings plus interest prior to 25 December 1776 the deed is void; signed: William Forster, William Johnston, Charles Bruce; witness: John Carrive, Thomas Fish; acknowledged February 1777 Term.

P. 388, 15 May 1777, John Hunter of Guilford to Edward Hunter & Elizabeth his wife of same, two hundred sixty seven pounds, 260 acres, part of a tract where John Hunter now lives, begin at a hicory a cor. of John Hunter's line on the N side of Dan R., down the river to the mouth of Little Whitestone, cross the river S to a Back Line of John Hunter's on the S side of the river, sd. line to the beginning, during the full term of Edward Hunter's & Elizabeth his wife's life together; signed: John Hunter; witness: John Leak, William Davison; acknowledged May 1777 Term.

P. 389, 10 October 1776, Samuel Watt Senr. of Guilford to Samuel Watt Junr. of same, one hundred pounds, 418 acres, on both sides of Woolf Island Cr., surveyed for Mark London & purchased by Samuel Watt Senr., [no metes and bounds description]; signed: Samuel (Z) Watt; witness: N. Williams, John Age; proved May 1777 Term by Nathl. Williams.

P. 390, 21 May 1777, John Clark & Mary his wife of Guilford to Francis McNairy of same, three hundred twenty nine pounds, 200 acres, begin at a black oak on James McCuistian's line & Samuel

Scott's line 70 rods from their cor., N 130 perches cross Richland Cr. to a white oak & black oak, W 250 perches to James' line, S 130 perches to his cor., E to the beginning, includes the Mill Place, part of 640 acres from Granville to James McCuistian Senr. 22 February 1759, 200 acres conveyed by his son James McCuistian to John Clark 9 October 1772, registered in Guilford Book A page 289; signed: Jno. (O) Clark, Mary (O) Clark; witness: Jno. Campbell, Arthur Forbus, Henry Reed; acknowledged May 1777 Term.

P. 392, 6 September 1776, John McCuistion, blacksmith, of Guilford to Thomas Lindsey of same, one hundred pounds, 20 acres, begin at James McCuistion's SW cor. at a white oak on a branch of Richland Cr., E 80 rods, begin again at the foresd. beginning white oak, N 80 rods to a red oak, a SE course to 2nd cor., James McCuistion to John McCuistion 5 October 1769, registered in Rowan Book 7 page 171, if John McCuistion makes a deed for 247 acres (it being the remainder of the tract John McCuistion bought of James McCuistion as reference to bill of sale from John McCuistion to Thomas Lindsey of same date of these presents will more fully appear) within four months after Earl Granville's Office shall be opened or as soon as a deed can be got out of sd. Office, then the above indenture to be void; signed: John McCuistion; witness: Benjamin McFarlin [also written Benjamin Farlin]; proved May 1777 Term by McFarlin.

P. 393, 20 November 1775, David Lowe & Mary his wife of Guilford to Philip Seller [also spelled Seler] of same, fifty pounds, 100 acres, part of a tract from Henry Eustace McCulloh to Lowe 23 February 1765 for 355 acres, begin at a black jack the end of the 6th line, N45W 80 perches to a white oak still with the out lines of sd. land reverst, N45E 200 perches, S45 80 perches to the end of 200 perches on the 7th line of aforesd. land, to the beginning; signed: David Lowe, Mary (+) Lowe; witness: Jacob Gobel, Wm. Dent Junr.; proved May 1777 Term by Dent.

P. 395, 7 July 1777, John Odeneal of Guilford to John Buster of same, one hundred thirty three pounds, six shillings eight pence, 86 acres, on N side of Hogans Cr., begin at a beech on the creek bank, W 74 p. to a hicory, N 113 p. to a hicory, E 175 p. to the creek, up the creek to the beginning, John McCollum to Odeneal; signed: Jn. Odeneal; witness: Thos. Rice, Nathl. Williams, Abraham Womack; proved August 1777 by Williams.

P. 396, 18 August 1777, Joshua Pendly of Guilford to Ambrose Nochlas [Nicholas] of Halifax County, Virginia, one hundred twenty six pounds, 199 acres, on both sides of Wolf Island Cr., begin at a post oak, N 60 p. to a pine on Byrd's line, along his line N75E 192 p. crossing the creek to a Brockman's cor. red oak, along his line S13E 180 p. to a small hicory near a path, along the line S5W 120 p. to a red oak, along the line S15W 40 p. to his cor. post oak, S87W 27 p. to an ash on a branch, down the branch N to a beech at the mouth of Wolf Island Cr., down the creek N60E 6 p. to a bent, down creek N7E to a white oak on the W side, a new line N64W 41 p. to a red oak, N75W 22 p. to the beginning, part of a tract surveyed for Joseph Dolittle 17 April 1762; signed: Joshua (P) Pendly; witness: John Buster, Thos. Owen, L. Harris; proved August 1777 by John Buster Esq.

P. 398, 11 July 1777, John Odeneal of Guilford to John Buster of same, two hundred sixty six pounds, 233 acres, on the S side of Hogans Cr., begin at a red oak on the creek, E 207 p. to a white oak, N 88 p. to a red oak saplin, W62N 90 p. to a white saplin, W30N 90 p. to a poplar on the creek bank, up creek to the beginning; signed: Jn. Odeneal; witness: Thos. Rice, Nathll. Williams, Abraham Womack; proved August 1777 Term by Nathaniel Williams.

P. 399, 15 August 1777, Thomas Baston of Caswell to Joshua Pendly of Guilford, nineteen pounds, 378 acres, on Wolf Island Cr. begin at a pine on Bird's line, S cross the creek 90 ch. to a white oak, E 176 p. to 3 post oaks on the W side of a Ridge Road, keeping to the Ridge Road to 3 red oak pointers in Bird's W line, with Bird's line W 154 p. to the first station, John Graves to Thomas Baston, recorded in Orange; signed: Thomas (T) Baston; witness: John Buster, Thos. Owens, L. Harris; proved August 1777 Term by John Buster Esq.

P. 400, 7 August 1777, John Tate son & executor of the will of Joseph Tate Decd. of Guilford to Alexander Hunter of same, seventy three pounds six shillings, 280 acres, on both sides of Beaver Island Cr., begin at a small black oak saplin the SW cor. of Charles Perkins, S 140 p. to a white oak, E 320 p. to a white oak, N 140 p. to a stake Charles Perkins cor., along Charles line to the beginning, the lower end of a tract from Granville to Robert Jones Esq., Jones to Joseph Tate; signed: John Tate; witness: Nath. Woygall, William (W) Covingtown; proved August 1777 Term by William Covington.

P. 401, 15 August 1777, Joshua Pendly of Guilford to Jacob Stillwell of same, five pounds, 3 1/2 acres, on Wolf Island Cr., begin at a white oak on Pendly's line, NE 27 p. to a pine, SE 28 p. to a black oak, SW crossing the creek 34 p. to an elm, crossing creek 18 p. N to the first station, Thomas Baston to Pendly; signed: Joshua (P) Pendly; witness: John Buster, Thos. Owen, L. Harris; proved August 1777 Term by John Buster Esq.

P. 402, 9 June 1777, William Buster of Montgomery County, Virginia, to Claudius Buster of Guilford, one hundred eighty pounds, 265 acres, on both sides of Wolf Island Cr., begin at a white oak on the E side of the creek a cor. of Hugh Churlish's [Challes'] land, along his line N 40 p. to a sugar tree, W 160 p. to a red oak, S 220 p. to a red oak, E 200 p. to a white oak, N 180 p. to a red oak in Charles' line, his line W to the beginning, John Ward to William Buster, registered in Orange; signed: William Buster; witness: John Buster, Elizabeth Buster, Thos. Owen; proved August 1777 Term by John Buster Esq.

P. 404, 29 July 1777, James McCuistian & Catherine his wife of Guilford to Thomas Lindsey of same, one hundred pounds, 50 acres, on Richland Cr. of Reedy Fork of Haw R., begin at a white oak on a branch of Richland Cr. James McCuistian's NW cor., S 150 perches along an Old Line to a stake, E45S along the Division Line between James McCuistian and John McCuistian 72 perches to a stake, N 56 perches to a stake E 8 perches to a stake, N 58 perches to a stake, W 36 perches to a stake, N 76 perches to a stake, 30 perches to the beginning, part of a tract from Granville to James McCuistian Senr. 18 December 1753, willed to James McCuistian Junr. by will dated 18 October 1765; signed: James McCuistian, Catherine (O) McCuistian; witness: Francis McNary, Benjamin McFarlin; proved August 1777 by McFarlin.

P. 405, 26 July 1777, John Buster of Guilford to Hugh Challes of Pittsylvania County, Virginia, four hundred pounds, 420 acres, on both sides of Wolf Island Cr., John Ward to John Buster, recorded in Orange, begin at a white oak on the W side of the creek, W 240 p. to a red oak, S 280 p. to a red oak, E 240 p. to a red oak, N to the first station; signed: John Buster; witness: Isham Dalton, Thomas Bryan, William King; proved Novem,ber 1777 Term by Dalton.

P. 407, 18 November 1777, James Presnell & Mary his wife of Guilford to William Asten of Charlotte County, Virginia, two hundred fifty pounds, 210 acres, on the S side of Dann R., see deed from Peter Perkins to James Presnell recorded in Rowan, [no metes and bounds description]; signed: James Presnell, Mary ( ) Presnell; witness: Baker Degraffenred, Nathl. Hogget, Jas. Martin; proved November 1777 Term by Col. James Martin.

P. 408, 10 October 1777, William Nunn Junr. of Guilford to Tyree Harris of Orange, four hundred pounds, 519 acres, land where William Nunn now lives, begin at a hicory on a line formerly Joseph Pinson's by High Rock Cr., N 85 ch. to a white oak, E 72 ch. to a white oak, S 85 ch. to a red oak on the side of a fork of High Rock Cr., W 72 ch. along the line formerly Joseph Pinson's to the first station; signed: William Nunn, Ede Nunn; witness: Richd. Simpson, John Peper; proved November 1777 Term by Peper.

P. 409, 8 November 1777, Isaac Thrasher of Guilford to Joseph Cloud Thrasher of same, one hundred thirty pounds, 218 acres, on both sides of Lick Fork of Hogans Cr., part of the land to John Thrasher Senr. December 1761 for 693 acres, begin at a white oak on the W side of the creek, S 272 p. to a cor. white oak, E 128 p. to a cor. white oak, N 201 p. to a red oak, W 50 p. to a dogwood, N 64 p. to a cor. white oak, W 28 p. to the beginning; signed: Isaac Thrasher; witness: John Guist, William Baley; proved November 1777 Term by Guist.

P. 410, 2 October 1777, Claudius Buster of Guilford to Hugh Challes of Pittsylvania County, Virginia, two hundred pounds, 265 acres, on both sides of Wolf Island Cr., begin at a white oak a cor. of Challes' land on the E side of the creek, his line N 40 p. to a sugar tree, W 160 p. to a red oak, S 220 p. to a red oak, E 200 p. to a white oak, N 180 p. to a red oak in Challes' line, along his line W to the beginning; signed: Cluadius Buster; witness: John Buster, Wyett Stublefield, Isam Dalton; proved

November 1777 Term by Dalton.

P. 411, 18 November 1777, Samuel Smith of Guilford to Robert Smith Junr. of same, seventy pounds, 75 acres, on both sides of North Buffaloe Cr., begin at a hicory, white oak & poplar on the N bank of the creek, N 24 ch. to a hicory on John Rankin's line, W 24 3/4 ch. to a hicory grub, S 10 ch. to a hicory, E 5 ch. to a black oak, S 37 ch. to a black jack cor. to Jacob Stricklin's land, N45E 23 ch. to a white oak, N 8 ch. to a white oak on the bank of the creek, E to the first station; signed: Samuel Smith; witness: [none listed]; acknowledged November 1777 Term.

P. 412, 18 October 1777, William Denny & Margarate his wife of Guilford to Samuel Smith of same, one hundred ten pounds, 278 acres, on the N side of Reedy Fork of Haw R., begin at George Finley's cor. maple by a branch, along his line W 10 ch. to a black oak bush, N 19 ch. 62 lk. to Thomas Fay's white oak cor., E 80 ch. along his line to his black oak cor., S 29 ch. 62 lk. to a red oak saplin, W 70 ch. to a stake on George Finley's line, N 10 ch. to the first station; signed: William Denny, Margarate Denny; witness: John Maxwell, Jodediah ( ) Alexander; proved November 1777 Term by Jediah Alexander.

P. 414, 12 March 1777, John Smith & Sarah his wife of Guilford to Ignatious Gann of same, thirty pounds, 200 acres, on the S side of East Mayo Mountain, begin at a red oak an Old Cor., N along the Old Line 228 p. to a white oak saplin, W 140 p. to a pine on the mountain side James Vernan's cor., S along the Division Line between Vernan & Gann 228 p. to a white oak saplin Vernon's cor., E 140 p. to the first station; signed: John (+) Smith, Sarah ( ) Smith; witness: Nehemiah Vernan, William Wright; proved November 1777 Term by Wright.

P. 415, 18 November 1777, Samuel Smith of Guilford to Jacob Stricklin of same, one hundred pounds, 115 acres, between North & South Buffaloe Cr. & on both sides of each, begin at a hicory, white oak, & poplar on the N bank of North Buffaloe, W 3 1/2 ch. to a white oak on the S bank of the creek, S 8 ch. to a white oak, S45W to a black jack, S 10 ch. to a post, W 14 1/2 ch. to a white oak bush, S 16 1/2 ch. to a post, E 48 1/2 ch. across South Buffaloe to a red oak, N 30 ch. to a white oak by the mouth of South Buffaloe, up John Rankin's line to the first station; signed: Samuel Smith; witness: [none listed]; acknowledged November 1777 Term.

P. 416, 10 April 1773, John Smith & Sarah his wife of Guilford to James Vernon of same, thirty pounds, 200 acres, on the S side of East Myo [Mayo] Mountain, begin at Ignatious Gann's cor. on the mountain side, S 228 p. along a Division Line between Gann & James Vernon to a white oak Gann's cor., W 140 p. to a red oak an Old Cor., N 228 p. to a spanish oak, E 140 p. to the beginning; signed: John (I) Smith, Sarah (S) Smith; witness: Nehemiah Vernon, Alexander McClaran, Elijah Joyce; proved November 1777 Term by McClaran.

P. 417, 1 January 1776, Levi McCollom & Mary his wife of Guilford, blacksmith, to Dunken McCollom of same, one hindred pounds, 275 acres, Granville to James Nicholson, Nicholson to Jonathon Paulk, Paulk to Isaac Jackson, Isaac Jackson to Daniel Jackson, Daniel Jackson to McCollom, begin at 3 marked hicorys a cor. of Herman Husband's land, E 76 ch., 7 1/2 ch., W 103 ch. to a black jack oak, N 81 ch. to an oak, E 27 ch. to a white oak & black jack oak, S on the Original Line to the beginning; signed: Levi McCollom, Mary McCollom; witness: William Welbourn, John Low, John Fruit, Robt. McClain; proved November 1777 Term by McClain.

P. 418, 21 November 1777, James Archer of Guilford to John Hamilton of same, one hundred pounds, 100 acres, where James Archer now lives, to James Archer 4 February 1777, begin at a white oak, S 80 perches, E 120, S 80, E 40, N 160 perches until it intersects a line drawn E from the beginning, W to the beginning; signed: James Archer; witness: Willi Dent, Benj. Starrat; proved November 1777 Term by Starrat.

P. 419, 9 November 1776, John Hanna of Guilford to Robert Hanna of same, two hundred pounds, 500 acres, on both sides of Beaver Cr., begin at a hicory tree, W 63 ch. to a post oak, S 38 ch. to a post oak, E 18 ch. to a hicory, S 10 ch. to a black oak, E 5 ch. to a hicory, S 27 1/2 ch. to a post oak, E 53 ch. to a saplin, N 115 ch. 50 lk. to the beginning; signed: John Hanna, Martha Hanna; witness: John Long, Charles Melarg, Moses Campbell; proved February 1778 Term by Campbell.

P. 420, 12 February 1778, Robert Donnell of Guilford to John Foster of same, one hundred seventy pounds, 307 acres, on both sides of South Buffaloe, begin at a white oak Hall's cor., along his line N 20 ch. to a hicory, W 26 ch. to a black oak, S 43 1/2 ch. to a black oak on John McAdow's line, along his line E 5 ch. 25 lk. to a white oak saplin, along his line S 36 ch. 50 lk. to a hicory, E 39 ch. to a post oak saplin, N 60 ch. to a black on Hall's line, along his line to the beginning; signed: Robert Donnell; witness: Daniel Donnell, George Denny; acknowledged February 1778 Term.

P. 421, 21 September 1777 James Archer of Guilford to Thomas Archer of same son of James Archer, fifty pounds, 150 acres, where James Archer lives, to James Archer 4 February 1765, begin at James Archer's cor. & Sarah Hunt's at a black oak, N 150 perches to a white oak, W 160 perches to a stone, S 150 perches to a water oak, E 160 perches to the beginning; signed: James Archer; witness: Jno. Hamilton, Benjamin Starret; proved November 1778 Term by Starret.

P. 422, 14 February 1778, Edward Moor of Anson to William Moor & Absalam Tatom of Caswell, two hundred ten pounds, 250 acres, on the waters of Carraway Cr., part of a larger tract where Samuel Lowe now lives, Lowe to Edward Moor, begin at a post oak E of Groggin's improvements, W 45 ch. 46 lk. to a red oak, S 50 ch. to a small post oak, E 45 ch. 46 lk. to a black jack, N 51 ch. to the first station; signed: Edward Moor; witness: Elijah Moor, Wm.

Campbell; acknowledged February 1778 Term.

P. 423, 29 August 1769, John Hunter & Edward Hunter of Rowan to Archibald Cary Esq. of Chesterfield County, Virginia, four hundred ninety six pounds eleven shillings five pence three fathings owed by John & Edward Hunter with interest from 2 November 1766 for value received by John Hunter from John Esdely, Walter Buchannan & Robert Hastie & Co. merchants in Virginia & paid by Cary 2 November 1766, 600 acres on the S side of Dan R., 380 acres on the same side of the river, 500 acres on the same side of the river being the plantation where John Hunter now lives, 940 acres on the N side of Dan R. known as Nealls Bent, 300 acres on the same side of the river, & 200 acres on the same side of the river [no metes and bounds description of any of the land], Robert Jones Junr. to John Hunter, also 21 slaves: Ceasar, Fan, Tom, Charles, Rainue, Juba, Moll, Rose, & Lucy, with Peter, Adam, James, & Jery children of Moll & Ceasar, Cicily, Kate, Isham, & Matthew children of Rose & Will, Ben, & Joe children of Lucy together with the future increase, if the money and interest is repaid by 15 November next the deed is void; signed: John Hunter, Edward Hunter; witness: John Walker, Robert Farguson, David Ross.

P. 425, 29 January 1778, Virginia, acknowledgement of receipt of full payment due by a deed of trust & relinquishes all claim; signed: Archibald Cary; witness: Gidion Johnson, Luke Kent; certificate proved February 1778 Term by Johnson.

P. 425, 29 January 1778, Archibald Cary of Chesterfield County, Virginia, to James Wray of Guilford, one hundred thirty pounds, 200 acres, on S side of Dan R., Wray had purchased the land from John Hunter decd. of Guilford & Edward Hunter his son of same but would not pay the consideration because the land was encumbered by the foregoing deed of trust, Cary has received full payment from the estate of John Hunter and for payment of one hundred thirty pounds by Gidion Johnson renounces all claim to the 200 acres; signed: Archibald Cary; witness: Edward Hunter, Luke Kent; proved February 1778 Term by Edward Hunter.

P. 426, 13 January 1778, Edward Hunter of Guilford to James Wray of same, one hundred fifty pounds, 200 acres, on N side of Dan R., known as Dead Timber, begin at a spanish oak on the bank of the river, 150 p. to a white oak, E 164 p. to a red oak on the river, up the river to the beginning; signed: Edward Hunter; witness: Gidion Johnson, Luke Kent; note indicates that the tract was security in a deed of trust to Archibald Cary; signed: Edward Hunter; acknowledged February 1770 [1778?] Term.

P. 427, 18 May 1778, John Dykes of Guilford to Nathaniel Hoggatt of same, two hundred sixty pounds, 250 acres, part of a tract from Edward Hunter to Dykes known as Neals Bent, on the N side of Dan R., begin at a linn on the river below the mouth of Little Reed Cr., N a new line 223 p. to a pine & white oak saplin on the Old E & W Line, E on the line 164 p. to the river, up the river to the beginning; signed: John ( ) Dykes; witness: [none listed]; acknowledged May 1778 Term.

P. 428, 20 May 1778, Peter Perkins of Pittsylvania County, Virginia, to John Chadwell of "sd. county", one hundred pounds, 300 acres, "rite & claim (and that only)", Baker Degravered to Robert Donald, on the N side of Dann R., begin at a persimon tree on the river, N 204 p. to a red oak, W 212 p. to a saplin, S 250 p. to a hicory on the river, down the river to the beginning; signed: Peter Pirkins; witness: [none listed]; acknowledged May 1778 Term.

P. 429, 23 April 1778, Robert Donald of Chesterfield County, Virginia, to Peter Perkins of Pittsylvania County, Virginia, one thousand pounds Continental money, 300 acres, on the N side of Dan R., begin at a persimon tree on the river, N 204 p. to a red oak, W 212 p. to a saplin, S 250 p. to a hicory on the river, down the river to the beginning; signed: Robert Donald; witness: Jesse Pope, Michael Coulter, John (+) Chadwell; proved May 1778 Term by Chadwell.

P. 429, 13 May 1778, Thomas Donnel of Guilford to John White of same, two hundred ninety three pounds, 293 acres, on borth sides of Reedy Fork of Haw R., part of a larger tract from Granville to George Black, Black to Donnell, begin at a stake a cor. to the land of Robert Donnell Junr., W 52 ch. to an ash a cor. to Donnell's land, S 56 1/2 ch. to a saplin stake, E 52 ch. to a stake a cor. to Robert Donnell, N 56 1/2 ch. to the beginning; signed: Thos. Donnell; witness: Alexr. Caldwell, Wm. Scott; acknowledged May 1778 Term.

P. 430, 15 April 1778, James Lorimer of Guilford to Francis Cook of same, four hundred pounds, 143 acres, on the S side of Dann R., begin at the river bank where the Old Line crosses, part of a tract surveyed for Peter Pirkins, joins Robert Joans Junr. on the lower end, E to a cor. black oak 60 ch., N to the river, up the river to the beginning; signed: James Laromore; witness: John Reagan, Jno. Hamilton; receipt for the consideration 21 April 1778 witnessed by John Kyes; proved May 1778 Term by Reagan.

P. 432, 9 May [no year given], John Buster of Guilford to John Cook [no residence given], five hundred pounds, 233 acres, on the S side of Hogans Cr., begin at a red oak on the creek, W62N 90 p. to a white saplin, W30 90 p. to a saplin on the creek bank, up the creek to the first station; signed: John Buster; witness: Mary (+) Mabry, Nathl. Williams, Danl. (D) McCollum; proved may 1778 Term by Williams.

P. 432, 13 May 1778, Thomas Donnell of Guilford to Robert Donnell of same, two hundred pounds, 154 acres, on both sides of Reedy Fork of Haw R., part of a larger tract from Granville to George Black, Black to Thomas Donnell, begin at William Scott's cor. white oak & red oak, N 56 1/2 ch. to a post oak & red oak, W 45 ch. to a stake, S 56 1/2 ch. to a stake on Scott's line, E along his line to the first station; signed: Thos. Donnell; witness: Alexr. Caldwell, Wm. Scott; acknowledged May 1778 Term.

P. 434, 20 April 1778, David Allison Senr. & Janet his wife of Guilford to his son John Allison of same, for love, goodwill & affection, 165 acres, begin at David Allison's NE cor. at the center between 2 white oaks set forth in his deed, S along Allison's line 22 ch. to a stake, W 75 ch. to his line, along his line N 22 ch. to his cor. black oak, E 75 ch. to the beginning, on the waters of North Buffaloe, Granville to Robert Donnell Sr. 21 December 1761, Donnell to William Trousdale, Trousdale to Allison; signed: David (C) Allison, Jennet ( ) Allison; witness: Joseph Hinds, Robert Barr; proved May 1778 Term by Joseph Hinds Esq.

P. 435, 9 March 1778, Samuel Thomson of Guilford to Thomas Bell of same, fifty two pounds, 232 acres, on the N side of Reedy Fork of Haw R., part of 460 acres from Granville to Robert Thompson 1755, bequeathed to Samuel Thompson by his father Robert Thompson, begin at a hicory on the N side of Reedy Fork of Haw R., a S cor. of John Cook's line, N 98 1/2 ch. to a stake, W 27 1/2 ch. to a white oak, S according to the original line to a hicory on the bank of Reedy Fork, down Reedy Fork to the first station; signed: Samuel Thompson; witness: James Bell, 'Robert Thompson, Samuel Bell Senr.; proved May 1778 Term by James Bell.

P. 436, 15 May 1778, John Fraizer & Abigal his wife of Guilford to Lewis Ashman of same, [torn] pounds, 60 acres, on the E side of Deep R., begin on the bank of the river, N53E to a post oak, N 60 p. to a black oak, W 100 p. to a hicory on the river bank, S2E 58 p. along the river bank, S9E 30 p., S20W 46 p., S12W 8 p. along the river bank to the beginning, part of a tract from Granville to John Fraizer; signed: John Fraizer, Abigail Fraizer; witness: Richardson Owen, Thomas Smith; proved May 1778 Term by Richardson Owen Esq.

P. 437, 6 March 1778, Edward Hunter of Guilford to John Dykes of same, two hundred fifty pounds, 250 acres, part of a tract from Robert Jones, known as Neals Bent containing in the whole 940 acres, on the N side of Dan R., begin at a linn on the river below the mouth of Little Reed Cr., N on a New Dividing Line 223 p. to a pine & white oak saplin on the Old E & W Line, E on the line 164 p. to the river, up the river to the beginning; signed: Edward Hunter; witness: [none listed]; there is a note that this is a repeat of a former deed given when the land was encumbered, this deed given at Hunter's expense; acknowledged May 1778 Term.

P. 438, 9 May 1778, John Buster of Guilford to John Cook of same, two hundred pounds, 86 acres, on the N side of Hognas Cr., begin at a beach on the creek bank, W 75 p. to a hicory, N 113 p. to a hicory, E 125 p. to the creek, up the creek to the beginning, land that John Odeneal had of John McCollam; signed: John Buster; witness: Danl ( ) McCullum, N. Williams, Mary Mabry; proved May 1778 Term by Williams.

P. 439, 18 May 1778, James Ross & Mary his wife of Guilford to Joseph Huskins of same, two hundred pounds, 150 acres, on Horsepen Cr. & on both sides of the Main Road, begin at a white oak saplin a cor. to Thomas White, N 22 ch. to a post oak on Hugh Foster's line, E 13 1/2 ch. along Foster's line to a white oak, N 16 ch. along Foster's line to a hicory, E to a white oak 32 ch. to Robert Mitchel Decd. line, S 38 ch. along Mitchell's line to a post a cor. to Thomas White, along Thomas White's line to the beginning; signed: James Ross, Mary Ross; witness: Thomas Black, Samuel Cummins; acknowledged May 1778 Term.

P. 441, 19 May 1778, George Hamilton & Jean his wife of Guilford to Ezekiel Wiggins of same, one hundred pounds, 110 acres, on Mairs Fork waters of Haw R., begin at a white oak on the S side of Mairs Fork in John Hallam's cor., W 40 ch. to a red oak bush, S30E 22 1/2 ch. to a spanish oak near the creek, S36E 44 ch. to Hallum's line, N to the beginning; signed: George Hamilton, Jean Hamilton; witness: Jno. Campbell, Richard Borton, John Porter; proved May 1778 Term by Campbell.

P. 442, 19 August 1778, Joseph Brown of Guilford to Andrew Donnell of same, six hundred pounds, 273 acres, on waters of North Buffaloe, begin at George Hamilton's black oak cor., along his line N 136 perches to Buffaloe Cr., up the creek to Hamilton's line, S along his line 170 perches to his cor. 3 black jacks & a white oak, E to the first station; signed: Joseph Brown, Mary (X) Brown; witness: [none listed]; acknowledged August 1778 Term.

P. 443, 17 August 1778, William Maben of Guilford to Samuel Maben his son of same, for love & regard, 130 acres, on the S side of South Buffaloe, begin at a red oak cor. of William Maben's land, N 19 ch. to a walnut, W 68 1/2 ch. to a hicory bush, S 19 ch. to a post oak cor., E 68 1/2 ch. to the beginning; signed: William Maben; witness: [none listed] acknowledged August 1778 Term.

P. 443, 18 August 1778, Thomas Donnell of Guilford to William Donnell of same, two hundred pounds, 350 acres, on both sides of North Buffaloe Cr., part of a larger tract from Granville to Thomas Donnell, begin at a post oak cor. to John Donnell's land, N 47 ch. to a hicory, W 20 ch. to a post, N 47 ch. to a post, E 47 ch. to a red oak, S94 ch. 70 lk. to a black oak, W 27 ch. to the beginning; signed: Thomas Donnell; witness: [none listed]; acknowledged August 1778 Term.

P. 444, 1 November 1775, John Odeneal to John McCollom [no residence given for either], twenty pounds, 37 acres, on the S side of Hogans Cr., begin at a sycamore on the creek bank, E 60 p. to 2 hicory saplins, S 90 p. to a whiote oak saplin, W30N 90 p. to a poplar on the creek bank, down the creek to the beginning, part of a tract from Patrick Mullen to Odeneal; signed: Jn. Odeneal; witness: Abraham Womack, Buchd [Richd.?] Stubblefield, William Prewitt; proved August 1778 Term by Womack.

P. 445, 31 March 1778, Alexander Hunter of Guilford to Robert Dearing of same, four hundred sixty six pounds thirteen shillings eight pence, 280 acres, on both sides of Beaver Island Cr., begin at a small black oak saplin the SW cor. of Charles Perkins' land,

S 140 p. to a white oak, E 320 p. to to a white oak, N 140 p. to a stake Charles Perkins' cor., along Charles line to the beginning, the lower end of a tract from Granville to Robert Jones Junr. Esq., Jones to Joseph Tate; signed: Alexr. Hunter; witness: J. Holdeness, James Gallaway, Rchd. Vernon; proved August 1778 term by Gallaway.

P. 446, 21 August 1778, William Maben of Guilford to John Maben his son of same, for love & regard, 150 acres, on the N side of South Buffaloe, part of the tract on which William Maben now lives, begin on the N bank of the creek on a place where the Old Line crosses South Buffaloe, N 7 ch. to a red oak cor. to William Meban's land, W 60 ch. to a pillar of stones near a marked white oak, S 43 ch. to an elm on the N bank of South Buffaloe, down the creek to the beginning; signed: William Maben; witness: [none listed]; acknowledged August 1778.

P. 447, 17 August 1778, William Farrow of Guilford to Leonard Barker of same, fifty pounds, 218 acres, on the N side of Dann R., begin at the mouth of Mayo R., N30E 50 p. to a gum, W 17 p. to a white oak, N30E 288 p. to a black oak on an Old Line formerly called Joneses Line, W 333 p. to the Mayo R. down the river to the beginning; signed: William Farrow; witness: Thos. Henderson, Turksfield Barnes; proved August 1778 Term by Henderson.

P. 448, 27 February 1778, Robert Hannah of Guilford to William Shaw, weaver, of same, forty pounds, 143 acres, on both sides of Beaver Cr., begin at a post oak, S 27 ch. to a post oak, E 53 ch. to a saplin cor., N 27 ch. to a stake, 53 ch. to the beginning, part of a tract where Robert Hannah lives; signed: Robert Hannah, Isbel Hannah; witness: John Forbiss, Andrew Finley; proved May [no year given] Term by Finley.

P. 450, 16 February 1778, Edward Hunter Exec. of Jno. Hunter decd. of Guilford to William Farrow & Leonard Barker of same, one hundred eighty pounds, 415 acres, on the N side of Dan R. & Mayo, begin in Hunter's line on the river, N by his line to a white oak his cor., W to Mayo R., down the river to Dan R., down the river to the beginning; signed: Edward Hunter; witness: Gidion Johnson, John Davice; acknowledged August 1778 Term.

P. 451, 7 August 1778, Hugh Wiley of Guilford to William Wiley his son of same, one hundred pounds, 200 acres, on the W side of Bever Cr., begin at a stake on Robert Warnah's line, E to a stake on Hugh Wiley Junr.'s line, N to Thos. Wiley, W to a stake on David Wiley's line, S to the first station; signed: Hugh (+) Wiley; witness: John Isley, John Forbiss, James Duff; acknowledged August 1778 Term.

P. 452, 31 July 1777, John Hunter of Guilford to Sarah Scott of same, one hundred thirty pounds, 200 acres, on the N side of Dan R., begin at spanish oak on the river at the letter "A", N 160 p. to a white oak, E 160 p. to a red oak on the river bank, up the river to the beginning; signed: John Hunter; witness: Ally Tate, W. Tate, Thos. (+) Carter; proved November 1777 Term by Mrs.

Ally Tate.

P. 453, 21 February 1778, Edward Hunter of Guilford to Nathaniel Hoggatt Junr. of same, forty six pounds eight shillings, 58 acres, on the S side of Dan R., part of a tract from Robert Jones to Edward Hunter for 600 acres, one of five tracts granted by Robert Jones & Daniel Weldon to Edward Hunter 30 January 1760, begin at an ash or hicory, E 90 p. to a post oak, N 162 p. to a black on the river, up the river to the beginning; signed: Edward Hunter; witness: [none listed]; acknowledged February 1778 Term.

P. 454, 13 February 1778, Thomas Tilworth of Guilford to Frederick Falkerson of same, three hundred pounds, 141 acres, on both sides of Lick Fork of Hogans Cr., begin at a white oak on the bank of the creek, W 72 p. to a hicory, S 200 p. crossing the creek to a red oak, E 120 p. to pointers, N 143 p. to a poplar, N37W to a beach on the creek bank, down the creek to the beginning, a survey from John Lea to William Chambers 6 February 1767, recorded in Orange; signed: Thomas (+) Tilworth; witness: Wm. Hubert, John (+) Halford, William Bethel; proved August 1778 Term by Bethel.

P. 455, 1 December 1777, Micagay Mills of Guilford to Thomas Archer of same, fifty pounds, 50 acres, begin at a white oak the NE cor. of Mills tract, W 17 ch. 25 lk. to a stake, S 29 ch. to a hicory, E 17 ch. 25 lk. to a hicory, N 29 ch. to the beginning, to Micagay Mills 28 February 1759; signed: Micajah Mills; witness: James Archer, Jno. Hamelton; proved February 1778 Term by Hamelton.

P. 457, 23 June 1778, George Hunt Allen of Buckingham County, Virginia, to James Hunter of Guilford, sixty three pounds fifteen shillings, 205 acres, on the N side of Dann R. below the mouth of Mayo, begin at a swamp or basket white oak on the river bank on Wm. Hunt Allen's line, N 276 P. to pointers on the Old Back Line on the road, W 157 p. to a post oak a new cor. on sd. line, S a new line 280 p. to a black oak on the river bank dividing James Hunter & John Whitworth, down the river to the beginning; signed: Geo. H. Allen; witness: Wm. H. Allen, John Whitworth; proved August 1778 Term by Whitworth.

P. 458, 3 November 1778, John Henderson and Sam Henderson Junr. Esqs. of Granville to James Marten esq. of Guilford, four hundred pounds, 200 acres, on the S side of Dann R., begin at a haw tree on the river, up the river 180 p. to an ash at the mouth of a gut below the Lone Island Ford, S 240 p. by the Dividing Line made by John Reagan & George Oliver to the Back Line, E 180 p. to a post oak, N 240 p. to the beginning, part of a tract from Granville to Anthony Hampton for 480 acres, this 200 acres from Hampton to John Reagan, Reagan to John & Samuel Henderson; signed: John Henderson, Samuel Henderson; witness: Bromfield Ridley; proved November 1778 term by Bromfield Ridley Esq.

P. 459, 17 November 1778, Robert Bell of Guilford to Christopher Ziglar of Culpeper County, Virginia, two hundred fifty pounds,

330 acres, begin at a red oak, S 80 ch. to a red oak, E 40 ch. to a white oak, N 80 ch. to the center of 3 white oaks, W 40 ch. to the first station, Granville to Patrick Hays; signed: Robt. Bell; witness: John Robertson, Samll. Bell; acknowledged November 1779 Term; Mary wife of Robert Bell relionquished her right of dower.

P. 460, 11 April 1777, Samuel Cannady & wife Sarah of Guilford to William Denny of same, one hundred pounds, 150 acres, on waters of Haw R., on the S side of the North Fork, begin at a red oak, 30 ch. to a white oak, 50 ch. to a white oak, W 30 ch. to a red oak, N to the first station; signed: Samuel Cannady, Sarah Cannady; witness: Walter Hill, William Cannady; proved November 1778 Term by William Cannady.

P. 461, 29 September 1777, William Walker of Guilford to James Walker of same, two hundred pounds, 124 acres, on the N side of Dann R., begin on Dann R. bank at a spreading white oak near a Cross Rock Shoal, N 160 p. to a maple on the bank of Road Cr. near John Glenn's field, E 156 p. to an elm on the river, up the river to the beginning; signed: William Walker; witness: John Glenn, Ann Porter, John Walker; proved November 1778 Term by John Glenn.

P. 462, 5 August 1778, Edward Clark of Guilford, planter, & Frances his wife to Samuel Moor of same, planter, one hundred pounds, 50 acres, on Moody Cr. waters of Deep R., begin at a post oak, E 11 ch. 13 to a white oak, N 45 ch. to a red oak, W 11 ch. 13 to a black jack, S to the beginning 45 ch.; signed: Edward Clark, Frances Clark; witness: Richardson Owen, Ely (+) Surry; proved November 1778 by Richardson owen Esq.

P. 463, 9 May 1775, Thomas Bullar of Guilford to Richardson Owen of same, eight hundred pounds, 198 acres, on Deep R. at the mouth of Muddy Cr., begin at a black oak, N53E 92 ch. to a stake, S 54 ch. to a black oak, W 73 ch. 55 lk. to the beginning; signed: Thomas Bullar; witness: John Clark, Thomas Smith, Francis Wallar; proved November 1778 Term by Smith.

P. 464, 19 August 1778, Edward Hunter & Elizabeth his wife of Guilford to Isaac Whitworth & Alexander McClaran of same, four hundred forty pounds, 386 acres, in Guilford & Surry Counties, on the S side of Dann R., begin at a white oak on the river, S 220 p. to a pine, W 260 p. to a red oak on the river, down the river to the beginning; signed: Edward Hunter, Elisabeth Hunter; witness: Isham Browder, Thos. Henderson; acknowledged August 1778 Term.

P. 465, 14 October 1778, Valuntine Allen of Guilford to Benjamin Gates of same, two hundred pounds, 100 acres, on the S side of Dann R., begin at a hicory Astom's line on the river bank, by Astom's line to a cor. black oak, by Benjamin Gates own line to a white oak, by a line of marked trees to the river bank to a cycamore [sic], down the river to the first station; signed: Valentine Allen; witness: Richd. Vernon, George ( ) Oliver, Anthony Reeseen; proved November 1778 Term by Vernon.

P. 466, 10 May 1778, John Ward of Bedford County, Virginia, to Isaac Hill of Guilford, three hundred fifty pounds, 500 acres, on both sides of Wolf Island Cr. begin at Hugh Chattles [Challes?] red oak, N 400 p. to an oak by the creek, W 400 p. to Chattles' cor, along his line cross the sd. S45E to the beginning; signed: John Ward; witness: John Martin, Henry Ward, John Yeates, London Harris; proved August 1778 Term by Harris.

P. 467, 21 March 1775, Simeon Hinds & Sarah his wife of Guilford to Joseph Hinds of same, nineteen pounds, 30 acres, on the SE forks of Polecat Cr., part of a tract from Granville to Zacharias Cox, begin at a white oak by the side of the Old Trading Road sd. white oak being the 6th cor. mentioned in Zacharias Cox's deed, W cross the Trading Road 24 ch. to the beginning cor. of Cox's land, S until it strikes one of the SE forks of Poulcat Cr., up the creek till it strikes the mouth of a small branch that runs from the E, up the SE fork of Poulcat Cr. 6 ch. 50 lk., a direct line near NE to the beginning, Joseph Hinds to Simeon Hinds 9 March 1770; signed: Simeon Hinds, Sarah (S) Hinds; witness: Robt. Field, James Hunter, John Hinds; proved November 1778 Term by John Hinds Esq.

P. 468, 1 October 1777, James Hunter of Guilford to Martha McGee of same, fifty pounds, 200 acres, on the head branch of Sandy Cr. & Stinking Quarter & on both sides of the Trading Path, begin at a hicory on the S side of the Trading Path, W 40 ch. to a chesnut tree, S 50 ch. to a black oak, E 50 ch. to a heap of stones or black jack, N 50 ch. to the first station, Granville to James Hunter 11 May 1760; signed: James Hunter; witness: John (X) Pugh, Elisha Mendenhall; "NB: it is the true intent & meaning of the above mentioned money Doubloons to be taken at six pounds, pistoles at thirty shillings & half jorg at three pounds four and this was wrote before the signing of the above; signed: James Hunter; witness: Elisha Mendenhall"; proved August 1778 Term by Mendenhall.

P. 470, 23 June 1778, George Hunt Allen of Buckingham County, Virginai, to John Whitworth of Guilford, sixty three pounds fifteen shillings, 205 acres, on the N side of Dan R. below the Mayo, begin on a hicory on Jones' Old Line on the river bank, N across 3 small branches 414 p. to a cor. white oak on the N side of a hill, E along the Old Back Line 167 p. to a post oak a new cor., S a new line 280 p. to a black oak on the river bank (Dividing John Whitworth & James Hunter), up the river to the beginning; signed: George H: Allen; witness: James Hunter, Wm. H. Allen; proved August 1778 Term by James Hunter Esq.

P. 471, 16 November 1778, William Foster of Guilford & Martha his wife to James Campbell of same, six hundred forty pounds, 207 1/2 acres, part of a tract from Granville to Hugh Foster 27 June 1751, formerly in Rowan now in Guilford, begin at a bounded black walnut on the N side of Horsepen Cr. about 40 yards from the creek & about 20 perches below a saw & grist mill built on the sad. creek by William Foster being the beginning of that part conveyed to William Dent, N50E 36 perches, N 148 perches the 2nd line of the whole tract, with the line according to the original & W 156 perches to a white oak, still with out lines of land the S line 140 perches to a stake in the Low Grounds of the creek, E with the line until it intersects a line drawn from the beginning black walnut S34W, with sd. line reverst to the beginning; signed: William Foster, Martha (+) Foster; witness: Tho. Henderson; proved February [no year given] Term by Henderson.

P. 472, 16 November 1778, William Foster of Guilford & Martha his wife to William Dent of same, one thousand pounds, 100 acres, aprt of a tract from Granville to Hugh Foster 27 June 1751, formerly in Rowan now in Guilford, begin at a bounded black walnut about 40 yards from the creek & about 20 perches below a saw & grist mill built on the creek by William Foster, N60E 36 perches, N to the 2nd line of the whole tract, with that line reverst according to the original deed E to a marked ash in a branch in the Line of Division between William Foster &. John & Samuel Foster, with the marked line S to the 4th or given line of the whole tract, reversing sd. line according to the original grant W until it intersects a line drawn from the black walnut S34W, with that line reverst to the beginnning; signed: William Foster, Martha (+) Foster; witness: Tho. Henderson; proved February 1779 Term by Henderson.

P. 474, 7 October 1778, Joseph Standly of Guilford, planter, to William Charles of same, sixteen pounds, 50 acres, part of a tract formerly belonging to "her Milles" [Mr. Mills?] & sold by Strangeman Standly to Joseph Standly, begin at the NW cor. of the original tract a marked scrubby white oak about 40 perches S from Joseph Standly's house, S 118 perches, E 68 perches, N 118 perches to a marked white oak, to the beginning; signed: Joseph Standly; witness: Leven Charles, Eli Fene; proved February 1779 Term [witness not given].

P. 475, 16 Decenmber 1778, North Carolina to Ralph Gorrell, fifty shillings per hundred acres, 200 acres, on the N side of South Buffaloe, begin on the cor. of his deeded land at a post oak, N with David Karr's line 108 p. to a post oak, W along a line of Wm. Duff's 189 p. to a post oak, N along Duff's line 80 p. to to apost oak, W 62 p. to a black oak, S 188 p. to a black jack on Daniel Gillespie's line, E 251 p. to the beginning; signed: Rd. Caswell; witness: J. Glasgow; no probate record.

P. 476, 16 December 1778, North Carolina to William Gowdy, fifty shillings per hundred acres, 560 acres, on the waters of Reedy Fork of Haw R., begin at Abraham Whitesisdes cor. spanish oak, along his line S 40 p. to a black oak Moses McCuistian's cor., his line W across Catetail Meadow Br. 158 p. to a red oak Thomas Anderson's cor., with his line N cross a branch and the Iron Works Road 240 p. to his xcor. post oak, N80E on Henry Ross' line 90 p. to a post oak bush near the Iron Works Road, N70E with his line 112 p. to a hicory bush, N33E with his line "to poles" to a hicory in a fork of Saw Pit & Long Br., E across the E fork of Long Br. 108 p. to a post oak saplin in the edge of a glade, S across Long Br. 265 p. to Abraham Whiteside's line, along his line W 157 p. to the first station; signed: Rd. Caswell; witness: J. Glasgow; no probate record.

P. 477, 16 December 1778, North Carolina to John Thom, fifty shillings per hundred acres, 300 acres, begin at a black saplin near the line of Henry Eustace McCulloh, N across Thoms Spring Br. 54.6 ch. to a small black jack, W to a white oak saplin 55 ch., S 54.6 ch. to a post oak, E across 2 branches 55 ch. to the first station; signed: Rd. Caswell; witness: J. Glasgow; no probate record.

P. 477, 16 February 1779, Martha McGee to Zebedee Wood [no residence given for either], receipt for "the within mortgage"; signed: Martha McGee; witness: John Wilburn; proved February 1779 Term by Wilburn.

P. 478, 1 September 1778, Edward Hunter of Guilford to Nathaniel Hoggatt of same, two hundred seventy five pounds, 542 acres, on the S side of Dann R., part of a tract Hunter purchased of Robert Jones Junr. containing in the whole 600 acres, the other having already been sold to Hoggatt, begin at a white oak on the river, S 160 p., W 320 p. to Hoggatt's cor., N to the river, down the river to the beginning; signed: Edward Hunter; witness: Nancy Wood Hunter, Judith Isold Hunter, Anthony Hoggat; acknowledged February 1778 Term.

P. 479, 1 March 1778, Moses McCuistian of Guilford to Henry Reed of same, one hundred pounds, 60 acres, part of 640 acres on both sides of Reedy Fork from Granville to Thomas McCuistian, Thomas McCuistian to Robert McCuistian Decd., begin at the SW cor. of the tract to the SD side of Reedy Fork & Horsepen Cr., N along the line 40 p. to a stake, E 240 p. to a stake, S 40 p. to a stake, W to the beginning; signed: Moses McCuistian; witness: Thos. McCuistian, James McCuistian; acknowledged February 1779 Term.

P. 480, 16 February 1779, John Stubblefield of Surry to Archibald Yarborough of Guilford, five hundred fifty three pounds six shillings eight pence, 164 acres & 137 poles, on the N side of Hogans Cr., begin at a white oak, S75W 11 p. to a red oak, N 215 p. to a white oak, E 140 p. to a hicory in Wyatt Stubblefield's Spring Br., E70S down the branch 30 p. to a maple, E down the branch 21 p. to a plum tree on the creek bank, up Hogans Cr. to the beginning; signed: John (I) Stubblefield, Elisabeth (X) Stubblefield; witness: Isham Dalton, John Odell; acknowledged February 1779 Term.

P. 481, 10 January 1779, Allen & Willie Jones to Valentine Allen [no residence given for any of the parties], fifty pounds, 200 acres, on the N side of Dan R., begin at a white oak Joseph Tate's cor., W 106 p. to a white oak, S 340 p. to the river, down the river to another cor. of Tate's, along his line to the beginning, part of 500 acres from Granville to Robert Jones Junr. Decd. 27 April 1751 registered in Granville County; signed: Allen

Jones, Willie Jones; witness: Turlyfield Barnes, R. Binnihan; proved February 1779 Term by Barnes.

P. 482, 13 October 1778, William Moreland & Catrin his wife of Guilford to John Hamilton of same, one hundred fifty pounds, 51 acres, on both sides of Horsepen Cr. waters of Haw R., begin at a white oak & sourwood Francis McNarry's cor., W 205 p. to an ash by a branch, S 40 p. to a stake, E 215 p. to a stake in Francis McNarry's line, N 40 p. to the beginning, the NE part of 615 acres from Granville to Hugh Foster 3 December 1753; signed: William (O) Moreland, Catrin (O) Moreland; witness: Joseph Huskins, John Ballenger; proved February 1779 Term by Huskins.

P. 483, 18 February 1779, William Williams of Guilford to Thomas Simpson of same, fifty pounds, 50 acres, on Mairs Fork waters of Haw R., begin at the mouth of Line Br. joining Richard Simpson's line, down the creek to a spanish oak, by a line of marked trees agreed upon between William Williams & Richard Simpson to the S line of William Williams' cornering on a red oak, part of a larger tract from Granville to George Jordan Junr. 29 October 1753, registered in Rowan, Robert Harris to William Williams 14 October 1758; signed: William (W) Williams; witness: William Dixson, Richd. Simpson, Sarah Dixson; proved February 1779 Term by Simpson.

P. 484, 16 February 1779, Rachel Hogatt & John Odeneal of Guilford to Peter Ford of same, four hundred forty three pounds fifteen shillings, 297 acres, on the N side of Dann R., begin on the river bank at a black walnut bush near the mouth of Red Bank Br., N along William Crump's line 268 p. to a pine, E 240 p. to a white oak, S 128 p. along Thomas Walker's line to a white oak on the river bank, up the river to the beginning; signed: Rachel Hoggatt, Jn. Odeneal; witness: Edward Hunter, Alex. Martain, Charles Perkins; acknowledged February 1779 Term.

P. 485, 16 Decemeber 1778, North Carolina to John Beasley, fifty shillings per hundred acres, 100 acres, on Burch Cr. waters of Allemance, begin at a post oak saplin cor. to his deeded land, W to a small black jack in Thomas Morgan's line 40 ch., S on Morgan's line to his own cor. 25 ch., E along his line to his cor. 40 ch., N along his line to the beginning 25 ch.; signed: Rd. Caswell; witness: J. Glasgow; no probate record.

P. 486, 16 December 1778, North Carolina to Andrew Finley, fifty shillings per hundred acres, 640 acres, on both sides of the North Fork of Allemance, begin at a post oak saplin joining William Armstrong, S2E 77 ch. to a post oak a cor. of land of William Wiley & Armstrong, N88E 10.5 ch. to a post oak cor. to Wiley, S2E 32 ch. to a black oak cor. to Wiley & crossing Allemance, N88E 58 ch. 25 lk. to a small post oak joining John Wiley's line & crossing his cor. on the bank on the N side 13 ch., N2:30W on Wiley's line 71.6 ch. to a small hicory, W to the beginning 58 ch. 25 lk.; signed: Rd. Caswell; witness: J. Glasgow; no probate record.

P. 487, 16 December 1778, North Carolina to William Mountgomery, fifty shillings per hundred acres, 500 acres, on the head branches of Rock Cr., begin at a hicory on the bank of the creek on John Philip Clap's line, N on his line 60 ch. to a spanish oak saplin, W 83.3 ch. to a stone in the head of a glade, S 60 ch. to a red oak, E 83.3 ch. to the beginning; signed: Rd. Caswell; witness: J. Glasgow; no probate record.

P. 488, 16 December 1778, North Carolina to Robert Allison, fifty shillings per hundred acres, 300 acres, on the S side of the North Fork of Allemance, begin at a black walnut on the bank of Haw Cr. on Jacob Summer's line near the bank of Allemance, S6E up the branch a conditional line with James Lett 71 ch. to a post oak saplin, W 51 ch. to a small ash on a branch a conditonal line with William Eken & John Wiley, down the branch N9W to a stake on the bank of the creek 47 ch., down the creek on Sampson Stuart's line to Summer's line to the beginning 57 ch.; signed: Rd. Caswell: witness: J. Glasgow; no probate record.

P. 489, 16 December 1778, North Carolina to Edward Holland, fifty shillings per hundred acres, 200 acres, on waters of North Buffaloe, begin on George Rankin's line at a black oak, W with Rankin's line 120 p. to a white oak, S on Rankin's line 100 p. to a spanish oak, W 1660 p. to a black oak, N 158 p. to James McCuistian's line cornering on a white oak, E on McCuistian's line 280 p. to Francis Wright's line, S on Wright's line 58 p. to the beginning; signed: Rd. Caswell; witness: J. Glasgow; no probate record.

P. 490, 16 December 1778, North Carolina to Thomas Hamilton, fifty shillings per hundred acres, 300 acres, on both sides of Rock Cr. waters of Allemance, begin at a hicory grub at Peter Larance's NW cor. on the stump of an oak near a creek, N75E on his line cross the creek 67 ch. to a black jack, N47W 38.5 ch. to a small post oak a conditional line with Michal Cocar, S88W on John Philip Clap's line to a cor. black oak & cross the creek 62 ch., S22E on a conditional line with Andrew Low 30 ch. to a black oak, S 40 ch. to a post oak, E 12 ch. to Larance's line at a black oak, N to the beginning; signed: Rd. Caswell; witness: J. Glasgow; no probate record.

P. 491, 16 December 1778, North Carolina to Finley Stuart, fifty shillings per hindred acres, 640 acres, on the N side of Allemance, begin at a red oak a cor. to Henry Eustace McCulloh, his line S44W 50.5 ch. to a red oak crossing a branch & coming past Stuart's house & the Persimon Br., W 25ch to a black jack, N 80.5 ch. to a black oak saplin, E 110 ch. to a black oak saplin, S 24 ch. to a black oak saplin, S45W 50 ch. on a conditional line with John Job to a hicory grub on McCulloh's line, N43W along his line to the beginning 20 ch.; signed: Rd. Caswell; witness: J. Glasgow; no probate record.

P. 492, 16 December 1778, North Carolina to James Wilson, fifty shillings per hundred acres, 300 acres, on a branch of North Buffaloe Cr., begin at a black oak cor. of Samuel Bell, W 240 p.

to a post oak cor. of John McNaight, N 200 p. to a post oak, E 240 p. to a white oak, S 200 p. to the beginning; signed: Rd. Caswell; witness: J. Glasgow; no probate record.

P. 493, 16 December 1778, North Carolina to Sampson Stuart, fifty shillings per hundred acres, 50 acres, on waters of Allemance on the N side of the North Fork, begin at a small post oak on Jacob Summer's line on Pissimon Br., N on his line cross the branch to a white oak 19 ch. 75 lk., W 25 ch. 38 lk. to a black saplin, S 19 ch. 75 lk. to a black oak saplin on his own line, N on his line 25 ch. 75 lk. to the beginning; signed: Rd. Caswell; witness: J. Glasgow; no probate record.

P. 494, "The oath of Elisabeth Davice - Elisabeth Davice being duly sworn saith that the Revd. Mr. David Caldwell asked Thomas Culver if James McCuistian struck him, she the deponent saith that he the said Culver answered: No, No, I do not know any further saith not, sworn before me July 13th 1779, Alexr. Caldwell."

P. 494, "Edward Holland being duly sworn saith that he was by James McCuistian all the time of the riot between Stephen Mahoney and Thomas Culver and the Gard and to the Court House from the Courthouse to John McCuistian's from thence to said Holland's from thenxce to sd. James McCuistian's & that the said McCuistain was not out of his sight all this time to the best of his knowledge and that he did not see the said James McCuistian strick or favor the stricking or hurting the sadi Thos. Culver nor no other person at that time or occation and further saith not, sworn before me July 13th, Alexr. Caldwell."

P. 494, "Catherine McNaight being duly sworn saith that she heard Amelia Bell say that when Thomas Culver was asked if James McCuistian struck or hurt him that he cleared him the said McCuistian and answered NO, NO & further saith not, sworn before me July 13th 1779, Alexr. Caldwell."

P. 494, 13 November 1779, North Carolina to William Dick, fifty shillings per hundred acres, 300 acres, on waters of Richland Cr., begin at his own cor. black oak in James McCuistian's line, W 230 p. to a chesnut in the S line of the Court House Tract, S on that line 90 p. to William Dent's cor. gum, on his line E 70 p. to a post oak near a pond, S along his line 160 p. to a black jack, E 269 p. to a post oak, N across a branch 90 p. to a black oak on James McCuistian's line, on his line W 109 p. to his cor. black oak, N on his line across 3 branches 160 p. to the first station, No. 234; signed: J. Glasgow, Secy.

P. 495, 16 December 1778, North Carolina to Thomas Morgan, fifty shillings per hundred acres, 400 acres, on waters of Allemance, begin at a stone near the bank of a branch of Burch Cr. on William Beasley's line, N on his line to a post oak 12.5 ch., E on the line 14 ch. 75 lk. to a black oak, N on Col. John Peasley's line 27.5 ch. to a black jack, E on his line 10 ch. to a black oak, N 25 ch. to a black oak, W 71 ch. to a black oak, S 71 ch. to a black jack, E 65 ch. to the beginning; signed: Rd. Caswell; witness: J. Glasgow; no probate record.

P. 496, 16 December 1778, North Carolina to John Anderson, fifty shillings per hundred acres, 300 acres, on the waters of North Buffaloe, begin on Robert Donnal's line, W 160 p. to a post oak John Burney's cor., N on Burney's line 300 p. to a post oak, E 160 p. to 2 white oaks on Hugh Brawley's line, S 300 p. on Brawley's line to the beginning; signed: Wm. Shepperd, Depty Sec.; no probate record.

P. 497, 16 December 1778, North Carolina to Andrew Low, fifty shillings per hundred acres, 200 acres, on waters of Rock Cr. of Allemance, begin at a small post oak on John Philip Clap's line, S on his line to a cor. black oak 29.5 ch., S22E a conditional line with Thomas Hamelton 30 ch. to a black oak, W 46 ch. to a black jack, N 57 ch. to a post oak, E 32 ch. to the beginning, No. 13; signed: Wm. Shepperd, Dep. Sec.; no probate record.

P. 497, 16 December 1778, North Carolina to Samuel Duff Junr., fifty shillings per hundred acres, 350 acres; on the N side of South Buffaloe, begin on Adam Leckey's deeded land on a spanish oak, N on Leckey's line & Samuel Duff Senr. 164 p. to a black oak, W on Samuel Duff Senr.'s line 60 p. to 2 black oaks, N on Duff's line 74 p. to a black oak, E with Duff's line 26 p. to a black oak, N partly along Duff's line 82 p. to a black oak, W 164 p. to a black jack, S 320 p. to a black jack, E 198 p. to the beginning, No. 48; signed: Wm. Shepperd, Dep. Sec.; no probate record.

P. 497, 16 December 1778, North Carolina to Susanna McGee, fifty shillings per hundred acres, 250 acres, on Buck Cr. a fork of Sandy Cr., begin at a chesnut near Henry Pickrale's improvements, S 49.5 ch. to a black oak cor. of Enuch Davices, on sd. line E 50.5 ch. to a post oak saplin crossing a branch, N 49.5 ch. to a black oak saplin, W 50.5 ch. to the beginning, No. 8; signed: J. Glasgow, Secy.

P. 498, 16 December 1778, North Carolina to Susanna McGee, fifty shillings per hundred acres, 400 acres, on waters of Sandy Cr., begin at a small hicory supposed to be on or near the line of deeded land that Martha McGee lives on, S 85.5 ch. cross a branch to a red oak saplin, W 55 ch. to a small hicory, N 17.5 ch. to a black oak on her own deeded land, E on her line to a black oak cor. 10.5 ch., on sd. line N to a black oak 68.5 ch., E 44.5 ch. to the beginning; signed: J. Glasgow, Secy.; no probate record.

P. 498, 16 December 1778, North Carolina to Samuel Shaw, fifty shillings per hundred acres, 200 acres, begin at a black jack saplin on Hugh Shaw's line in the side of a glade near Falling Run, W on his line & continued 50 ch. to a stake, N 40 ch. to a small black jack, E 50 ch. to a red oak, 40 ch. to the beginning, No. 5; signed: J. Glasgow, Secy.; no probate record.

P. 498, 16 December 1778, North Carolina to Thomas Landreth, fifty shillings per hundred acres, 475 acres, on the waters of Allemance, begin on the N side of a creek on Alexander Maben's deeded land at a black jack, W along the claim of William Moor 220 p. to a post oak, S along a claim of William Barnhill 346 p. to a hicory, E along a claim of Hugh Drennan 220 p. to a post oak, N 346 p. to the beginning, No. 45; signed: Wm. Shepperd, Dep. Sec.; no probate record.

P. 499, 16 December 1778, North Carolina to Samuel Long, fifty shillings per hundred acres, 300 acres, begin near Alexander Breeden's cor. post oak, S 219 p. to a post oak, W 220 p. to a post oak, N 219 p. to a black jack, E 220 p. to the beginning, No. 60; signed: Wm. Shepperd, Dep. Sec.; no probate record.

P. 499, 16 December 1778, North Carolina to Robert Axton, fifty shillings per hundred acres, 170 acres, begin at a chesnut oak, E 20 p. to a black oak on James Vernon's claim, N45E 40 p. along Vernon's claim to a white oak, N55E 20 p. along Vernon's claim to a pine, N48E 40 p. along Vernon's claim to a spanish oak, N58E 164 p. along Vernon's claim to a white oak, N 42 p. along Vernon's claim to a white in Sarah Powell's line, N along her line 30 p. to a white oak on the river, down the river (the opposite side being property of sundry persons) to the first station, No. 4; signed: J. Glasgow, Secy.; no probate record.

P. 499, 16 December 1778, North Carolina to William Gowdy Esq., fifty shillings per hundred acres, 433 acres, on Haw R., begin at a chesnut tree near the river, S 294 p. to a white oak, W across sundry branches 324 p. to a post oak in Thomas Person's line, with his line N 134 p. to a box elder on the bank of the river, down the river to the first station; signed: William Shepperd, Dep. Sec.; no probate record.

P. 500, 16 December 1778, North Carolina to Hannah McCrory, fifty shillings per hundred acres, 640 acres, on both sides of Mairs Fork of Haw R., begin at a post oak in James Stuart's line, N 205 p. across Mairs Fork to his cor. white oak, W 16 p. to his cor. black oak saplin, N 20 p. to his cor. white oak, E 18 p. to a black cor. of James Barr's old survey, N along that line across Simpsons Br. 220 p. to a black oak saplin, W across the branch & Bruces Road 233 p. to a post oak saplin, S 185 p. to a chinquepin grub in Peter Garrison's line, with his line 2 p. to a black oak, along his line S 235 p. across Mairs Fork to a black jack, W 2 p. to a hicory grub, S 25 p. to a black oak, E 231 p. to the first station, No. 102; signed: Wm. Shepperd, Dep. Sec.; no probate record.

P. 500, 16 December 1778, North Carolina to James Stuart, fifty shillings per hundred acres, 365 acres, on both sides of Mairs Fork of Haw R., begin at a white oak in Hannah McCrory's line, E to & along James Barr's line of his old survey across Mairs Fork 260 p. to a white oak saplin, S across a branch 220 p. to a post oak saplin, W 40 p. to a post oak, S 22 p. to a hicory, W 204 p. to a post oak saplin Hannah McCrory's cor., along her line N 220 p. across Mairs Fork to a white oak, W along her line 16 p. to a black oak saplin, along her line N 20 p. to the first station, No. 85; signed: Wm. Shepperd, Dep. Sec.; no probate record.

P. 501, 16 December 1778, North Carolina to William Duff, fifty shillings per hundred acres, on the N side of South Buffaloe Cr., begin on David Kerr's cor. white oak, E along Kerr's line 80 p. to a post oak, N along Kerr's line 212 p. to a post oak, W 160 p. to a post oak, S along John Gillespie's line 20 p. to a post oak, W along Gillespie's line 109 1/2 p. to a white oak, S 240 p. to Ralph Gorrel's line to a post oak, E along Gorrel's line 189 p. to a post oak, N 40 p. to the beginning, No. 33; siogned: Wm. Shepperd, Dep. Sec.; no probate record.

P. 501, 16 December 1778, North Carolina to Archibald McIntir, fifty shillings per hundred acres, 417 acres, on waters of Reedy & Mairs Fork of Haw R., begin at a post oak on John Blair's & John Anderson's line, N with John Anderson's line across a branch 285 p. to a cor. post oak in James Stuart's line, with his line W 64 p. to his & Hannah McCrory's cor. post oak, S 22 p. to a post oak, W crossing sundry branches 236 p. to a white oak, S 210 p. to a white oak, E across Cornfield Br. 180 p. to a red oak saplin, 120 p. E to the first station, No. 72; signed: Wm. Shepperd, Dep. Sec.; no probate record.

P. 502, 16 December 1778, North Carolina to William Anderson, fifty shillings per hundred acres, 250 acres, on waters of Reedy Fork of Haw R., begin at a black in John Anderson's line, E 164 p. to a grub, N across the Dann River Road & the Long Br. 142 p. to a post oak, W 36 p. to a post oak, N 143 p. to a black oak, W 128 p. cross the road to a black oak, S to & along John Anderson's line 285 p. to the first station, No. 64; signed: Wm. Shepperd, Dep. Sec.; no probate record.

P. 502, 16 December 1778, North Carolina to Henry Ross, fifty shillings per hundred acres, 400 acres, on waters of Reedy Fork of Haw R., begin at a grub William Anderson's cor., E 56 p. to a post oak Thomas Anderson & William Gowdy's cor., along Gowdy's line N80E 90 p. to a post oak bush near the Iron Works Road, N70E 112 p. to a hicory bush, N33E 10 p. to a hicory in a fork of Sawpit & Long Br., E 12 p. to an alder bush, N 180 p. to to a black oak, W 74 p. to 2 post oaks, N70W 92 p. to a black oak, W 100 p. across Long Br. to a post oak, S 286 p. to the first station, No. 96; signed: Wm. Shepperd, Dep. Sec.; no probate record.

P. 503, 16 December 1778, North Carolina to James Bell, fifty shillings per hundred acres, 500 acres, on Reedy Fork of Haw R., begin at a hicory in Thomas Bell's line on the bank of Reedy Fork, up the fork (land on the opposite side property of John McClintock) to James Barr's line, his line W to a stone 68 p., S to an ash on his line to the bank of the creek 40 p. (land on the opposite side entered by William Scott) to Robert Donald's line, along his line N to his cor., same course continued (in all) 400 p. to a grub, E 236 p. across a branch to Thomas Bell's line, S along his line 291 p. to the first station, No. 91;

signed: Wm. Shepperd, Dep. Sec.; no probate record.

P. 503, 16 December 1778, North Carolina to James Barr, fifty shillings per hundred acres, 350 acres, on both sides of Mairs Fork of Haw R., begin at a white oak, W 200 p. to 3 chesnut trees, S to & along Hannah McCrory's line across Simpsons Br. 280 p. to a black oak in James Stuart's line, E along his line across Mairs Fork 200 p. to a white oak, N across the creek 280 p. to the first station, No. 77; signed: Wm. Shepperd, Dep. Sec.; no probate record.

P. 503, 16 December 1778, North Carolina to Hugh Shaw, fifty shillings per hundred acres, 300 acres, begin at a post oak on the E of falling Run on the N side of Great Allemance near the creek, S58W on the line of Henry Eustace McCulloh 60.5 ch. to a red oak cor., S87W on a conditional line with John Job 15.5 ch. to a post oak, N. to Finley Stuart's cor. & along his line & beyond it 56 ch. 17 lk. to a stake, E 68 ch. to a post oak crossing Falling Run, S 25 ch. to the beginning, No. 9; signed: J. Glasgow Secy.; no probate record.

P. 504, 16 December 1778, North Carolina to Samuel Duff Senr., fifty shillings per hundred acres, 400 acres, on waters of South Buffaloe, begin at Charles Burn's cor. on Adam Lackey's line on the S side of the creek on the bank at a white oak bush, W 276 p. along Adam Lackey's line to a post oak, N along Samuel Duff Junr.'s line 100 p. to a black oak, W along Duff's line 60 p. to 2 black oaks, N along Duff's line 74 p. to a black oak, E 26 p. along Duff's line to a black oak, N along Duff's line 55 p. to a post oak, E 210 p. to a black jack on John Duff's line, S on John Duff's line 55 p. to a post oak, E along John Duff's line 100 p. to a hicory, S 174 p. across the creek to the beginning, No. 34; signed: Wm. Shepperd, Dep. Sec.; no probate record.

P. 504, 16 December 1778, North Carolina to Moses McClain, fifty shillings per hundred acres, 200 acres, begin at a black jack on Robert Rankin's line, W along Jonas Touchstone's line 120 p. to a white oak, N alonfg Robert Rankin's line 90 p. to a black oak, E along David Allison's line 30 p. to a black oak, N along Allison's line 180 p. to a post oak, E along Robert Rankin Junr.'s line 144 p. to a black oak, S 96 p. to a post oak, W along Robert Rankin Senr.'s line 44 p. to a white oak, S along Rankin's line 174 p. to the beginning, No. 83; signed: Wm. Shepperd, Dep. Sec.; no probate record.

P. 505, 16 December 1778, North Carolina to David Russel, fifty shillings per hundred acres, 640 acres, on waters of Allemance, on the N side of the North Fork of sd. creek, begin at a post oak cor. of Isaiah McBride, E on sd. line 82 ch. to a small post, S 23 ch. to a hicory, E 30 ch. to a black jack saplin, N 56.5 ch. to a small hicory on William Beasley's line, W on his line to a stake 36.5 ch., N on his line 50 ch. to a stake, W 40 ch. to a post oak saplin, S 48 ch. to a black oak saplin a conditional line with William Thrasher, W 35 ch. to a maple a conditional line with Thrasher, S 35 ch. to the first station, No. 7; signed:

J. Glasgow, Secy.; no probate record.

P. 505, 7 June 1779, Adam Mitchel Junr. of Guilford to Revd. David Caldwell [no residence given], ten pounds & full consent of Margarate Mahoney, 1 acre, bounded on S by the road leading to Salisbury, on the E by confiscated land late the property of Edmund Fanning, on W & N by land of Adam Mitchel, [no metes and bounds description]; signed: Adam Mitchel, Margarate (+) Mahoney; witness: [illegible signature], William Strain; acknowledged August 1779 Term.

P. 506, 16 December 1778, North Carolina to William Dick, fifty shillings per hundred acres, 640 acres, on waters of Beaver Cr. of Allemance, begin at a black oak saplin on John Forbes' line joining to Joseph Kennedy, N 30 ch. to a black jack, E on Forbes' line 52.5 ch. to a white oak, n on Robert Hannah's line 42.5 ch. to a post oak, W on David Wiley's line to a stake in sd. Dick's field 4 ch. 70 lk., N on David Wiley's line 59 ch. to a red oak, W on William Cusick's line cross Beaver Cr. to a black walnut on the bank on the N side 24 ch., S on James McAdoo's line across the creek 34.5 ch. to a post oak, W on McAdoo's line 23 ch. to a white oak, S on Benjamin Starrat's line 27 ch. to a red oak, W along Starrat's line 29.5 ch. to a small white oak on the bank of the creek, S on Starrat's line 37 ch. to his cor. & continued to a black saplin in all 70 ch., E to the beginning, No. 42; signed: Wm. Shepperd, Dep. Sec.; no probate record.

P. 506, 16 December 1778, North Carolina to John Burney, fifty shillings per hundred acres, 640 acres, on both sides of Sugar Tree Cr. waters of North Buffaloe, begin on John Nix's line at a white oak, E 124 p. to a post oak on Robert Donnel's line, N along Donnel's line 154 p. cross Sugar Tree Cr. to a post oak, E along Donnel's line 96 p. to apost oak, N om John Anderson's line 379 p. to a spanish oak, W 220 p. to a black oak, S 533 p. to the beginning, No. 42; signed: Wm. Shepperd, Dep. Sec.; no probnate record.

P. 506, 16 December 1778, North Carolina to Patrick Dimm, fifty shillings per hundred acres, 320 acres, on both sides of Arwin Br., begin at a black oak, W 210 p. to a post oak, S across a branch 244 p. to a post oak, E 210 p.to a post oak, N 240 p. to the first station, No. 61; signed: Wm. Shepperd, Dep. Sec.; no probate record.

P. 507, 16 December 1778, North Carolina to John Anderson, fifty shillings per hundred acres, 597 acres, on waters of Mairs Fork & Reedy Fork of Haw R., begin at a post oak & black John Blair's cor., N 80 p. to a post oak, W 46 p. to a black, N 240 p. to a black jack, W 124 p. to a spanish oak in James Stuart's line, his line S 13 p. to his cor. post oak, along his line W 40 p. to a post oak, along his line S 22 p. to a hicory, along his line W 140 p. to a post oak, S 285 p. across a branch to a post oak in John Blair's line, along his line E 350 p. to the first station, No. 58; signed: Wm. Shepperd, Dep. Sec.; no probate record.

P. 507, 16 December 1778, North Carolina to Thomas Anderson, fifty shillings per hundred acres, 264 acres, on waters of Reedy Fork of Haw R., begin at Moses McCuistian's cor. black oak, E across a branch & Dann R. & Iron Works Road 176 p. to a black oak saplin William Gowdy's cor., along his line N across Cattail Meadow Br. & Iron Works Road 240 p. to a post oak saplin, W across the Dann River Road 176 p. to John Blair's line, his line S 240 p. to the first station, No. 94; signed: Wm. Shepperd, Dep. Sec.; no probate record.

P. 507, 11 March 1778, William Foster & Polly his wife of Guilford to Charles Bruce of same, sixty six pounds seventeen shillings eight pence, 307 acres, on both sides of Horse Pen Cr. & part of a tract from Granville to Hugh Foster 3 December 1753, begin at an ash on the W side of Horsepen Cr. in or near a branch, W 205 p. to a white oak (alias) a post oak, S 240 p. to a stake in the Low Ground of the creek, E 205 p. to a black oak, N 240 p. to the first station, deed void if Foster pays Bruce sixty six pounds seventeen shillings eight pence plus six per cent interest by 1 November 1778; signed: William Foster, Martha (+) Foster, Charles Bruce; witness: Tho. Henderson; proved August 1779 Term by Henderson.

P. 509, 16 December 1778, North Carolina to Benjamin Parratt, fifty shillings per hundred acres, 500 acres, on both sides of Wolf Island Cr. waters of Dann R., begin at a white oak Mr. Hill's NW cor., N across Wolf Island Cr. 260 p. to a red oak on Farrow's line, S82W 268 p. to a white oak on Jesse Gamman's claim, S36W 165 p. to a black on sd. claim, S 100 p. to a red oak on or near Hill's line, E along sd. line across the creek to the beginning, No. 84; signed: Wm. Shepperd, Dep. Sec.; no probate record.

P. 510, 16 December 1778, North Carolina to James Coots, fifty shillings per hundred acres, 200 acres, on waters of Reedy Fork of Haw R., begin at a black oak, N 200 p. to Samuel Thompson's SE cor. white oak, W on his line 160 p. to a white oak, S 200 p. to a black oak saplin, E 160 p. to the beginning, No. 100; signed: Wm. Shepperd, Dep. Sec.; no probate record.

P. 510, 16 December 1778, North Carolina to Samuel Thompson, fifty shillings per hundred acres, 422 acres, on both sides Poplar Br. waters of Reedy Fork, begin at a black oak Samuel Thompson's cor., S 260 p. to a black oak, E 260 p. to a black oak, N 260 p. to a white oak on sd. Thompson's line, W the same line to the beginning, No. 66; signed: Wm. Shepperd, Dep. Sec.; no probate record.

P. 510, 16 December 1778, North Carolina to John Genn, fifty shillings per hundred acres, 453 acres, on both sides of Reed Cr., begin at James Walker's cor. poplar stump near the mouth of Reed Cr., along James Walker's line W across the creek twice 288 p. to a pine, N across the creek 278 p. to a pine, E across 2 branches 180 p. to a pine in John Wolson's [Wilson's?] line, his line S 68 p. to his cor. pine, along his line E 180 p. to a pine,

S across Reed Cr. 210 p. to the first station, No. 38; signed: Wm. Shepperd, Dep. Sec.; no probate record.

P. 510, 16 December 1778, North Carolina to Charles Garner, fifty shillings per hundred acres, 200 acres, begin on the S side of Bever Island Cr. at a black oak, S 206 p. to a black oak saplin a cor. of Thomas Scale's claim, W 156 p. across a branch to a pine, N 206 p. to a pine, E 106 p. to the beginning, No. 26; signed: Wm. Shepperd, Dep. Sec.; no probate record.

P. 511, 16 December 1778, North Carolina to John White, fifty shillings per hundred acres, 640 acres, on both sides of Long Br. of Reedy Fork of Haw R., begin at a post oak on Thomas Donnel's line, W across Long Br. 204 p. to an ash, along his line S 18 p. to a post oak, along his line W 92 p. to a white oak in Abraham Whiteside's line, along his line N 42 p. to a black oak, along his line 124 p. to 3 black oaks, across Long Br. 223 p. to a post oak, E across Arwins Br. 420 p. to a black oak, S across a branch 247 p. to the first station, No. 95; signed: Wm. Shepperd, Dep. Sec.; no probate record.

P. 511, 16 December 1778, North Carolina to Robert McKemie, fifty shillings per hundred acres, 200 acres, on waters of Lick Br. of Haw R., begin at a black oak saplin in his own line, along his line S across Bruces Road & 2 branches of Mairs Fork 226 p. to a post oak in James Barr's line, along his line W 142 p. to a small maple in a branch, N along McKemie's line 226 p. to a grub, E along his line 142 p. to the first station, No. 63; signed: Wm. Shepperd, Dep. Sec.; no probate record.

P. 511, 16 December 1778, North Carolina to Robert McKemie, fifty shillings per hundred acres, 640 acres, on waters of Haw R., begin at a black oak on Thomas Blair's cor., N 62 p. along his line to John Porter's cor. white oak, along his line E across Lick Br. 155 p. to a black oak, S crossing a fork of sd. branch 200 p. to a black oak saplin, W 137 p. along his line to a grub, S 226 p. to a maple in a branch on James Barr's line, along his line W 36 p. to his cor. 3 chesnut trees, S along his line 66 p. to Hannah McCrory's cor. black oak, along her line W across Simpsons br. 138 p. to a post oak, N across Bruce Road 430 p. to Thomas Blair's line 156 p. to the first station, No. 95; signed: Wm. Shepperd, Dep. Sec.; no probate record.

P. 512, 16 December 1778, North Carolina to James Hays, fifty shillings per hundred acres, 416 acres, on both sides of Haw R., begin at a white oak Samuel McCracken's cor., W along his line 80 p. to a grub, N bounded by William Mortimore's claim 280 p. to a grub on Isaac Wright's line, E on his line 60 p. to a white oak, N 80 p. to a red oak, E 12 p. to a white oak, S 200 p. to a white oak, E79S bounded by Frederick Dill's claim to the mouth of Cains Br. crossing Haw R. to an elm on the river bank 185 p., S 45 p. to a hicory, E 63 p. to a white oak on McCaminy's line, S along his line 120 p. to a white oak, W bounded by Nathaniel Swain's claim 211 p. to a white oak on Samuel McCracken's line, N along his line across Haw R. to the beginning, No. 97; signed: Wm.

Shepperd, Dep. Sec.; no probate record.

P. 512, 16 December 1778, North Carolina to George Alexande [Alexander?], fifty shillings per hundred acres, 557 acres, on both sides of 2 creeks known by the name of Brushy Fork & on the S side of Allemance, begin at John Alexander's cor. black oak bush, S 381 p. to a black jack, E 234 p. across Brushy Fork to a white oak, n 381 p. across the 2 Brushy Forks to a black on William Doaks' line & Charles Harden's cor., W along Doaks' line 234 p. to the beginning, No. 49; signed: Wm. Shepperd, Dep. Sec.; no pronate record.

P. 513, 16 December 1778, North Carolina to Robert Arvin, fifty shillings per hundred acres, 150 acres, on both sides of Arvins Br., begin at a black oak in Patrick Diman's line, E 150 p. along his line to a post oak, S 160 p. to a white oak, W 150 p. across a branch to a post oak, N 160 p. to the first station, No. 56; signed: Wm. Shepperd, Dep. Sec.; no probate record.

P. 513, 16 December 1778, North Carolina to Zachariah Williamson, fifty shillings per hundred acres, 200 acres, 'on waters of haw R., begin at a beach in a branch in Thomas Blair's alias David Peoples line, W 206 p. across a branch to a post oak, n 157 p. to a black jack, E across 2 branches 206 p. to a post oak, S to & along Thomas Blair's alias David Peeples line 157 p. to the first station, No. 93; signed: Wm. Shepperd, Dep. Sec.; no probate record.

P. 513, 16 December 1778, North Carolina to Samuel Sharp, fifty shillings per hundred acres, 450 acres, on the W side of Mayo R., begin on James Scale's line, n 273 p. to a black oak, E 240 p. to a white Ruben Cook's cor., S along his back line 37 p. to a white oak, S70E along Cook's line 76 p. to a black oak, E along Cook's line 67 p. across a branch to a rock in the river, S 80 p. to a black oak on John Sharp's line, W on Sharp's line 178 p. to a stump in a field, S along Sharp's line 138 p. to a post oak, W on Joshua Smith's line & James Scale's 210 p. to the beginning, No. 28; signed: Wm. Shepperd, Dep. Sec.; no probate record.

P. 514, 16 December 1778, North Carolina to Valuntine Allen, fifty shillings per hundred acres, 320 acres, on the N side of Dann R., begin at a mulberry tree, n 250 p. across a branch to a white oak his own line, W along his line cross 2 forks of Sharps Cr. 448 p. to a white oak, N 3 p. to a spanish oak James Holderness' cor., along his line W 206 p. to a white oak, S 83 p. to a white oak, E across Sharps Cr. 600 p. to a post oak, S across a branch 180 p. to a white oak on the river bank, down the river (land on the opposite side property of Alexander Martin) to the first station, No. 57; signed: Wm. Shepperd, Dep. Sec.; no probate record.

P. 514, 16 December 1778, North Carolina to Valuntine Allen, fifty shillings per hundred acres, 380 acres, on both sides of Sharps Cr., begin at William Hunt Allen's cor. red oak, N 190 p. to a white oak in James Holderness' line, along his line W across

Sharps Cr. 360 p. to a spanish oak, S across the creek 146 p. to a black oak John Whitworth's & James Hunter's cor., along Hunter's line E 148 p. to a black oak, along Hunter's line S 44 p. to a post oak in William Hunt Allen's line, along his line E 212 p. to the first station, No. 71; signed: Wm. Shepperd, Dep. Sec.; no probate record.

P. 514, 16 December 1778, North Carolina to John Fields, fifty shillings per hundred acres, 300 acres, begin at a black oak, E along Richard Vernon's claim 300 p. across Mountain Run to a black oak, N 160 p. across a branch to a black, W 300 p. across Mountain Run & a branch to a black oak, S 160 p. to the beginning, No. 62; signed: Wm. Shepperd, Dep. Sec.; no probate record.

P. 515, 16 December 1778, North Carolina to Charles Bruce, fifty shillings per hundred acres, 337 acres, on both sides of Great Branch of Reedy Fork of Haw R., begin at a post near John Garry's plantation, W across Great Br. 180 p. to a black oak in James Hays' old line, along his line 68 p. to his cor. black oak, W along his line across James Br. 66 p. to a white oak, N 170 p. across James Br. & Bruces Road to a black oak; E across the road & sd. Great Br. 246 p. to a post oak in Charles Bruce's own line, along his line S to his cor. & same course (in all) 238 p. to the first station, No. 65; signed: Wm. Shepperd, Dep. Sec.; no probate record.

P. 515, 16 December 1778, North Carolina to Henry Mitchell, fifty shillings per hundred acres, 367 acres, on the S side of Haw R., begin at a box elder on the bank of Lowrys Br. on Thomas Blair's line, along his line W 92 p. to his cor. black oak, N 43 p. along his line to Haw R., up the river (the opposite side entered by Sarah & Mary Blair) to a chesnut tree the beginning cor. of a tract surveyed for William Gowdy Esq. in Trust for the Orphans of John Pyate Decd., their line S across a branch 194 p. to William White's cor. post oak, S65E 40 p. to a black oak, S50E 80 p. to a post oak, E 17 p. to a black oak, S65E across a branch 100 p. to a post oak, S 32 p. to a black oak Charles Bruce's cor., E along his line 70 p. to a chesnut oak on the Moravian Road side, N 26 p. to a white oak at the head spring of Lowrys Br., down the branch to the first station, No. 89; signed: J. Glasgow, Secy.; no probate record.

P. 515, 16 December 1778, North Carolina to Pleasant Henderson, fifty shillings per hundred acres, 600 acres, on both sides of Long Br. of Beaver Island Cr., begin at William Crump's cor. black oak, E across 2 branches 270 p. to 2 poplars, n across Long Br. 356 p. to a white oak, W across a branch 270 p. to a spanish oak, S 356 p. to the first station, No. 22; signed: Wm. Shepperd, Dep. Sec.; no probate record.

P. 516, 16 December 1778, North Carolina to Samuel McCracken, fifty shillings per hundred acres, 640 acres, on both sides of Haw R., begin at a white oak, S across the river & a branch 360 p. to a post oak, W across a branch 199 p. to his own cor. white oak, N along his line 86 p. to his cor. black oak, N across the river & a branch 276 p. to a black oak, E across a road & 2 branches 311 p. to the first station, No. 59; signed: Wm. Shepperd, Dep. Sec.; no probate record.

P. 516, 16 December 1778, North Carolina to James Leeper, fifty shillings per hundred acres, 500 acres, on both sides of Reedy Fork of Haw R., begin at 2 white oak saplins, N across Reedy Fork to & along Benjamin Britain's line 325 p. to a black oak saplin on James Hays' line, W along his line 112 p. to his cor. post oak, S 41 p. to a post oak saplin, W 154 p. to James Britain's cor. hicory, along his line S across Reedy Fork 284 p. to a black oak, 266 p. to the first station, No. 58; signed: Wm. Shepperd, Dep. Sec.; no probate record.

P. 516, 16 December 1778, North Carolina to Elijah Joyce, fifty shillings per hundred acres, 200 acres, begin at a white on his father's deeded line, S 285 p. across Mountain Run to a spanish oak on Joshua Smith's line, E 57 p. to a sower wood on Mary Fields' line, N along Mary Fields' line 104 p. across the creek to a hicory bush, E along Mary Fields' line 70 p. across a creek to a black oak, N along Mary Fields' line 194 p. across the creek to a white oak, E along Mary fields' line 40 p. to a black oak, N 77 p. to a black oak, W 167 p. to the beginning, No. 67; signed: Wm. Shepperd, Dep. Sec.; no probate record.

P. 517, 16 December 1778, North Carolina to Elijah Joyce, fifty shillings per hundred acres, 640 acres, on the W side of Mayo R. & both sides Sheppards Cr., begin at Philoman Deatherage's cor. black oak, W 80 p. to a hicory, S along Alexander Joyce's line 78 p. to a hicory Benjamin Cook's cor., W along Cook's line 373 p. across Sheppards Cr. to a black oak, N 24 p. across 2 branches to a black oak, E 453 p. to a post oak bush, S 227 p. to the first station, No. 86; signed: Wm. Shepperd, Dep. Sec.; no probate record.

P. 517, 16 December 1778, North Carolina to Robert Wright, fifty shillings per hundred acres, 326 acres, on waters of Reedy Fork of Haw R., begin at a white oak near the road leading from Kings Mill to the Court House of sd. county, E 160 p. across 2 branches to John McMurry's cor. black oak, N along his line 68 p. to his cor. black oak, E along his line 55 p. to his cor. black oak, N 148 p. across a branch to a black oak, W 261 p. to a hicory near the road on Jeremiah Johnston's claim, along Jeremiah Johnston's claim S12E 220 p. to the first station, No. 82; signed: Wm. Shepperd, Dep. Sec.; no probate record.

P. 517, 16 December 1778, North Carolina to Hezekiah Gates, fifty shillings per hundred acres 300 acres, on both sides of Hogans Cr. a branch of Dann R., begin at a white oak, N 233 p. across creek to a black oak, E 206 p. to a spanish oak in Josiah Gates line, S 233 p. across the creek to 2 black jacks, W 206 p. to the beginning, No. 90; signed: Wm. Shepperd, Dep. Sec.; no probate record.

P. 518, 16 December 1778, North Carolina to Igntius [Ignatius]

Gann, fifty shillings per hundred acres, 341 acres, begin on the Mayo Mountain at Sarah Powell's cor. white oak, S along Sarah Powell's & James Vernon's line 372 p. to a post oak, E along William Farrow's line 147 p. to a post oak, N along John Pratt's line 372 p. to a white oak, W along Sarah Powel's line 372 p. to the beginning, No. 76; signed: Wm. Shepperd, Dep. Sec.; no probate recoerd.

P. 518, 16 December 1778, North Carolina to William Crump, fifty shillings per hundred acres, 327 acres, on both sides of Red Bank Br. of Dann R., begin on a branch of Dann R., N 74 p. to a spanish oak in Nathaniel Hoggatt's line, his line W across a branch 132 p. to a pine in Surry County line, the county line N 318 p. to a pine, E 160 p. to a pine, S 330 p. to a black oak on the bank of the river, up the river (land on the opposite side property of Nathaniel Hoggatt) to the first station, No. 46; signed: Wm. Shepperd, Dep. Sec.; no probate record.

P. 518, 16 December 1778, North Carolina to Henry Scales, fifty shillings per hundred acres, 400 acres, on both sides of Buff Island of Dann R., begin at a black saplin in John Hill's line, E along his line across a branch 200 p. to a spanish oak in Thomas Bridges' line, along his line S 70 p. to a black oak, E along his line 34 p. to a black, S across Buff Island Creek 215 p. to 2 white oaks, W 234 p. across Otter Br. to a white oak, N across the creek 285 p. to the first station, No. 30; signed: Wm. Shepperd, Dep. Sec.: no probate record.

P. 519, 16 December 1778, North Carolina to Charles Bruce, fifty shillings per hundred acres, 587 acres, on waters of Mairs & Reedy Fork of Haw R., begin at a white oak on Lick Br., E across Cross Creek Road & 2 forks of Lick Br. 270 p. to a spanish oak, N across Mairs Fork 358 p. to a chesnut & black oak, W 38 p. to a black saplin in Nathan Peeples line, S along his line 20 p. to a post oak saplin near a branch, W along his line 338 p. to the first station, No. 101; signed: Wm. Shepperd, Dep. Sec.; no probate record.

P. 519, 16 December 1778, North Carolina to John Watson, fifty shillings per hundred acres, 550 acres, begin on the N side of Dan R. on Lacy's line, N along Lacy's line 400 p. across Beaver Island Cr. to a pine & black oak on John Davice'sline, W along Davice's line 258 p. across the creek to a pine Thomas Scale's cor., S 280 p. to a black oak on John Glenn's line, E along Glenn's line 96 p. to a white oak, S 118 p. to a white oak on the bank of Reed Cr. near the mouth of the creek, down the creek & river to the beginning, No. 53; signed: Wm. Shepperd, Dep. Sec.; no probate record.

P. 519, 16 December 1778, North Carolina to Samuel McCrackin, fifty shillings per hundred acres, 60 acres, on waters of Haw R., begin at a grub his own cor., S along his line 86 p. to his cor. white oak, W 112 p. across a branch to a white oak saplin, N 86 p. to his own cor. black oak, E along his line across a branch 112 p. to the first station, No. 52; signed: Wm. Shepperd, Dep.

Sec.; no probate record.

P. 520, 16 December 1778, North Carolina to Sarah Powell, fifty shillings per hundred acres, 293 acres, on waters of Mayo & Dan R., begin at a white oak on the bank of Mayo R., E 172 p. to a white oak, N 46 p. to a white oak, E 147 p. across a branch to a white oak, N 140 p. to a white oak, W 260 p. to a rock in the river, down the river (land on the opposite side property of Joshua Smith) to the first station, No. 68; signed: Wm. Shepperd, Dep. Sec.; no probate record.

P. 520, 16 December 1778, North Carolina to Josiah Gates, fifty shillings per hundred acres, 350 acres, begin on the N side of Hogans Cr. a branch of Dan R. at a white oak, N 280 p. to a post oak, E 200 p. to a black oak, S 280 p. across the creek to a black oak, W 200 p. across the creek to the beginning, No. 54; signed: Wm. Shepperd, Dep. Sec.; no probate record.

P. 520, 16 December 1778, North Carolina to John Alexander, fifty shillings per hundred acres, 66 acres, on waters of Allemance, begin at Joseph Dason's cor. post oak, along the deeded line of Alexander N 78 p. to a black oak, 77 p. to a post oak on Joseph Dabson's line, E along Dabson's line 138 p. to the beginning, No. 39; signed: Wm. Shepperd, Dep. Sec.; no probate record.

P. 521, 16 December 1778, North Carolina to Thomas Cook, fifty shillings per hundred acres, 350 acres, begin at a white oak, W 220 p. to 2 dogwoods & a white oak on James Lier's line, N 255 p. across a branch to a black oak, E 220 p. to a black on Ben Cook's line, S 255 p. across a branch to the beginning, No. 31; signed: Wm. Shepperd, Dep. Sec.; no probate record.

P. 521, 16 December 1778, North Carolina to Thomas Blair, fifty shillings per hundred acres, 629 acres, on both sides of Haw R., begin at a black oak Henry Mitchel's cor., N 340 p. across the river to a white oak, E across a branch 296 p. to a gum, S across the river 340 p. to a hicory, W 296 p. to the first station, No. 78; signed: Wm. Shepperd, Dep. Sec.; no probate record.

P. 521, 16 December 1778, North Carolina to Benjamin Cook, fifty shillings per hundred acres, 620 acres, begin at a black Joshua Smith's cor., N 348 p. across Big Br. & Shepperds Cr. to a hicory & post oak, W 286 p. across Big Br. to a black oak, S 348 p. across a branch to a chesnut & gum, E 286 p. to the beginning, No. 35; signed: Wm. Shepperd, Dep. Sec.; no probate record.

P. 521, 16 December 1778, North Carolina to Samuel Young, fifty shillings per hundred acres, 200 acres, on the S side of Troublesome, begin at a cor. of his old survey at a black oak, S 200 p. to a post oak, E 160 p. across 2 branches to a black oak, N 200 p. to a white oak, W 160 p. to the first station, No. 74; signed: Wm. Shepperd, Dep. Sec.; no probate record.

P. 522, 16 December 1778, North Carolina to Reuben Cook, fifty shillings per hundred acres, 350 acres, on the W side of Mayo R., begin at a gum & post a cor. of Joshua Smith, W 106 p. along Joshua Smith's claim to a black oak, S 126 along the claim of Smith to Samuel Sharpe's cor. rock in the river, W along Sharpe's line 67 p. to a black oak, N70W along Sharpe's line 76 p. to a white oak, N along Sharpe's line 48 p. to a white oak, N28W along James Lier's line 40 p. to a white oak, E along Lier's line 88 p. to a white oak, N along Lier's line 168 p. across a branch to a chesnut Benjamin Cook's line, E along Benjamin Cook's line 196 p. to a black oak Joshua Smith's cor., S along Smith's line 168 p. across a branch to the beginning; signed: Wm. Shepperd, Dep. Sec.; no probate record.

P. 522, 16 December 1778, North Carolina to Francis Wright, fifty shillings per hundred acres, 300 acres, begin at a poplar George Rankin's cor., W along Rankin's line 40 p. in Edward Holland's line, N along Edward Holland's line 230 p. to a black jack, E 197 p. across a branch to a white oak on James Wilson's line, S along Wilson's line 250 p. across a branch to a white oak on Widow McKnight's line, her line W 157 p. across a branch to a hicory in George Rankin's line, N along George Rankin's line 20 p. to the beginning, No. 12; signed: Wm. Shepperd, Dep. Sec.; no probate record.

P. 523, 16 December 1778, North Carolina to Jonas Touchstone, fifty shillings per hundred acres, 75 acres, begin at Alexander Breaden's cor. black oak, N 104 p. to a black jack, W along Moses McClain's line 120 p. to a white oak, S 104 p. to a post oak, E 120 p. to the beginning, No. 79; signed: Wm. Shepperd, Dep. Sec.; no probate record.

P. 523, 16 December 1778, North Carolina to Moses Campbell, fifty shillings per hundred acres, 516 acres, on both sides of Troublesome Cr., begin at a white oak in Samuel Young's line, W across 3 branches 245 p. to a post oak, S across 2 branches 337 p. to a black oak, E across a branch 245 p. to a post oak, N 337 p. to the first station, No. 32; signed: Wm. Shepperd, Dep. Sec.; no probate record.

P. 523, 16 December 1778, North Carolina to George Stuart, fifty shillings per hundred acres, 600 acres, on waters of Allemance, begin on Benjamin Starrat's cor. black oak, E along Starrat's line 164 p, to a post oak, S a Contable [?] line 586 p. to a black oak, W 164 p. to a black oak, n 586 p. to the beginning, No. 29; signed: Wm. Shepperd, Dep. Sec.; no probate record.

P. 523, 16 December 1778, North Carolina to William Shaw, fifty shillings per hundred acres, 450 acres, on both sides of Beaver Cr., begin at a post oak a cor. to deeded land of his own formerly property of Robert Hanna, S across the creek 61.5 ch. to a post oak, E 73.5 ch. to a black oak saplin, N 61.5 ch. to a post oak, W to the beginning, No. 27; signed: Wm. Shepperd, Dep. Sec.; no probate record.

P. 524, 16 December 1778, North Carolina to John Job, fifty shillings per hundred acres, 150 acres, on the S side of Allemance, begin at a white oak in Henry Eustace McCulloh's line, McCulloh's line S55W 60 p. to a white oak, S43W McCulloh's line 190 p. to a black oak in the line of Christian Forest, S45E along Forest's line 18 p. to a black oak a cor. of James Powel, N78E along Powel's line 244 p. to a black oak, N29W 120 p. to the beginning, No. 48; signed: Wm. Shepperd, Dep. Sec.; no probate record.

P. 524, 16 December 1778, North Carolina to Charles Harden, fifty shillings per hundred acres, 640 acres, on both sides of Brushy Fork of Allemance, begin on William Doaks' line, E 320 p. across Allemance 3 times to a rock, S 320 p. to a black oak, W 320 p. to a black oak, N 320 p. across Brushy Fork to the beginning, No. 73; signed: Wm. Shepperd, Dep. Sec.; no probate record.

P. 524, 16 December 1778, North Carolina to Edward Wetherly, fifty shillings per hundred acres, 453 acres, on the N side of Reedy Fork of Haw R., begin at a white oak on the Dividing Br., E 340 p. to a post oak, N 230 p. to a black jack, W 280 p. to a black oak on Robert Russel's line, S along his claim 60 p. to a white oak, S40W to a small gum on Dividing Br. between Wetherly & Robert Russel 95 p., S down the branch to the beginning, No. 75; signed: Wm. Shepperd, Dep. Sec.; no probate record.

P. 525, 16 December 1778, North Carolina to John Reagan, fifty shillings per hundred acres, 640 acres, begin on the N side of Dan R. at a beach George Olliver's cor., S 360 p. across Hogans Cr. at Jas. Robert's Mill Pond to a chesnut, W 258 p. across a branch & Hogans Cr. to a white oak, N 77 p. to a black oak, W 135 p. along Francis Cook's claim to a post oak, N along Francis Cook's claim 135 p. to a black oak, E along Cook's claim 185 p. to a black oak, N 140 p. along a deeded line of Cook to a walnut tree on the river, down the river (the opposite side property of James Hunter & William Allen) to the beginning, No. 50; signed: Wm. Shepperd, Dep. Sec.; no probate record.

P. 525, 16 December 1778, North Carolina to William White, fifty shillings per hundred acres, 320 acres, on waters of haw R. & Reedy Fork, begin at a post oak Henry Mitchel's cor., along his line S65E 40 p. to a black, S50E 80 p. along his line to a post oak, E 17 p. to a black oak, S65E along Mitchel's line across a branch 100 p. to a post oak, S along his line 32 p. to a black oak Charles Bruce's cor., same course on his line (in all) 202 p. across a branch to a white oak in James Hays' line, W along Hays' line across a branch 204 p. to a white oak, N to & along the line of a tract surveyed for William Gowdy Esq. in Trust for the Orphants of John Pyatt Decd. 313 p. to the first station, No. 99; signed: Wm. Shepperd, Dep. Sec.; no probate record.

P. 526, 16 December 1778, North Carolina to John Maxwell, fifty shillings per hundred acres, 280 acres, on waters of Reedy Fork on the N side of sd. cr., begin at a black oak on George Finley's line, N 320 p. to a black oak, W 160 p. to a maple, S 160 p. to a black oak at Jeremiah McFadgen's claim, E 40 p. to a white oak, S 160 p. along McFadgen's claim to a black oak on George Finley's line, E along his line to the beginning, No. 55; signed: Wm. Shepperd, Dep. Sec.; no probate record.

P. 526, 16 December 1778, North Carolina to Robert Russel, fifty shillings per hundred acres, 500 acres, on the N side of Reedy Fork of Haw R., begin at a white oak at or near Robert Thompson's line, W on or near Thompson's line 190 p. to 2 white oak saplins, N 370 p. to a stone in a glade, E 267 p. to a white oak, S 90 p. to a black oak on Wetherly's line, W along his line 10 p. to a red [oak?] a cor., S 60 p. to a white oak, S40W 95 p. to a gum beach on Dividing Br., S down the branch to the beginning, No. 69; signed: Wm. Shepperd, Dep. Sec.; no probate record.

P. 526, 16 December 1778, North Carolina to Moses Craner, fifty shillings per hundred acres, 235 acres, on waters of Nelsons Cr. of South Buffaloe, begin at a white oak on Isham Harris' line, E 234 p. across Nelsons Cr. to a white oak on Nelson's line, S along Nelson's line & David Barnhill's line 161 p. to a spanish oak, W 234 p. to a black oak, N 161 p. to the beginning, No. 44; signed: Wm. Shepperd, Dep. Sec.; no probate record.

P. 527, 16 December 1778, North Carolina to Josiah Finley, fifty shillings per hundred acres, 640 acres, on both sides of Reedy Fork & Haw R., begin at a white on the bank on the S side of Reedy Fork, S 120 p. to a spanish oak, E 120 p. to a post oak, N across Reedy Fork 400 p. to a hicory, W 222 p. to a white oak on George Finley's old line, along his line S 169 p. to a white on Reedy Fork, up Reedy Fork to the beginning, No. 80; signed: Wm. Shepperd, Dep. Sec.; no probate record.

P. 527, 16 December 1778, North Carolina to John McMurry, fifty shillings per hundred acres, 396 acres, on waters of Horsepen Cr., begin on Francis McNarie's line at a black oak, N 230 p. across 2 branches to a black oak Robert Wright's cor., W along Wright's line 55 p. to a black oak, S along Wright's line 68 p. to a black oak, W along Wright's line 227 p. across 2 branches & the Waggon Road to a white oak, S 212 p. across a branch to a black oak, E 282 p. to the beginning, No. 40; signed: Wm. Shepperd, Dep. Sec.; no probate record.

P. 527, 16 December 1778, North Carolina to James McMurry, fifty shillings per hundred acres, 114 acres, on waters of Horsepen Cr., begin at a hicory on Francis McNarie's line, N along his line 130 p. to a red oak on John McMurry's line, W along John McMurry's line across a branch 141 p. to a white oak, S 130 p. to Hugh Foster's line, along his line E 141 p. to the first station, No. 37; signed: Wm. Shepperd, Dep. Sec.; no probate record.

P. 528, 27 May 1778, John Duffel of Guilford, farmer, to Reese Porter of same, two hundred twenty pounds, 217 acres, formerly in Orange now in Guilford, on the S side of Buffaloe Cr., part of a tract from Granville to William Black Wood [Blackwood] 14 March 1755, all that part on the S side of Buffaloe, begin at a black oak on the S side & near Buffaloe Cr. the 3rd bound tree, N to the creek, down to the third line, along the third line S to the cor., W to the beginning; signed: John Duffel, Elizabeth (3) Duffel; witness: James Brown, William Peasley, David Hamilton; acknowledged May 1779 Term.

P. 529, 18 August 1779, Isaac Whiteworth & Alexr. McClean of Guilford to John & James Dearing of same, sixteen hundred pounds, 380 acres, in Guilford & Surry, on the S side of Dann R., begin at a white oak on the river, S 220 p. to a pine, W 260 p. to a red oak on the river, down the river to the beginning; signed: Isaac (I) Whitworth, Alexr. McClain; witness: Anthony Dearing, Robert Dearing, Hezikiah Gates; proved August 1779 Term by Anthony & Robert Dearing.

P. 530, 12 March 1779, John Cook of Guilford to David Philpott of same, eight hundred pounds, 233 acres, on the S side of Hogans Cr., begin at a red oak on the creek, E 207 p. to a white oak, N88 p. to a red oak saplin, W62N 90 p. to a white saplin, W 30 degrees 90 p. to a poplar on the creek bank, up the creek to the first station; signed: John Cook; witness: John Philpott' William Stubblefield, Warran Philpott, William Weatherford; proved May 1779 Term by John & Warran Philpott.

P. 530, 7 October 1779, Samuel Hargrove & Susannah his wife of Guilford to John Ledforsd & Grizzallah his wife of Rowan, ten shillings, 229 acres, on both sides of Deep R., part of a tract given Grizzellah Ledford & Shusannah Hartgrove by their Honoured Father William Buise by his will recorded in Salisbury, begin at a post oak on the N side of Deep R. in Robert Linsey's line, S42E 31 ch. to a red oak being the dividing line agreed upon between the parties, S22W 5 ch. to a beech on the N bank of Deep R., S66E across the river 10 ch. to a post oak in Garris Chipman's line, N40E 45 ch. to a white oak, N 30 ch. to a white oak, W 34 ch. to Robert Lindsey's line, along sd. line to the beginning; signed: Samuel Hartgrove, Susannah Hartgrove; witness: Robt. Lindsey, Henry Davis; proved [no date given] by Robert Lindsey Esq.

P. 532, 12 March 1779, John Cook of Guilford to David Philpott of same, four hundred pounds, 86 acres, on the N side of Hogans Cr., begin at a beech on the creek bank, W 74 p. to a hicory, N 113 p. to a hicory, E 152 p. to a beech, up the creek to the beginning, John McCollum to Odeneal, Odeneal to John Buster; signed John Cook; witness: John Philpott, William Stubblefield, Warran Philpott, William Weatherford; proved May 1779 Term by John & Warran Philpott.

P. 533, 1 June 1778, Edward Hunter heir at law & executor with James Martin & James Hunter surviving Ext. nominated in John Hunter Deceased his last Will & Testament of Guilford to Charles May of Buckingham County, Virginia, three hundred pounds by a bond bearing date 27 December 1772 also by an accompt of one hundred sixty pounds amounting in the whole to four hundred sixty pounds a debt due from my Father John Hunter Decd. to Charles May, 150 acres, on the N side of Dan R., part of a tract from Joseph Tate to John Hunter, begin on Watkin's line on the river, up the river on sd. line 1 ch. to his cor., along sd. line 3 ch.

to a hicory, W 50 ch. 25 lk. to a white oak, S a new line to David Walker's line, E along Walker's line to the river, down the river to the beginning, sold as directed in the will of John Hunter to pay debts; signed: Edward Hunter; witness: John May, John Simon, Richard (R) Sharp; proved May 1779 Term by John May & John Lemmon.

P. 535, 22 March 1778, Samuel Thompson of Guilford to Robert Thompson of same, fifty pounds, 230 acres, a tract taken out of a tract formerly belonging to James Gamble (Deceased), begin at Ralph Gorrel's cor at a pond on Reedy Fork the N side, down Reedy Fork to Gamble's cor., E 3 ch. 25 lk. to a white oak, N 39 ch. to a black oak, W to Gorrel's cor., S along Gorrel's line to the beginning; signed: Samuell Thompson; witness: John Coots, Thomas Thompson; acknowledged August 1779 Term.

GUILFORD COUNTY DEED BOOK 1

PERSONAL NAME INDEX

Citations are to the page number of the original deed book and not to the page numbers of this volume. The user is encouraged to check for alternative spellings of the surname.

Abraham, 222
Age, John, 389
Agnew, Robert (Robt.), 304, 341
Aldredg, William, 41
Aldridge, James, 165
   William, 41, 165
   see also Eldridge
Alexande, George, 512
Alexander, Francis, 196
   George, 249, 512
   Jas., 249
   Jediah, 412
   Jodediah, 412
   John, 249, 512, 520
Allen, George Hunt, 274, 457, 470
   John, 93, 346
   Phebe, 93
   Samuel, 346
   Valentine, 374, 465, 481
   Valuntine, 465, 514
   William, 525
   William (Wm.) Hunt (H.), 457, 470, 514
Allison, David, 40, 434, 504
   Janet, 434
   Jennet, 434
   John, 434
   Robert, 488
Allred, Mary, 58
   Soloman, 58
Alston, George, 182
   John, 182
Amy, Nicholas, 352
Anderson, John, 139, 146, 496, 501, 502, 506, 507
   Thomas, 476, 502, 507
   William (Wm.), 139, 146, 256, 264, 274, 281, 502, 365
Archer, James, 418, 421, 455
   Thomas, 421, 455
Armfield, James, 209
Armstead, Moses, 360
   Moss, 350
Armstrong, William, 486
Arvin, Robert, 513
Ashman, Lewis, 436

Ashmore, William, 340
Asten, William, 407
Astom, 465
Avery, Waightstill, 374
   Wi., 288
Axton, Robert, 499
Bailes, 14
Bailles, John, 14
   Sarah, 14
Baldwin, John, 210, 265
   William, 210, 348(A) 349
Bales, Boater, 244
   Sarah, 279
   Thomas, 279
Baley, William, 409
Ballenger, Henry, 193, 226, 275, 344
   John, 482
Bankston, Lawrence, 149
Barden, Willm., 235
Barker, Leonard, 447, 450
   Samuel, 161
Barnes, Riley, 21
   Turksfield, 447
   Turlyfield, 481
Barnhill, David, 526
   William, 498
Barr, James, 500, 503, 511
   Robert 434
Barringer, Paul 97
Bartan, see Barton
Barten, see Barton
Barton, 354, 357
   Elizabeth, 49
   John, 21, 49, 352
   Martha, 377
   Richard, 377
   Thos., 321
   William, 21, 352
   see also Burton
Baston, Thomas, 399, 401
Bates, Jno., 233
   John, Jr., 222
Beals, John, 14
Beard, John Lewis, 97
Beasley, John, 485
   William, 495, 505

Beck, Jeffrey 348
Beeson, Beniamin (Benjamin), 127
   Isaac, 210, 229
Beles, Sarah, 14
Bell, Amelia, 494
   Francis, 215
   James, 435, 503
   Mary, 459
   Robert, 215, 306, 459
   Sampson, 149
   Samuel (Samll.), 215, 459, 492
   Samuel, Sr. 435
   Thomas, 435, 503
Bethel, Sampson, 350, 360
   William, 454
Beuis, see Buis
Billups, Christopher, 332
Binnihan, R., 481
Birbeck (Birkbeck), Morris, 368
Bird, 399
Black, George 429, 432
   Thomas (Thos.), 87, 256, 439
Blackwood, William, 179, 528
Blagge, John, 324, 328
Blair, Mary, 515
   John, 501, 507
   Sarah, 515
   Thomas, 511, 513, 515, 521
Boddington, Sarah, 321, 323, 324
   William, 321, 323, 324
Boilstone, Robert, 37
Bond, Edward, 270
Boon, Martin, 90
Borden, William, 239
Borton, Richard, 379, 441
Bostick, William, 265
Boyd, John, 3
   Mary, 321
   Rebbecca (Rebekah), 3, 306
Braley (Braly), Hugh 191
   Jno., 282
   see also Brawley
Branson, Levi, 311
   Thos., 242
Braselton, Wm., 155
Brashear, Baxel, 1
   Robt., 190
Brawley, Hugh, 496
   see also Braley
Breaden (Breeden), Alexander, 499, 523
Breden, Robt., 179

Bridhes, Thomas, 518
Britain, Benjamin, 516
   Daniel, 156, 347
   James, 199, 516
   William, 347
Brittain, see Britain
Britton, see Britain
Brockman, 396
Brooks, David, 223, 224, 301, 302, 303
Browder, Isham, 74, 149, 198, 207, 350, 360, 464
   Tabitha, 149
Brown, Daniel, 52
   Elizabeth, 11
   Frederick, 200, 353
   James, 57, 62, 206274, 528
   Jane, 206
   Joseph, 66, 442
   Mary, 442
   Michael, 200, 353
   Robert, 62
   Samuel, 11, 209, 252
   William, 206, 256
Bruce, Charles, 377, 386, 507, 515, 519, 525
Bryan, Anna, 203
   John, 203
   Thomas, 405
Brylo, Constant, 49
Buchanan, James, 105
   Samuel (Sam), 67, 88, 375
   Walter, 423
   William, 268, 269
Buchannan, see Buchanan
Buffington, Joseph 97
Buis, John 210, 265
   Martha 210, 265
   William (Willm.) 210, 265, 348(A), 349, 530
Buise, see Buis
Bull, Frederick (Fred.), 321, 322, 323, 324
Bullar, Thomas, 463
Burke, Thos., 182
Burks, Saml., 359
Burney, John, 496, 506
Burns, Charles, 504
Burton, John, 352
   see also Barton
Buster, Claudius, 402, 410
   Elizabeth, 402
   John, 395, 396, 398, 399, 401, 402, 405, 410, 432, 438, 532

Buster, William, 381, 402
Butler, John, 76, 180, 220, 347(A)
Byrd, 396
Caldwell, Alexander (Alexr.), 53, 55, 184, 312, 365, 429, 432, 494
  David 53, 55, 505
Callahan, Darby, 363
  Forster, 363
Campbell, Archibald, 379
  James (Jas.), 357, 379, 471
  John (Jno.), 76, 126, 219, 379, 390, 441,
  Mary, 379
  Mes., 23
  Moses, 419, 523
  Sarah, 371
  William, 3, 20, 371, 422
Cannady, Samuel, 460
  Sarah, 460
  William, 460
Cantrell, Abraham, 125
Carlin, William, 87
Carr, Jane, 188
  Jean, 188
  Joseph, 188, 225, 352
  see also Kerr
Carrive, John, 386
Carter, Thos., 452
Carteret, 227
  see also Granville
Cary, Archibald, 423, 425, 426
Caswell, Rd., 475, 476, 477, 485, 486, 487, 488, 489, 490, 491, 492, 493, 495,
Cather, Robert, 53
Cayton, James M., Jr., 15
Ceepy, Robert, 55
Chadwell, John, 428, 429
Challes, Hugh, 381, 405, 410, 466
Chambers, John 214
  William 123, 124, 125, 454
Chapman, Peres, 348(A), 349
Charles, Hugh, 402
  Leaven, 474
  William, 474
Chattles, Hugh, 466
Cheedle, Jno., 245
Chipman, Garris, 530
Churlish, Hugh, 402
Churton, William, 321, 323, 324, 328
  see also Curten

Cimmons, Robert, 194
Cladwell, David, 494
  see also Chadwell, Caldwell
Clap, Barbery, 251
  Barnaby, 251
  George Tobias, 251
  George Valentine, 251
  John Philip, 487, 490, 497
  Ludwig, 356
  Philip, 251
  Tobias, 251
Clark, Edward, 462
  Francis, 462
  John, 273, 289, 390, 463
  Mary, 390
  William (Wm.), 197, 227
Cloud, Joel, 72
Coabel, see Coble,
Cobaen, Samuel, 227
Coble, Anthony, 85, 216
  John, 83, 85
  Mary, 85
  see also Goble
Cocar, Michael, 490
Coffee, see Keaughy
Coffin, Barnabus, 378
  Benjamin, 222
  Samuel, 382
  William, 223, 224, 244, 378, 382
Cole, William, 340
Coleman, James, 207, 280
Collier, John, 78, 202, 203
Coltrane, Abigal, 177
  David, 177
  Jacob, 177
  James, 177
  Mary, 177
  Rachel, 177
  William, 177
Conner, John, 340
  Nicholas, 321, 323, 324
Conway, James, 280
  Henry, 280
Cook, Benjamin (Ben), 517, 521, 522
Cook, Francis, 430, 525
Cook, John, 432, 435, 438, 530, 532,
  Reuben (Ruben), 513, 522
  Thomas, 521
Coory, John (Jno.), 121, 258
Coots, James, 510
  John, 535
Corry, John, 26

Cotner, George, 356
Coulter, Michael, 429
Covington, William, 400
Cowan, Edward, 300
   Elias, 317
   Mary, 300, 332
   Thomas, 300
   William 332
Cowen, see Cowan
Cowper, Wells 341
Cox, Benjamin, 262
   David, 346
   Harmon (Hearman), 235, 311, 346
   Isaac, 64, 93, 242, 346
   John (Jno.), 93, 242
   Juliatha(s), 52
   Naomi, 340
   Phebe, 307, 308
   Sarah, 66
   Solomon, 340
   Thomas (Thos.), 66, 240, 340
   William, 52, 66, 93, 161, 311
   Zachariah (Zacharias) 317, 467
Crabtree, John, 75
Craner, Moses, 526
Creson, Hannah, 81
   John, 81
Crump, William, 484, 515, 518
Culver, Thomas, 494
Cuming, Maryan, 194
   Thomas, 194
Cummin(g)s, Francis, 184, 312
   Marian, 194
   Samuel, 439
   Thomas 130, 190, 194, 312
Cuntz, Mary, 142
   Nicholas, 142
Curry, Jane, 234
   Samuel, 234
Curtain, William, 26
Curten, William, 26
Cusick, William, 506
Dabson, Joseph, 520
Dalton, Isham, 405, 410, 480
Dannal, William, 179
Dason, Joseph, 520
Davice, Enuch, 497
   Elizabeth, 494
   John, 450, 519
Davis, Deborah, 252
   Elizabeth ,311
   Enoch, 72, 153, 161
   Henry, 530
   James, 265

Davis, John, 15, 29, 67, 256
   Thomas, 311
Davison, William, 388
Deane, William, 324, 328
Dearing, Anthony, 529
   James, 529
   John, 529
   Robert, 445, 529
Deatherage, Philoman (Phil), 74, 517
Degraffenred, (Degraffenreidt, Degraffenreitt, Degravered)
   Baker, 332, 359, 407, 428
   Francis, 332
   William, 332
Denny, George, 264, 365, 420
   James, 139, 146, 214, 264, 365
   Margarate, 412
   Margaret, 205
   William, 121, 186, 205, 214, 412, 460
Dent, William Willm., Wm.), 217, 243, 393, 418, 471, 472, 494
Deviney, Samuel, 253
Dick, William, 331, 494, 506
Dickison, Richd., 359
Dicks, Nathan, 138, 234, 366
   Zacharias (Zach.), 17, 19, 25, 134, 136, 138, 139, 153, 163, 193, 199, 212, 252, 347, 366
Dickson, William, 377
   see also Dixon
Dill, Frederick, 512
Dillion, Daniel, 276
Dillon, Peter, 183
Diman, Patrick, 513
Dimm, Patrick, 506
Diques, John, 358
Dixon, Charles, 262
   Henry, Jr., 360
Dixson, Sarah, 483
   William, 483
   see also Dickson
Doak, Hannah, 266
   John, 23, 249, 260
   Robert, 23, 260, 266
   William, 23, 512, 524
Dolittle, Joseph, 396
Donnell (Donald, Doneld, Donnal Donnall, Donneal, Donnel, Donnel, Andrew, 442
   Daniel, 420

Donnell, John, 110, 443
   Robert, 139, 146, 257, 359,
      365, 420, 428, 429, 432,
      434, 496, 503, 506
   Thomas (Thos.), 40, 110, 257,
      429, 432, 443, 511
   William, 186, 443
Douglas, William, 368
Downing, John, 364
Draper, William (Wm.), 35, 236
Drennan, Hugh, 498
Dudley, Thos., 210
Duff, Agness, 257
   James, 106, 119, 257, 384,
      451
   John, 504
   Samuel, 189, 204, 497, 504
   William (Wm.), 475, 501
Duffel, Elizabeth, 528
   John, 528
Dunn, Bartholomew, 354, 357
   Elizabeth, 354
Dupues, Isaac, 324, 328
Duskins, Sarah, 57
   Sarea, 57
Dykes, John, 427, 437
Edwards, 53
   David, 11, 212
   Joshua, 25
   Isaac, 209
Eken, William, 488
Eldredge, Thomas, 163
Eldreg, Thomas, 163
Eldreg, see also Aldridge
Elliot, Abraham, 272
   Jacob, 229
   Joseph, 272
Ellis, Benjamin, 113, 340
Emack, John, 216
Engel, Jacob, 356
England, Daniel, 214, 232
Esdely, John, 423
Espey, Mary, 375
Falkerson, Frederick, 454
Fanning, Colonel (Col.) Edmund,
   321, 323, 324, 328, 505
Ferguson, Jeremiah, 118
   Robert, 423
Farlin, Benjamin, 392
   see also McFarlin
Farlow, Michael, 349
Farrow, 509
   William, 447, 450, 518
Fay, Thomas, 412
Fene, Eli, 474

Few, James, 108
Field, Ann, 232
   Jane, 211
   Jeremiah, 217, 232
   Joseph, 129, 144
   Mary, 516
   Robert (Robt.), 144, 232,
      467
   William, 38, 45, 129, 213,
      330
Fields, John (Jno.), 265, 514
Finley, Andrew, 304, 448, 486
   George, 412, 526, 527
   Josiah, 527
Finly, Andrew, 191
   George, 205
Fish, Thomas, 386
Flack, Jane, 214
   Jean, 214
   Thomas, 121, 214
Flanen, John, 348
Flemming, William, 132
Fletcher, Aaron, 286, 287
Forbish (Forbes, Forbess, Forbis,
   Forbiss, Forbus, Forbush),
   Arthur, 130, 191, 219, 331,
      390
   John, 189, 448, 451, 506
   Lydia, 191
Ford, Peter, 484
Forest, Christian, 524
Forster (Foster), 276, 285
   Hugh, 288, 374, 386, 439, 471,
      472, 482, 507, 527
   James, 374
   John, 126, 288, 384, 420, 472
   Martha, 288, 374, 471, 472,
      507
   Polly, 507
   Samuel, 288, 472
   William (Willm.), 234, 288,
      374, 386, 471, 472, 507
Fothergill, John, 368
Fouse, Christian, 81
Fox, David, 367
Fraizer, 35
   Abigal, 436
   John, 436
Frazier, Aaron, 35, 78, 273
   Samuel, 107, 108, 307, 308
   Sarah, 35
Fruit, John, 107, 108, 209, 417
Fulton, David, 3

Funkhauser (Founkhauser, Funkhausen, Funkhousen, Funkhowser), Christian, 90, 130, 194
   Christopher, 237
Gallaway, James, 371, 445
Galloway, Chas., 359
Gamble, James, 535
Gamman, Jesse, 509
Gann, Ignatious, 414, 416, 518
   Igntius, 518
Garner, Charles, 510
Garrison, Peter, 500
Garrott, Sarah, 149
   William, 149
Garry, John, 515
Gates, Benjamin, 261, 374, 465
   Hezekiah, 517, 529
   James, 374
   Josiah, 517, 520
   Phillip, 261
Genn, John, 510
George III, 49, 81, 83, 85, 142, 216, 271, 356
Gillespie, Daniel, 119, 314, 384, 475
   David, 351
   John, 501
Glasgow, J., 331, 475, 476, 477, 485, 486, 487, 488, 489, 490, 491, 492, 493, 494, 495, 497, 498, 499, 505, 515
Glenn, John, 20, 371, 461, 519
Gobel, Jacob, 393
Goble, Anthony, 83
   Mary, 83
   Nicholas, 83
   see also Coble
Gorrel(l), Mary, 90
   Ralph, 90, 119, 132, 207, 230, 246, 254, 257, 274, 314, 475, 501, 535
Gowdy, 502
   William, 476, 499, 507, 515, 525
Granville, 11, 25, 26, 32, 34, 35, 41, 52, 58, 61, 62, 66, 72, 75, 76, 78, 86, 88, 93, 94, 100, 107, 108, 116, 123, 124, 134, 136, 138, 141, 144, 151, 153, 160, 161, 165, 167, 178, 179, 184, 190, 191, 193, 199, 201, 206, 209,

Granville, 211, 214, 215, 226, 229, 267, 242, 246, 248, 253, 256, 258, 262, 264, 265, 268, 269, 270, 273, 274, 275, 279, 281, 288, 289, 300, 301, 303, 304, 306, 309, 311, 315, 317, 336, 338, 340, 343, 346, 347(A), 348, 348(A), 351, 352, 353, 354, 355, 362, 364, 366, 367, 374, 375, 379, 386, 390, 400, 404, 417, 429, 432, 434, 435, 436, 443, 445, 458, 459, 467, 468, 471, 472, 479, 481, 482, 483, 507, 528
   Earl 357, 392
   see also Carteret
Graves, James, 188, 352
   John, 399
   Thomas, 352
Gray, Robert (Robt.), 115, 202
   William, 301, 302, 303, 309, 316, 348(A), 349
   see also Grey
Green, Thomas, 34
Green, Robert, 35
   William, 348
Greer, Robert, 273
Greeson, Jacob, 271
Gregg, Jacob, 242, 307, 308
   Joshua, 93
Greson, Hannah, 81
Grey, Robert, 99
   see also Gray
Griffeth, Rebekah, 17
Grinley, Alexander, 182
Grizsel, William, 350, 360
Grog(g)in, 116, 422
Guist, John, 409
Gwin(n), Isbell, 3
   Robert 1, 3, 26, 121
Habkns, Thomas, 57
Haley, Elizabeth, 21
   Martin, 21
Halford, John, 454
Hall, 119, 257, 420
   Andrew (Andw.), 246, 314
   Ann, 254, 384
   Isabellah, 314
   John, 254, 384
   William, 206
Hallum (Hallam), Elizabeth, 379
   John, 377, 379, 441
Hamilton (Hamelton), David 528

Hamilton, George, 375, 441, 442
   Jean, 441
   John (Jno.), 418, 421, 430,
      455, 482
   Ninian 201, 217
   Thomas 347(A), 490, 497
   William, 215, 304
Hammond, Moses, 32, 52, 66
Hampton, Anthony, 458
Hanna(h), Isbel, 448
   John 170, 189, 419
   Martha 170, 419
   Robert (Robt.) 170, 189,
      260, 419, 448, 506, 523
Hannon, John, 132
Hanshato, Absolom, 52
Harden, Charles, 512, 524
Hargrave (Hargrove, Hartgrove),
   Richard, 183
   Samuel, 347, 530
   Susannah 530
   Thomas 17
Harken, Natt, 113
Harris, Isham, 526
   John, 170
   L., 396, 399, 401
   London, 466
   Nathaniel, 363
   Obidiah, 245, 348(A)
   Robert, 483
   Tyree, 408
   William, 151
Hastie, Robert, & Co. 423
Hawkins, John 7, 43, 81, 211
Haworth, Richard 156
Hays, James, 379, 512, 515,
      516, 525
   John, 258
   Patrick, 306, 459
   Thomas, 205
Henderson, 373
   John, 96, 458
   Pleasant, 515
   Richard, 183, 220, 97
   Samuel, 96, 207, 261, 458
   Thos., 96, 132, 134, 136,
      138, 373, 374, 447, 464,
      471, 472, 507
   William, 207
Hendricks, James, 282
Herrons, David, 1
Hiatt, Christopher, 234
   see also Hyatt
Hidgins, Robert, 57
Hill, Isaac, 466

Hill, John, 518
   Mr., 509
   Thos., 94
   Walter, 460
Hindman, Saml., 87
   William, 87
Hinds, John, 467
   Joseph, 92, 317, 318, 434,
      467
   Levi, 317
   Sarah, 317, 318, 467
   Simeon, 317, 318, 467
   Simon, 92
   Susannah, 92
Hinshaw, Jacob, 220, 242
   James, 209
   Joseph, 209
   Rebecca, 209
   William, 34, 200, 353
Hodgen, Robert, 57, 62
   Theodeat, 57
Hodges, Robert, 62
Hog(g)at(t), Anthony, 270, 478
   Mary, 270
   Nathaniel (Nathl.), 37, 38,
      407, 427, 453, 478, 484,
      518
   Rachel, 484
   Samuel, 270
Holdeness, J., 445
Holderness, James, 514
Holland, Edward, 489, 494, 522
Hollingsworth, Jacob, 161
   Jesse, 307, 311
Holloway, John, 368
Holt, Michael, 357
Hoots, Michael, 237
Hopkins, 58
Hopper, 363
Hotsz, Michael, 237
House, John, 81
Howard, M., 180, 324, 328
Hubert, Wm., 454
Hudgins, Theodate, 57
   Theodet, 57
Hughes, John, 368
Hughs, Archibald, 178
Hunt, Abner, 226
   Eleazer, 193, 199, 212, 226,
      344, 378
   Jacob, 226
   Mary, 226
   Sarah, 421
   Thos., 226
Hunter, Alexander, 400, 445

Hunter, Edward, 20, 74, 280, 358,
    388, 423, 425, 426, 427,
    437, 450, 453, 464, 478,
    484, 533
  Elizabeth, 388, 464
  James (Jas.), 175, 176, 201,
    217, 253, 265, 273, 457,
    467, 468, 470, 514, 525,
    533
  John, (Jno.), 20, 37, 38,
    388, 423, 425, 450, 452,
Hunter, John, 533
  Judith Isold, 478
  Nancy Wood, 478
  Samuel, 175
Husband, E., 34
  Harman (Herman), 32, 34, 41,
    86, 107, 108, 144, 180,
    182, 190, 201, 209, 220,
    242, 253, 265, 307, 308,
    343, 353, 417
  John, 107, 242
  Mary, 308
  William, 108
Huskins, Joseph, 439, 482
Hussey, John, 51, 57, 62
  Stephen, 340
Hutchins, Thomas, 383
Hutton, Lewis, 266
Hyat, Willm., 167
  see also Hiatt
Ingleson, Sarah, 141
  William, 141
Irving, Eve, 356
  Ludewick, 356
  Mary Eve, 356
Isley, John, 451
  Lodiwick, 90
  Ludowick, 237
Jackson, Daniel, 417
  David, 32, 41
  Elizabeth, 32
  Isaac, 41, 417
  Jabse, 32
  Jess, 32
  Jobe, 41
  Margaret, 256
  Mary, 41
  William, 206, 256
Jamison, Thomas, 382
Jay, James, 368
Jenkins, David, 57, 62
Jessop, Ann, 17, 19, 51, 155,
    199
  Caleb, 275, 279

Jessop, Calep, 155
  Joseph, 19, 193, 275, 347
  Priscilla, 275
  Thomas, 17, 19, 51, 155,
    199, 212, 275, 279, 347
  Timothy, 17, 19, 51, 193,
    221, 235, 275
  William (Willm.), 17, 19,
    226, 235, 275, 347
Jessup, Timothy 51
Joans, see Jones
Job, John, 491, 503, 524
Johnson, Gidion, 425, 426, 450
Johnston, James, 155, 167, 289
  Jeremiah, 517
  John, 202, 348
  Lancelot, 142
  William, 341, 386
Jones, 470
  Agnes. 253
  Allen, 481'
  Aquila, 201, 265
  Elizabeth, 201, 253
  Robert (Robt.), 176, 339,
    400, 423, 430, 437, 445,
    453, 478, 481
  Stephen, 220, 242, 253, 265,
    273, 343
  Willie, 481
  see also Joans
Jordan, George, Jr., 483
Joyce, Alexander, 517
  Elijah, 416, 516, 517
Jude, George, 37, 38
  John, 38
Julian, Ann, 216
  Peter, 6, 9, 141, 211, 216
Karr, see 1
  OCarr, Kerr
Keaughy, Matt:, 341
Kennedy, John, 11
  Joseph, 506
  Judith, 105, 106
  Samuel, 105
  William, 105, 106
Kent, Luke, 425, 426
Kerr, David, 475, 501
  John, 230
  Jos., 53, 55
  Nathaniel, 78, 79, 203, 273
  see also Carr
Kersey, Christofer, 57
Kimbrough, John, 383
  Mary, 383
Kimmons, see Cimmons

Kinchen, John, 182
King, Benajah, 113
   William, 405
Kinman, James, 215
Kiser, Nathaniel, 35
Knapp, Jno. C., 324, 328
Koontz, see Cuntz
Kyes, John, 430
Lacey, Theops., 381
Lackey, Adam, 504
Lacy, 519
Lamb, Henry, 229
   Joseph, 229, 235
   Josiah, 127, 218, 272
   Reuben, 218
   Robert, 70
   Sarah, 127
   Thomas, 127, 218, 272
Landreth, Thomas, 498
Lane, Jesse, 270
   William, 245
Larance, see Lawrence
Laromore, see Lorimer
Larrance, see Lawrence
Lashley, Charles, 118
Lau, Daniel, 43
   Daolin, 7
Lawrence, Adam, 252, 259
   John, 336, 338
   Peter, 347(A), 490
   Peter, Sr., 347(A)
Lea, John, 125, 454
Leak, John, 207, 388
Leckey, Adam, 497
Ledford, Grizzallah, 530
   John, 369, 372, 530
Leeper, James, 516
Lemmon, John, 533
Lett, James, 488
Lewis, David, 38, 291
   Enoch, 198
   George, 107, 108, 343
   Jacob, 291
   John, 38, 45, 58, 61, 127
     129, 213, 291
   Priscilla, 127, 291
Lienbarger, Catherine, 271
   Francis, 271
   George, 271
   Jacob, 271
Lier, James, 521, 522
Linderman, Henry, 61, 367
Lindsey, Robert, 265, 530
   Thomas, 288, 392, 404
Linsey, Robert, 530

Linterman Margaret, 151
   Henry, 151
Little, Hannah, 364
   Jacob, 94, 364
Littlejohn, William, 182
London, Mark, 389
Long, John, 118, 419
Long, Samuel, 499
Lorimer, James, 430
   see also Laramore
Lovelatty, Leah, 360
   Simeon, 350
   Thomas, 3, 198, 350
   Thomas, Jr,. 360
Lowe (Low), Andrew, 490, 497
   Conrad, 252, 341
   David, 6, 9, 243, 252, 393
   John, 417
   Lydia, 7, 43
   Mary, 243, 393
   Rosannah; 252
   Samuel, 116, 243, 422
   Tabitha, 116
   Thomas, 6, 7, 9, 43, 217
Lowther, William, 324
Lynam, Andrew, 339
   Richard, 339
Maben, Alexander, 498
   John, 446
   Samuel, 442
   William, 443, 446
Mabry, Mary, 432, 438
Mackey, William, 67, 88, 268
Mackie, William, 268, 269
Macky, David, 138
Macy, Abijah, 138
   Anna, 138
   David, 134, 136, 138, 153,
     163, 199, 209, 234, 252,
     263, 276, 366
   Enoch, 134, 136, 138, 160,
     163, 193, 199, 209, 212,
     252
Maddock, Joseph, 72
   Nathan, 144
Mahoney, Margarate, 505
   Stephen, 494
Major, Nicholas, 197, 274
Mann, Josiah, 274
Marley, William, 201
Martin, Alexander (Alex, Alexr.), 230, 375, 514, 484
   Col. James, 407
   James (Jas.), 182, 407, 458, 533

Martin, John, 466
  Sam., 100
Marton, James, 182
Mateer, Robert, 121
Mathies, Jno., 249
Matthews, Isaac, 230
  James, 119, 170, 260, 266
  Mary, 119, 260
  Moothman, 254
  Oliver, 234
  Walter, 344
  William, 170, 254
Maxwell, John, 186, 205, 412, 526
May, Charles, 533
  John, 533
McAdam, Hugh, 197
McAdoo, James, 506
  John, 119, 257, 351
McAdow, John, 420
McBride, Isaiah, 505
McCain, James, 280
McCallum, Kenneth, 197
McCaminy, 512
McCarroll (McCarrel), James, 142
McCarthy, Jeremiah, 258
McClain, Alexr., 529
  Moses, 504, 523
  Robt., 417
McClaran, Alexander (Alex.), 96, 261, 373, 374, 416, 464
McClean, see McClain
McClintock, John, 503
McCollum (McCollom), Daniel (Danl.), 112, 173, 432, 438
  Dunken, 417
  James, 173
  John, 395, 438, 444, 532
  Levi, 32, 417
  Mary, 417
McCracken, Samuel, 512, 516, 519
McCrory, Hannah, 500, 501, 503, 511
McCuistion (McCuistian, McCuiston), Catherine, 289, 404
  James, 29, 110, 219, 256, 289, 331, 390, 392, 404, 479, 489, 494
  John, 219, 289, 392, 404, 494
  Moses, 476, 479, 507
  Robert, 479
  Thomas, 40, 53, 479
McCullock, 217

McCullock, Thos., 142
McCulloh, 21, 85, 90, 130, 142, 194, 232, 347(A), 352, 354
  B., 357
  Henry, 7, 49, 83, 216, 271, 356
  Henry Eustace, 81, 204, 237, 243, 282, 354, 357, 372, 393, 477, 491, 503, 524
McDaniel, Absalom, 165
  Daniel, 94, 165
  John, 76
McFadgen, Jeremiah, 516
McFarlin, Benjamin, 392, 404
  see also Farlin
McFarson, William, 93
McGee, John (Jno.), 78, 141, 144, 151, 209, 216, 230, 249, 291, 354, 357
  Martha, 273, 300, 343, 468, 477, 498
  Saml., 209
  Susanna, 497, 498
McGown, Jas., 105
McIlroy, Samuel, 1
  see also Mickleroy
McIntir, Archibald, 501
McKemie, Robert, 511
McKnight, Widow, 522
McMurry, James, 527
  John, 517, 527
McNaight, John, 492
McNair, John, 362
McNairy, Andrew, 321
  Catherine, 321
  Francis, 219, 321, 374, 390, 404, 482, 527
  James, 321
  John, 321
  Mary, 321
  Robert, 321
McNeight, Catherine, 494
McNight, Alexander, 179
  John (Jno.), 179, 215
McQuiston, Thomas, 40
Mebane, 246
  William, 351
Melarg, Charles, 419
Mendenhall, Charity, 100, 103, 156
  Elisha, 468
  Jas., 223, 224
  John (Jno.), 64, 70, 224, 330
  Mary, 330

Mendenhall, Mordicia, 100, 103, 138, 156, 366
  Moses, 64, 70, 223, 224, 233, 245, 330, 378, 382
  Stephen, 100, 103
Meteer, Robert, 121
Mickleroy, James, 165
  see also McIlroy
Mier, Leonard, 151
Miller, Andrew, 182
Millikan, Jane, 99, 115
  Samuel, 99, 115
  William (Will:, Wm.), 14, 36, 38, 45, 99, 115, 116, 369, 372
Mills, Aaron, 309
  Henry, 167, 362
  Hus, 315
  John (Jno.), 36, 222, 233
  Micagay, 455
  Micajah, 315, 455
  Mr., 474
  Reuben, 316
  Richard, 167
  Rubin, 167
  Sarah, 36
  Thomas (Thos.) 223, 224, 309, 315, 316
Millsaps, Ellender, 236
  Robt., 236
  Thos., 236
Milner, James, 220
Miner, Leonard, 367
  Mary Madeleena, 367
  Mary Magdalene, 367
Mitchell (Mitchel), Adam, 87, 175, 176, 178, 191, 281, 505
  Agness, 175, 176
  Henry, 515, 521, 525
  Isabel, 176
  John, 230, 281
  Margaret, 126, 284, 285
  Mary, 281
  Robert, 126, 284, 285, 288, 310, 439
Mock, Peter, 86
Moffet, William, 66
Moody, Alexr., 219, 284, 285
Moon, John, 352
  Richard, Sr., 160
  Simon, 160
Moor (Moore), Cam, 362
  Edward, 116, 422
  Elijah, 422
  M., 182

Moor (Moore), Samuel, 462
  William, 422, 498
Moreland, Catrin, 482
  William, 482
Morgan, James, 204, 343
  Jno., 256
  Mehetabel, 248
  Soloman, 248
  Thomas, 132, 485, 495
Morgh, Conzoyt, 21
Morphew, James, 349
Morphus, James, 348(A)
Morris, Henry, 368
  Hugh, 167
Morrow, David, 190
  Martha, 190
Mortimore, William, 512
Mountgomery, William, 487
Mucklehatton, Abraham, 256
Mullen (Mullin, Mullins), John, 123, 124
  Patrick, 125, 173, 444
  Thomas, 123
Murphey (Murphy), Mary 86
  Roger, 86, 242
Nash, Abner, 180, 182
Nation, Bethyyuk, 235
  Capt., 211
  Christopher, 229
  Eleanor, 235
  Elizabeth, 229
  John, 229
  Joseph, 235, 239
Neal, Judith, 178
  Sarah, 178
  Thos., 178
Needham, John, 352
Nees, George, 204
Negroe - Abraham, 332
Negroe - Absalom, 332
Negroe - Adam, 423
Negroe - Ben, 423
Negroe - Cato, 332
Negroe - Ceasar, 423
Negroe - Charles, 423
Negroe - Cicily, 423
Negroe - Cremy, 332
Negroe - Esther, 332
Negroe - Fan, 423
Negroe - Guilford, 260
Negroe - Isham, 423
Negroe - James, 423
Negroe - Jery, 423
Negroe - Joe, 423
Negroe - Juba, 423

Negroe - Judah, 332
Negroe - Julias, 332
Negroe - Kate, 332
Negroe - Lucy, 423
Negroe - Matthew, 423
Negroe - Moll, 423
Negroe - Peter, 423
Negroe - Rainus, 423
Negroe - Rose, 423
Negroe - Silva, 332
Negroe - Tom, 423
Negroe - Will, 423
Negroe - Winny, 332
Nelson, 526
  Moses, 151, 348, 367
Nesbitt, James, 121
Nicholas, Ambrose, 396
Nicholson, James, 32, 41, 61, 94, 364, 417
Nickell, Ealsie, 258
  John, 258
Nickoll, James, 258
Nickolls, John, 281
Nicks, see Nix
Nilson, John, 28
  Levina, 28
Nix, John, 97, 139, 146, 215, 264, 506
  Margaret, 146
Nochlas, see Nicholas
Nogget, Anthony, 70
Noris, Thomson, 118
North Carolina, 331, 475, 476, 477, 485, 486, 487, 488, 489, 490, 491, 492, 493, 494, 495, 496, 497, 498, 499, 500, 501, 502, 503, 504, 505, 506, 507, 509, 510, 511, 512, 513, 514, 515, 516, 517, 518, 519, 520, 521, 522, 523, 524, 525, 526, 527
Norton, Richard, 317
  William, 92, 218
Nunn, Ede, 408
  William (Wm.), 227, 408
Odell, John, 480
  William, 123, 173
Odeneal, 532
  John (Jno.), 100, 112, 113, 173, 230, 260, 360, 395, 398, 438, 444, 484, 498
  Sarah, 360
Ogle, Hercules, 127
  Mary, 127

Oliver, George, 96, 373, 458, 465, 525
Oneal, John, 173
Osbun, John, 64
  see also Ozbun
Osburn, 64
Overby, John, 61, 94, 364
Owen (Owens, Owings), Ann, 61
  John, 61, 94, 364
  Richardson, 436, 462
  Samuel 86
  Thos., 396, 399, 401, 402
Ozbun, John, 330
  see also Osbun
Park, George, 274
Parks, Anna, 207
  George, 207
  Samuel, 113, 383
Parratt, Benjamin, 509
Patrick, Ebenezer, 268
Patrick, Hugh, 268, 269
  James, 268
  Mary, 88, 268, 269
  Nicholas, 130
  William, 15, 29, 67, 88, 268, 269, 375
  William Armstrong, 269
Patten, Hugh, 311
Paulk, John Athen, 32
  Johnathan, 41
  Jonathon, 417
Payne, John, 344, 347
  Mary, 344
Pearce, Mary, 336, 337, 338
  Windsor, 188, 241, 248, 241, 336, 345
Peasley, John, 495
  William, 528
Peasly, Wm., 304
Peay, George, 74
Pendly, Joshua, 396, 399, 401
Peoples (Peeples), David, 513
  Nathan 519
Peper, John, 408
Perkins, Charles, 175, 400, 445, 484
  Joseph, 276
  Peter, 381, 407, 428, 429, 430
Perry, William, 153
Person, Thomas, 180, 183, 499
Phifer, John, 97
  Martin, 97
Philpott, David, 530, 532
  John, 530, 532
  Warran, 530, 532

Pickrale, Henry, 497
Pickrell, Catherine, 161
  John, 52, 66, 161
Pierpoint, Larkin, 198
Piggot, Benjamin, 288
Pike, Elizabeth, 348
  John, 348
  Nathan, 348
Pinson, Joseph, 408
Pirkins, see Perkins
Plunkett, William, 243
Pope, Jesse, 429
Porter, Ann, 461
  Hugh, 1
  John, 441, 511
  Rees, 206
  Reese, 528
Potter, Ephriam 198, 350, 360
Powell (Powel), Abraham, 14, 233, 278
  Jane, 233
  James (Jas.), 194, 524
  John, 14, 36
  Sarah, 499, 518, 520
Presnell (Presnel), 374
  James, 407
  Mary, 407
Prewitt, William, 444
Pritchett, Joseph, 258
Pugh, James, 107, 108, 307, 308
  John, 468
  Thomas, 108, 242
Puntrick, Nicholas, 130, 194
Pyatt (Pyate), John, 515, 525
Quaill, William, 246
Ralstone, Robert, Jr., 74
Ramage, Alexander, 355
Ramfield, William, 11
Rankin, George, 191, 301, 302, 489, 522
  John (Jno.), 179, 196, 411, 415
  Lydia, 191
  Robert, 15, 29, 191, 281, 504
  William, 179, 196
Rayl, George, 25
Read (Reade), Arthur, 240, 241
  Henry, 105
  Lombard, 248
  Martha, 240
  William, Sr., 241
Reagan, John 96, 430, 458, 525
  Mary 96
Rear, Robt., 237
Redock, Benjamin, 265

Reece (Rease, Rees), John, 311
  Thomas, 41
  William, 276, 277
Reed, Henry, 390, 479
Reeseen, Anthony, 465
Reynolds, David, 291
  Henry, 213
  Jeremiah, 38, 45, 58, 129, 213, 291
  Rachel, 38, 45, 129, 213
  Susanna, 129
  William (Wm.), 38, 45, 129, 213, 222, 266
Rhoades, William, 348
Rice, Thos., 395, 398
Richeson, 248
Ricter, Michael, 282
Ridge, Thomas, 100
Ridley, Bromfield, 458
Right, Richard, 144
  see also Wright
Roark, Bryan, 246
Roberts, James, 280, 373, 525
Robertson, John (Jno.), 121, 227, 459
Robinson, John, 25
  William, 25
Robyson, John, 25
Rogers, Robert, 312
Ross, David, 368, 423
  Henry, 284, 285, 310, 476, 502
  James, 284, 285, 310, 439
  Margaret, 310
  Mary, 439
Rowland, George, 3
Rudolph, Andrew, 83, 85
Russel(l), David, 132, 505
  James, 207
  Robert, 524, 526
  Timothy, 234, 252, 263, 366
  William, 106
Sallinger, Peter, 194
Salmon, Jno., 381
Sanders, Hezekiah, 167, 362
  Isaac, 184
  Joel, 362
  John, Sr., 362
  Martha, 167
Savage, Elizabeth, 118
  Thomas, 364
  William, 118, 197, 274, 339
Scales, Henry, 518
  James (Jas.), 256, 513
  Joseph, 256, 363

Scales, Mary, 256
  Thomas, 510, 519
Scott, Samuel, 184, 289, 331, 390
  Sarah, 452
  William (Wm.), 184, 214, 429, 432, 503
Searcy, William (Willm., Wm.), 188, 225, 240, 241, 248, 336, 338, 345, 352
Sel(l)er, Philip, 393
Sharp, Edward, 78, 79, 99, 115, 203
  John, 513
  Richard, 533
  Samuel, 513, 522
Shaver, William, 347(A)
Shaw, Hugh, 498, 503
  Samuel, 498
  William, 448, 523
Shepherd, Jacob, 336, 338
Shepperd, Charles, 372
  John, 369, 372
  Peter, 369
  Wm., 496, 497, 498, 499, 500, 501, 502, 503, 504, 505, 507, 509, 510, 511, 512, 513, 514, 515, 516, 517, 518, 519, 520, 521, 522, 523, 524, 526, 527
Shore, Thos., 368
Shruiel, William, 110
Sigfret, Henry, 212
Simon, John, 533
Simpson, Richard (Richd.), 227, 408, 483
  Thomas, 483
Skipworth, Henry, 220
Smalley, Jno., 234
Smith, Adam, 200
  George, 282
  Hugh, 243
  John, 130, 341, 414, 416
  Joshua, 513, 516, 520, 521, 522
  Robert, 196, 411
  Samuel, 196, 411, 412, 415
  Sarah, 414, 416
  Thomas, 436, 463
  William (Wm.), 1, 227
Sothberry, George, 180
Southerland, 240
  Ransom, 262, 336, 338, 345, 352
Southwell, 227

Spinks, Enoch, 240
  John, 352
Spruiel, William, 110
Stabler, Edward, 368, 375
Stal(l)ey (Stally, Staly, Stealy)
  Barbara, 352
  Conrad, 34, 83, 200, 353
  Elizabeth, 21
  Jacob, 21, 34, 49, 352, 354
  Martin, 21, 352, 353, 354
Stalker, George, 315
Stanl(e)y (Standlly), 64
  John, 233
  Joseph, 245, 315, 474
  Martha, 344
  Strangeman, 474
  W. Strangeman, 315
  Zachariah, 64, 70, 245, 330
Stanton, Jno. 310
Starbuck (Strabuck, Straybuck), 263
  Gayer, 155, 366
  George, 226
  William, 263, 366
Starns, Anne, 265
  Ebenezer, 265
Starr, Adam, 190, 252, 259
Starrat(t), Benjanin (Benjn.), 189, 254, 418, 421, 596, 523
Stewart, John, 245
  see also Stuart
Stillwell, Jacob, 401
Stone, Mervil, 178
Strain, William, 505
Stricklin, Jacob, 411, 415
Stringfellow, Mary, 6, 9
  William, 6, 7, 9, 43
Stroud, Abraham, 62
Stuart, Finley, 491, 503
  George, 523
  James, 500, 501, 503, 507
  Sampson, 488, 493
  see also Stewart
Stubblefield, Buchd., 444
  Elizabeth, 480
  John, 360, 480
  Richd., 444
  Seth, 198
  William, 530, 532
  Wyatt, 360, 480
  Wyett, 410
Stubbs, Esther, 72
  John, 72
Sumner, Jacob, 488, 493

GUILFORD COUNTY DEED BOOK 1

Sumner, Joshua, 275
   Robert, 284, 310
Surry, Ely, 462
Suther, Samuel, 356
Swain, Nathaniel, 4512
Swift, Flower, 32
   Thomas, 6, 9
Syfret, Frederick, 311
Tate, Ally, Mrs., 452
   John (Jno.), 381, 382, 400
   Joseph, 20, 37, 74, 178, 400, 445, 481, 533
   Sarah, 260
   W., 452
Tatom (Tatum), Absalam, (Ab.), 35, 116, 422
Taylor, Esther, 276, 277
   Simeon, 153, 263, 276, 277
   Simon, 153, 163
   Thomas, 153
Terrel (Terril), Mary, 38, 45, 213, 291
   Timothy, 38, 45, 213
Thackstone, Saml., 383
Thom, John, 477
Thomas, William 186
Thompson (Thomson), Dorithy, 321
   Dorothy, 323, 324
   Elizabeth, 225
   James, 321, 323, 324
   Jennings, 188, 225
   John, 339
   Latice, 29
   Lawrence, 274
   Robert (Robt.), 11, 15, 29, 88, 212, 268, 269, 435, 526, 535
   Samuel, 274, 435, 510, 535
   Thomas, 535
   Victor, 202
   William, 307
Thornberry, 53
Thornburgh (Thornborough, Thornbrough, Edward, 35
   Henry, 155
   James, 136
   Joseph, 134
   Thomas, 134, 136, 160
   William, 99
Thrasher, Isaac, 286, 287, 409
   John, 286, 287, 409
   Joseph Cloud, 286, 287, 409
   William, 505
Tilswort(h), Thomas, 124, 125,
Tisworth, Thomas, 454

Tompkins, Robert, 67
Touchstone, Jonas, 504, 523
Townsend, James, 368
Tracks, John, 262
Triplett(e), Eleanor, 227
   Willm, 227
Trousdale, Agness, 40
   Ann, 40
   William, 40, 434
Underhill, Hannah, 222
   John (Jno.), 222, 233
Underwood, Henry, 354
United Synod of New York & Philadelphia, 121
Unthank, Allen, 301, 303
   John, 302, 303
   Joseph, 301, 302, 303
Vernon, Isaac, 346
   James, 414, 416, 499, 518
   Nehemiah, 414, 416
   Richard (Richd., Rchd.), 445, 465, 514
Wade, Henry, 236
Walker, David, 126, 533
   James, 461, 510
   John, 215, 423, 461
   Samuel, 308
   Thomas, 256, 484
   Warren, 371
   William, 371, 461
Wallace, William, 1
Wallar, Francis, 463
Ward, Henry, 466
   John, 381, 402, 405, 466
Ward, William, 86, 107
Warnah, Robert, 451
Warnock, James, 227
Watkins, 533
Watson, John, 519
Watt, 119
   Samuel 118, 197, 274, 389
Weatherford, William, 532
Weldon, Daniel, 453
Wel(l)bo(u)rn, Edward, 75, 300
   John, 477
   William, 165, 300, 417
Wells Cowper Company, 341
Wells, Frank, 363
West, Issac, 58
Wetherly, 526
   Edward, 524
Whaitsell, Henry, 259
   Mary, 259
White, Issac, 51
   John, 429, 511

White, Thomas, 310, 439
   William, 368, 515, 525
Whiteside, Abraham, 476, 511
Whiteworth, Isaac, 529
Whitsel, Henry, 204, 252
   Mary, 204
Whitworth, Isaac, 464
   John, 457, 470, 514
Wheeler, John, 309
Wiggins, Ezekiel, 441
Wilcocks, John, 307
Wiley, David, 364, 451, 506
   Hugh, 304, 355, 364, 451
   John, 355, 488
   Mary, 130
   Robert, 304
   Thomas (Thos.), 355, 451
   William, 130, 207, 304, 355, 364, 451, 486
Williams, C., 321
   Charles, 322, 323, 324
   Edmd., Jr., 340
   Emas, 203
   Jesse, 244
   Jno., 339
   Jonathon, 124
   N., 438
   Nathl., 339, 389, 395, 398, 432
   R., 381
   Richard, 244, 303, 378
   William, 483
Williamson, Jere, 274.
   Zachariah, 513
Wil(l)son, James, 11, 207, 330, 492, 522
   John (Jno.), 381, 510
   Thomas, 88, 127
Wimbish, John, 178
Winters, Daniel, 262
Wolson, John, 510
Womack, Abraham, 395, 398, 444
Wood, John, 92
   William Black, 528
   Zebedee, 253, 343, 477
Woodleif, John, 383
Work, Henry, 26, 88, 97, 268, 269
   John, 26, 67
Worley, Henry, 279
Worth, Daniel, 222
Worthington, Rachel, 177
Woygall, Nath., 400
Wray, James, 425, 426
Wright, Ann, 144

Wright, Francis, 489, 522
   Isaac, 512
   Richard, 220
   Robert, 517, 527
   William, 414
   see also Right
Wymie, Willm., 112
Yarborough, Archibald, 480
Yeates, John, 466
York, Francis, 61
   Henry, 300
   Jeremiah, 75, 165
   John, 364
   Semore, 75
   Simon, 165
   Simone, 165
   Simor, 141
Young Miller & Co., 182
Young, James, 182
   Francis, 28
   Samuel, 521, 523
Youngblood, Peter, 52, 161, 311
Zigler, Christopher, 459

PLACE NAME INDEX

Citations are to the page numbers in the original deed book and not to the page numbers of this volume.

Allamance (Allemance), 211, 216, 230, 232, 246, 260, 266, 485, 486, 488, 490, 491, 493, 495, 497, 498, 505, 506, 512, 520, 523, 524
Allamance Creek, 216
Anson County, 116, 422
Arvins Branch, 513
Arwin(s) Branch, 506, 511
Back Line, 188, 225, 262, 388
Bailey's Place, 282
Balesses Branch, 199
Barber Tract, 307
Be(a)ver Creek, 153, 163, 170, 189, 263, 304, 364, 419, 448, 451, 506, 523
Be(a)ver Island Creek, 175, 176, 178, 256, 400, 445, 510, 515, 519
Bedford County, VA, 381, 466
Belews Creek, 306
Big Branch, 521
Big Troublesome, 97
Bleating Branch, 266
Bleating-house Land, 266
Blumery, 97
Bottom, 180
Broad Mouth Creek, 52, 161
Bruce Road, 511, 515
Brush Creek, 72, 134, 136, 156, 302, 303, 348
Brushy Fork, 512, 524
Buck Creek, 497
Buckingham County, VA, 457, 470, 533
Buff Island, 518
Buffaloe Creek, 11, 139, 179, 190, 207, 281, 528
Burch Creek, 485, 495
Cabbin Tract, 242
Cab(b)in Branch, 118, 197, 274
Cains Branch, 512
Caroline County, VA, 347
Carraway, 99, 115, 116, 202, 372
Carraway Creek, 369, 422
Carteret County, 235, 239
Caswell County, 399, 422

Cattail Meadow Branch, 476, 507
Cedar Creek, 90, 130, 194, 237
Challes Land, 410
Charlotte County, VA, 407
Chatham County, 194, 248, 271, 311, 332, 348, 383
Chesterfield County, VA, 359, 423, 425, 429
Church of Scotland, 121
Clift of Rock, 107, 220, 242
Confiscated Land, 505
Contable Line, 523
Cornfield Branch, 501
County Line, 274
Court House, 494
Court House Road, 173, 517
Court House Tract, 494
Cox Mill Creek, 93
Coxes Creek, 346
Crafords Path, 72
Cross Creek Road, 519
Cross Rock Shoal, 20, 371, 461
Culpeper County, VA, 459
Cumberland County, VA, 37, 38
Dan (Dann) River, 20, 37, 74, 96, 261, 280, 358, 359, 360, 363, 371, 373, 374, 388, 407, 423, 425, 426, 427, 428, 429, 430, 437, 447, 450, 452, 453, 457, 458, 461, 464, 465, 470, 478, 481, 484, 509, 514, 517, 518, 519, 520, 525, 529, 533
Dann River Road, 502, 507
Dead Timber Tract, 426
Deep River, 35, 51, 52, 57, 58, 62, 66, 70, 72, 99, 115, 161, 188, 210, 223, 224, 225, 240, 241, 245, 248, 265, 270, 273, 307, 309, 311, 315, 316, 330, 336, 338, 340, 345, 348(A), 349, 352, 362, 382, 436, 462, 463
Dennys Branch, 186
Dividing Branch, 524, 526
Division Line, 414, 416
East Fork, 20, 72, 270, 476
East Mayo Mountain, 414, 416

Enoe Settlement, 274
Falling Run, 498, 503
Flat(t) Creek, 188, 225
Fork Creek, 240
Fountain Head, 199
Fraizers Fork, 35, 78
Frazier's Tract, 273
Georgia, 72, 346
Goochland County, VA, 245
Granville County, 183, 458, 481
Granville's Line, 237, 354, 357
Great Allamance (Allemance) Creek, 23, 81, 204, 259, 347(A), 503
Great Branch, 515
Great Brittain, 368
Great Road, 345
Guilford County, 1, 3, 17, 19, 21, 26, 28, 35, 37, 38, 45, 49, 51, 52, 53, 55, 57, 58, 62, 66, 67, 72, 75, 76, 78, 79, 81, 83, 85, 86, 87, 88, 90, 93, 94, 97, 99, 100, 103, 105, 106, 110, 112, 115, 116, 118, 119, 123, 124, 125, 126, 127, 129, 130, 132, 134, 136, 138, 139, 141, 142, 144, 146, 149, 151, 153, 155, 156, 160, 161, 163, 165, 167, 170, 175, 176, 178, 179, 180, 186, 188, 189, 190, 191, 193, 194, 195, 197, 198, 199, 200, 201, 202, 203, 204, 205, 206, 207, 209, 210, 211, 212, 213, 214, 215, 216, 217, 218, 219, 220, 222, 223, 224, 225, 226, 227, 229, 230, 232, 233, 234, 235, 236, 237, 240, 241, 243, 244, 246, 248, 249, 251, 252, 253, 254, 256, 257, 258, 259, 260, 261, 262, 263, 264, 265, 266, 268, 269, 270, 271, 272, 273, 274, 275, 276, 277, 279, 281, 282, 284, 285, 286, 287, 288, 289, 291, 300, 301, 302, 303, 304, 306, 309, 310, 311, 312, 314, 315, 316, 317, 318, 330, 332, 336, 338, 339, 340, 341, 343, 345, 346, 347(A), 348(A), 349, 350, 351, 352,

Guilford County, 353, 354, 355, 356, 358, 359, 360, 362, 363, 364, 365, 366, 367, 368, 369, 371, 372, 373, 374, 375, 377, 378, 379, 382, 383, 384, 386, 388, 389, 390, 392, 393, 395, 396, 398, 399, 400, 401, 402, 404, 405, 407, 408, 409, 410, 411, 412, 414, 415, 416, 417, 418, 419, 420, 421, 425, 426, 427, 429, 430, 432, 434, 435, 436, 437, 438, 439, 441, 442, 443, 445, 446, 447, 448, 450, 451, 452, 453, 454, 455, 457, 458, 459, 460, 461, 462, 463, 464, 465, 466, 467, 468, 470, 471, 472, 474, 478, 479, 480, 482, 483, 484, 505, 507, 528, 529, 530, 532, 533, 535
Halifax County, 180, 182, 220
Halifax County, VA, 261, 396
Haw Creek, 488
Haw River, 1, 3, 15, 29, 67, 81, 88, 266, 121, 134, 136, 153, 156, 163, 183, 190, 205, 214, 215, 258, 263, 268, 269, 274, 288, 347(A), 374, 377, 379, 404, 412, 429, 432, 435, 441, 460, 476, 482, 483, 499, 500, 502, 503, 507, 510, 511, 512, 513, 515, 516, 517, 519, 521, 524, 525, 526, 527, 501
Head Spring, 515
Hewwary, 202
  see also Uwarry
Hickory Creek 64, 330
High Rock Creek 408
Hillsborough 321
Hock Stone 93
Hogans Creek 113, 123, 124, 125, 173, 274, 286, 287, 339, 360, 373, 395, 398, 409, 432, 438, 444, 454, 480, 517, 520, 525, 530, 532
Horsepen Creek 17, 126, 155, 193, 199, 234, 275, 279, 284, 285, 302, 303, 310, 344, 347, 366, 374, 386, 439, 471, 479, 482, 507, 527

Hunting Creek, 331
Huwary, see Uwarry
Iron Works, 97
Iron Works Road, 476, 502, 507
Jacobs Creek, 28, 74
James Branch, 515
Jas. Roberts' Mill Pond, 525
John Glenn's Field, 371, 461
Jones Old Line, 470
Joneses Line, 447
Kennedy Cr., 105, 106
Kings Mill, 517
Lancaster, 321
Lancaster County, PA, 184
Level Tract, 86, 201
Lick Branch, 511, 519
Lick Fork, 123, 124, 125, 286, 287, 409, 454
Line Branch, 483
Little Allamance Creek, 252
Little Branch, 366
Little Reed Creek, 358, 427, 437
Little Whitestone, 388
London, 322, 324, 368
Lone Island Ford, 96, 458
Long Branch, 70, 270, 476, 502, 511, 515
Lot #15, 6, 43
Lot #22, 7, 9
Low Grounds, 263, 386, 471
Lowrys Branch, 515
Lunenburg County, VA, 332
Lynam Tract, 339
Main Branch, 23
Main Road, 253, 284, 285, 310, 343, 439
Mairs Fork, 377, 379, 441, 483, 500, 501, 503, 507, 511, 519,
Manor Plantation, 240
Mars Fork, 377
Massachusetts Bay, 222
Matrimony Creek, 363
Mayo Mountain, 518
Mayo River, 447, 450, 457, 470, 513, 517, 520, 522
McCullo(c)h Tract, 357
  Line, 347(A), 491, 524
  Tract # 38, 90
  Tract # 11, 232
McGown's Place, 105
Mebanes Mill Creek, 351
Mecklenburgh County, 97
Meeting House, 121

Middlesex, 323
Middlesex County in the Island of Great Britain, 321
Mill & Mill Seat, 362
Mill, 373
Mill Creek, 29, 57, 62, 67, 88, 149, 383
Mill Place, 390
Mill Pond, 15, 88, 243, 348(A)
Mill Tract, 311
Mill-falls, 220
Mine Hill, 97
Mistoney Ridge, 26
Montgomery County, VA, 402
Moody Creek, 462
Moons Creek, 160
Moravian Road, 515
Morgans Creek, 112
Mount Pleasant Creek, 165
Mountain Run, 514, 516
Muddy Creek, 463
Nansemond County, VA, 341
Nantucket County, MA, 222
Neals (Neels) Bent, 358, 423, 427, 437
Neels Field, 176
Nelsons Creek, 526
New Bern, 324, 328
New Bond Street, 323
New England, 222
New Garden, Guilford Co., 368
New York, 324, 328
Nixes Creek, 191
North Branch, 15
North Buffaloe Creek, 87, 110, 146, 191, 196, 206, 256, 264, 281, 365, 411, 415, 434, 442, 443, 489, 492, 496, 506
North Carolina, 189, 200, 237, 321, 368
North Fork, 3, 26, 38, 45, 70, 127, 129, 149, 183, 213, 223, 224, 243, 246, 256, 260, 306, 309, 315, 316, 362, 382, 460, 486, 488, 493, 505
Obidiah Harris' Mill Pond, 348(A)
Old Back Line, 457, 470
Old Corner, 416
Old County Line, 274
Old Line, 362, 364, 414
Old Mill Dam 220, 242
Old Road 112

Old Trading Path 92, 317, 467
Orange County 1, 6, 7, 9, 32, 34, 38, 40, 41, 43, 45, 58, 61, 72, 74, 81, 107, 108, 113, 121, 130, 142, 173, 180, 211, 213, 217, 220, 242, 274, 307, 308, 321, 339, 350, 357, 360, 399, 402, 405, 408, 454, 528
Orange Courthouse Old Road, 112
Parish of St. Luke, 11, 78
Pearces Creek, 336
Pee Dee, 72
Pennsylvania, 67, 184, 227
Penny Branch, 197
Persimon (Pissimon) Branch, 491, 493
Petersburg, VA, 368, 375
Philadelphia, 67
Pine Branch, 118
Piney Branch, 274, 315, 362
Pittsylvania County, VA, 178, 350, 360, 373, 381, 405, 410, 428
Polecat Creek, 14, 36, 38, 45, 92, 129, 213, 222, 229, 233, 291, 317, 467
Poplar Branch, 510
Quaker Fork, 211
Reads Island, 336, 338
Ready Fork, 263
Red Bank Branch, 484, 518
Reed Creek, 371, 510, 519
Reedy Fork, 1, 25, 153, 163, 184, 205, 214, 217, 274, 276, 404, 412, 429, 432, 435, 476, 479, 501, 502, 503, 507, 510, 511, 515, 516, 517, 519, 524, 525, 526, 527, 535
Rich Fork, 184
Richland Creek, 219, 262, 289, 331, 340, 390, 392, 404, 494
Richland Fork, 282
Ridge Road, 399
Road, 336
Road Creek, 461
Rock Creek, 341, 487, 490, 497
Rock River, 348
Rocky Creek, 20
Rocky River, 151, 348, 367
Rowan County, 3, 11, 14, 15, 20, 23, 25, 29, 36, 38, 40, 45, 64, 70, 92, 184, 206, 209, 215, 219, 236, 274,

Rowan County, 279, 280, 282, 344, 347(A), 392, 423, 471, 472, 483, 530
Salisbury, 505, 530
Salisbury Road, 301, 373
Samuel Walker's Mill Dam, 308
Sandy Creek, 32, 58, 61, 75, 86, 94, 107, 108, 141, 144, 165, 200, 201, 209, 220, 242, 253, 265, 300, 308, 343, 353, 354, 468, 497, 498
Saw & Grist Mill, 472
Saw Pit Branch, 199, 347, 476, 502
Settle, York County Great Britttain, 368
Sharps Creek, 514
Sheppards Creek, 517, 521
Simpsons Branch, 500, 503, 511
South Buffaloe Creek, 40, 76, 119, 196, ' 209, 212, 252, 254, 257, 312, 314, 351, 384, 415, 420, 443, 446, 475, 497, 501, 504, 526
South Carolina, 265
South East Fork, 467
South Fork, 149, 216, 232, 256
Spring Branch, 142, 211
St. James Place, 323
St. Pauls Parish, GA, 72, 346
Standley's House, 474
Stinking Quarter Creek, 7, 21, 49, 83, 85, 142, 243, 352, 356, 408
Stonehouse, 240
Straight Fork, 366
Stuart's House, 491
Sugar Tree, 215
Sugar Tree Creek, 506
Surry County, 176, 206, 235, 239, 244, 274, 275, 279, 348, 464, 480, 518, 529
Tann-house, 375
Tann-yard, 375
Thicket Tract, 201
Thoms Spring Branch, 477
Thrashers Fork, 149
Tract No. 11, 81, 142, 232
Tract No. 38, 90
Trading Path, 92, 217, 468
Trading Road, 317, 467
Troublesome, 521
Troublesome Creek, 523
Troublesome, Big, 97

Twp. of Little Brittain, PA, 184
Uwarry (Uharee) Creek, 202, 236, 282, 383
Virginia, 37, 38, 178, 245, 261, 332, 339, 341, 347, 350, 359, 368, 373, 375, 381, 396, 402, 405, 407, 410, 423, 425, 428, 429, 457, 459, 466, 470, 533
Waggon Road, 527
Wake County, 57
Walnut Branch, 214
Weak (Wake) County, 57
Westminster County, Middlesex, 323
William Dennys Branch, 186
Wolf Branch, 245
Wolf Island Creek, 149, 198, 360, 381, 389, 396, 399, 401, 402, 405, 410, 466, 509
Wrightsboro Twp,, GA 72
Wyatt Stubblefield's Spring Branch, 480
Wyatt's Spring Branch, 360
York County, Great Brittain, 368
York County, PA 227

www.ingramcontent.com/pod-product-compliance
Lightning Source LLC
Chambersburg PA
CBHW020656300426
44112CB00007B/409